365

Favorite Brand Name ™

CASSEROLES

▪ & ONE-DISH MEALS ▪

PUBLICATIONS INTERNATIONAL, LTD.

365
Favorite Brand Name ™
CASSEROLES
■ & ONE-DISH MEALS ■

CHICKEN & TURKEY FAVORITES   4

PRIME-TIME MEATS   60

TREASURES FROM THE SEA   126

MAKE IT MEATLESS   160

PASTA MANIA   218

BREAKFAST & BRUNCH BUFFET   294

ACKNOWLEDGMENTS   326

INDEX   327

Chicken & Turkey
Favorites

1 CHICKEN ENCHILADAS

1³/₄ cups fat free sour cream
¹/₂ cup chopped green onions
¹/₃ cup minced fresh cilantro
1 tablespoon minced fresh jalapeño chili
    pepper
1 teaspoon ground cumin
1 tablespoon vegetable oil
12 ounces boneless, skinless chicken
    breasts, cut into 3×1-inch strips
1 teaspoon minced garlic
8 flour tortillas (8-inch)
1 cup (4 ounces) shredded ALPINE LACE®
    Reduced Fat Cheddar Cheese
1 cup bottled chunky salsa (medium or
    hot)
1 small ripe tomato, chopped
    Sprigs of cilantro (optional)

1. Preheat the oven to 350°F. Spray a 13×9×3-inch baking dish with nonstick cooking spray.

2. In a small bowl, mix together the sour cream, green onions, cilantro, jalapeño pepper and cumin.

3. Spray a large nonstick skillet with the cooking spray, pour in the oil and heat over medium-high heat. Add the chicken and garlic and sauté for 4 minutes or until the juices run clear when the chicken is pierced with a fork.

4. Divide the chicken strips among the 8 tortillas, placing them down the center of the tortillas. Top with the sour cream mixture, then roll them up and place them, seam side down, in the baking dish.

5. Sprinkle with the cheese, cover with foil and bake for 30 minutes or until bubbly. Spoon the salsa in a strip down the center and sprinkle the salsa with the tomato. Garnish with the sprigs of cilantro, if you wish. Serve hot!   *Makes 8 servings*

Chicken Enchiladas

2 SPANISH–STYLE CHICKEN & RICE

2 tablespoons olive or vegetable oil
1 clove garlic, finely chopped
1 cup uncooked regular rice
1 envelope LIPTON® Recipe Secrets®
    Onion Soup Mix
2½ cups hot water
1 cup frozen peas, partially thawed
½ cup chopped red or green bell pepper
8 green olives, sliced
1 chicken (2½ to 3 pounds), cut into
    serving pieces

Preheat oven to 400°F.

In 13×9-inch baking or roasting pan, combine oil with garlic; heat in oven 5 minutes. Stir in uncooked rice until coated with oil. Add onion soup mix blended with hot water; stir in peas, pepper and olives. Press chicken pieces into rice mixture. Bake 35 minutes or until chicken is done and rice is tender. Cover and let stand 10 minutes before serving.   *Makes about 4 servings*

MENU SUGGESTION: Serve with cooked green beans and fresh fruit for dessert.

Chicken in French Onion Sauce

3 CHICKEN IN FRENCH ONION SAUCE

1 package (10 ounces) frozen baby
   carrots, thawed and drained, *or*
   4 medium carrots, cut into strips
   (about 2 cups)
2 cups sliced mushrooms
½ cup thinly sliced celery
1 can (2.8 ounces) FRENCH'S® French
   Fried Onions
4 chicken breast halves, skinned and
   boned
½ cup white wine
¾ cup prepared chicken bouillon
½ teaspoon garlic salt
½ teaspoon pepper
   Paprika

Preheat oven to 375°F. In 12×8-inch baking dish, combine vegetables and *½ can* French Fried Onions. Arrange chicken breasts on vegetables. In small bowl, combine wine, bouillon, garlic salt and pepper; pour over chicken and vegetables. Sprinkle chicken with paprika. Bake, covered, at 375°F for 35 minutes or until chicken is done. Baste chicken with wine sauce and top with remaining onions. Bake, uncovered, 3 minutes or until onions are golden brown.

Makes 4 servings

MICROWAVE DIRECTIONS: In 12×8-inch microwave-safe dish, combine vegetables and *½ can* onions. Arrange chicken breasts, skinned side down, along sides of dish. Prepare wine mixture as above, except reduce bouillon to ⅓ cup; pour over chicken and vegetables. Cook, covered, on HIGH 6 minutes. Turn chicken breasts over and sprinkle with paprika. Stir vegetables and rotate dish. Cook, covered, 7 to 9 minutes or until chicken is done. Baste chicken with wine sauce and top with remaining onions; cook, uncovered, 1 minute. Let stand 5 minutes.

4 INDIVIDUAL CHICKEN RICE CASSEROLES

1 bag SUCCESS® Rice
4 tablespoons reduced-calorie margarine,
   divided
½ pound fresh mushrooms, sliced
1 cup pasteurized process cheese cubes
1 cup evaporated skim milk
1 teaspoon white wine Worcestershire
   sauce
½ teaspoon salt
½ teaspoon white pepper
1½ cups chopped cooked chicken
1 package (10 ounces) frozen peas,
   thawed and drained
½ cup fresh bread crumbs

Prepare rice according to package directions.

Preheat oven to 350°F.

Add 2 tablespoons margarine to hot rice; mix lightly until margarine is melted. Melt remaining 2 tablespoons margarine in medium skillet. Add mushrooms; cook and stir until tender. Set aside. Combine cheese, milk, Worcestershire sauce, salt and pepper in medium saucepan. Cook, stirring constantly, over medium heat until cheese is melted. Remove from heat.

Layer half of rice in bottoms of six individual casseroles; cover with layers of chicken, mushrooms and peas. Top with remaining rice and cheese sauce; sprinkle with bread crumbs. Bake until hot and bubbly, 15 to 20 minutes. *Makes 6 servings*

5 SAVORY CHICKEN & BISCUITS

2 tablespoons olive or vegetable oil
1 pound boneless skinless chicken breasts, cut into 1-inch pieces (about 2 cups)
1 medium onion, chopped
1 cup thinly sliced carrots
1 cup thinly sliced celery
1 envelope LIPTON® Recipe Secrets® Savory Herb with Garlic Soup Mix
1 cup milk
1 package (10 ounces) refrigerated flaky buttermilk biscuits

Preheat oven to 400°F.

In 12-inch skillet, heat oil over medium-high heat and cook chicken, stirring occasionally, 5 minutes or until almost done. Stir in onion, carrots and celery; cook, stirring occasionally, 3 minutes. Stir in savory herb with garlic soup mix blended with milk. Bring to a boil over medium-high heat, stirring occasionally; cook 1 minute. Turn into lightly greased 2-quart casserole; arrange biscuits on top of chicken mixture with edges touching. Bake 10 minutes or until biscuits are golden brown.   *Makes about 4 servings*

MENU SUGGESTION: Serve with a mixed green salad and LIPTON® Iced Tea.

NOTE: Also terrific with LIPTON® Recipe Secrets® Golden Onion or Golden Herb with Lemon Soup Mix.

Savory Chicken & Biscuits

6 FANCY CHICKEN PUFF PIE

4 tablespoons butter or margarine
1/4 cup chopped shallots
1/4 cup all-purpose flour
1 cup chicken broth or stock
1/4 cup sherry
    Salt to taste
1/8 teaspoon white pepper
    Pinch ground nutmeg
1/4 pound ham, cut into 2×1/4-inch strips
3 cups cooked PERDUE® chicken, cut into 2 1/4-inch strips
1 1/2 cups coarsely chopped fresh asparagus *or* 1 (10-ounce) package frozen asparagus pieces
1 cup (1/2 pint) heavy cream
    Chilled pie crust for a 1-crust pie *or* 1 sheet frozen puff pastry
1 egg, beaten

In medium saucepan, melt butter over medium-high heat. Add shallots; cook and stir until tender. Stir in flour; cook 3 minutes, stirring constantly. Add broth and sherry. Heat to boiling, stirring constantly; season with salt, pepper and nutmeg. Reduce heat to low; simmer 5 minutes, stirring occasionally. Stir in ham, chicken, asparagus and cream. Pour chicken mixture into ungreased 9-inch pie plate.

Preheat oven to 425°F. Cut 8-inch circle from crust. Cut hearts from extra dough with cookie cutter, if desired. Place circle on cookie sheet moistened with cold water; pierce with fork. Brush with egg. Decorate pastry with hearts; brush hearts with egg.

Bake crust and filled pie plate 10 minutes. Reduce heat to 350°F. Bake additional 10 to 15 minutes or until pastry is golden brown and filling is hot and set. With spatula, place pastry over hot filling and serve immediately.
        Makes 4 servings

CHICKEN & TURKEY FAVORITES

7 DAIRYLAND CONFETTI CHICKEN

1 cup diced carrots
¾ cup chopped onion
½ cup diced celery
¼ cup chicken broth
1 can (10½ ounces) cream of chicken soup
1 cup dairy sour cream
3 cups cubed cooked chicken
½ cup (4 ounces) sliced mushrooms
1 teaspoon Worcestershire sauce
1 teaspoon salt
⅛ teaspoon pepper
Confetti Topping (recipe follows)
¼ cup (1 ounce) shredded Wisconsin Cheddar cheese

For casserole: In saucepan, combine carrots, onion, celery and chicken broth. Simmer 20 minutes. In 3-quart casserole, mix soup, sour cream, chicken cubes, mushrooms, Worcestershire sauce, salt and pepper. Add simmered vegetables and liquid; mix well. Prepare Confetti Topping. Drop tablespoons of topping onto casserole. Bake in 350°F oven for 40 to 45 minutes or until golden brown. Sprinkle with cheese and return to oven until melted. Garnish as desired.   *Makes 6 to 8 servings*

CONFETTI TOPPING
1 cup sifted all-purpose flour
2 teaspoons baking powder
½ teaspoon salt
2 eggs, slightly beaten
½ cup milk
1 tablespoon chopped green bell pepper
1 tablespoon chopped pimiento
1 cup (4 ounces) shredded Wisconsin Cheddar cheese

In mixing bowl, combine flour, baking powder and salt. Add eggs, milk, green pepper, pimiento and cheese; mix just until well blended.

Favorite recipe from **Wisconsin Milk Marketing Board**

8 BROWN RICE CHICKEN BAKE

Vegetable cooking spray
3 cups cooked brown rice
1 package (10 ounces) frozen green peas
2 cups chopped cooked chicken breasts
½ cup cholesterol-free, reduced-calorie mayonnaise
⅓ cup slivered almonds, toasted (optional)
2 teaspoons soy sauce
¼ teaspoon ground black pepper
¼ teaspoon garlic powder
¼ teaspoon dried tarragon leaves

Spray 3-quart baking casserole with nonstick cooking spray. Combine rice, peas, chicken, mayonnaise, almonds, soy sauce, and seasonings in large bowl; mix well. Spoon into prepared casserole; cover. Bake at 350°F for 15 to 20 minutes or until heated through.   *Makes 6 servings*

Favorite recipe from **USA Rice Council**

Dairyland Confetti Chicken

CHICKEN & TURKEY FAVORITES

9 LATTICE–TOP CHICKEN

1 can (10¾ ounces) condensed cream of potato soup
1¼ cups milk
½ teaspoon seasoned salt
1½ cups (7 ounces) cubed cooked chicken
1 bag (16 ounces) frozen vegetable combination (broccoli, carrots, cauliflower), thawed and drained
1 cup (4 ounces) shredded Cheddar cheese
1 can (2.8 ounces) FRENCH'S® Fried Onions
1 cup biscuit baking mix*
¼ cup milk
1 egg, slightly beaten

*1 package (4 ounces) refrigerated crescent rolls may be substituted for baking mix, ¼ cup milk and egg. Separate dough into 2 rectangles; press together perforated cuts. Cut each rectangle lengthwise into 3 strips. Arrange strips on hot chicken mixture to form lattice. Top as directed. Bake, uncovered, at 375°F for 15 to 20 minutes or until lattice is golden brown.

Preheat oven to 375°F. In large bowl, combine soup, 1¼ cups milk, seasoned salt, chicken, vegetables, ½ cup cheese and ½ can French Fried Onions. Pour into 12×8-inch baking dish. Bake, covered, at 375°F for 15 minutes. Meanwhile, in small bowl, combine baking mix, ¼ cup milk and egg to form soft dough. Stir casserole and spoon dough over hot chicken mixture to form lattice design. Bake, uncovered, 20 to 25 minutes or until lattice is golden brown. Top lattice with remaining cheese and onions; bake, uncovered, 3 minutes or until onions are golden brown.

Makes 4 to 6 servings

MICROWAVE DIRECTIONS: Prepare chicken mixture as directed; pour into 12×8-inch microwave-safe dish. Cook, covered, on HIGH 10 minutes or until heated through, stirring chicken mixture halfway through cooking time. Prepare biscuit dough and spoon over casserole as directed. Cook, uncovered, 7 to 9 minutes or until lattice crust is done in center, rotating dish halfway through cooking time. Top lattice with remaining cheese and onions; cook, uncovered, 1 minute or until cheese melts. Let stand 5 minutes.

10 OVEN CHICKEN & RICE

1 package (4.3 ounces) RICE-A-RONI® Long Grain & Wild Rice Pilaf
4 bone-in chicken breast halves
½ teaspoon dried thyme leaves *or* dried basil
¼ teaspoon garlic powder
1 tablespoon margarine or butter, melted
½ teaspoon paprika
1 cup chopped tomato or red bell pepper

1. Heat oven to 375°F. In 11×7-inch glass baking dish or 1½-quart casserole, combine 1¼ cups water, rice and contents of seasoning packet; mix well.

2. Place chicken over rice. Sprinkle evenly with thyme and garlic powder. Brush with margarine; sprinkle with paprika.

3. Cover with foil; bake 45 minutes. Stir in tomato. Bake, uncovered, 15 minutes or until liquid is absorbed and chicken is no longer pink inside. *Makes 4 servings*

Microwaved Garlic and Herb Chicken

11 MICROWAVED GARLIC AND HERB CHICKEN

8 broiler-fryer chicken thighs
   (about 2 pounds)
½ cup olive oil
1 large tomato, chopped
1 rib celery, thinly sliced
2 tablespoons parsley flakes
6 cloves garlic, chopped
1 teaspoon salt
½ teaspoon ground black pepper
½ teaspoon dried oregano leaves
¼ teaspoon dried basil leaves
⅛ teaspoon ground nutmeg

Microwave Directions: In 1½-quart microwave-safe baking dish, mix together olive oil, tomato, celery, parsley, garlic, salt, pepper, oregano, basil and nutmeg. Microwave on HIGH 3 minutes; stir. Add chicken; mix well. Cover; refrigerate 3 hours or overnight. Cover baking dish with waxed paper; microwave on HIGH 10 minutes. Turn chicken over; cover again with waxed paper. Microwave on HIGH 10 minutes or until chicken is no longer pink in center. Let stand 5 minutes. Remove garlic; discard. Spoon sauce over chicken.   *Makes 4 servings*

Favorite recipe from **National Broiler Council**

12 CHICKEN À LA BOURGUIGNONNE

4 pounds skinless chicken thighs and
   breasts
Flour
Nonstick cooking spray
2 cups defatted low sodium chicken broth
2 cups dry white wine or defatted low
   sodium chicken broth
1 pound whole baby carrots
¼ cup tomato paste
4 cloves garlic, minced
½ teaspoon dried thyme leaves
2 bay leaves
¼ teaspoon salt
¼ teaspoon pepper
8 ounces fresh or thawed frozen pearl
   onions
8 ounces whole medium mushrooms
2 cups hot cooked white rice
2 cups hot cooked wild rice
¼ cup minced fresh parsley

Preheat oven to 325°F. Coat chicken very
lightly with flour. Generously spray nonstick
ovenproof Dutch oven or large nonstick
ovenproof skillet with cooking spray; heat
over medium heat until hot. Add chicken;
cook 10 to 15 minutes or until browned on
all sides. Drain fat from Dutch oven.

Add chicken broth, wine, carrots, tomato
paste, garlic, thyme, bay leaves, salt and
pepper to Dutch oven; heat to a boil. Cover;
transfer to oven. Bake 1 hour. Add onions
and mushrooms. Uncover; bake about
35 minutes or until vegetables are tender
and chicken is no longer pink in center and
juices run clear. Remove bay leaves.
Combine white and wild rice; serve with
chicken. Sprinkle with parsley.

Makes 8 servings

Chicken à la Bourguignonne

13 CHICKEN POT PIE

2 tablespoons butter or margarine
1 pound boneless skinless chicken thighs,
  cut into 1-inch pieces (about 2 cups)*
2 ribs celery, sliced
2 carrots, cut lengthwise in half and sliced
1 medium onion, diced
1 cup frozen cut green beans, thawed
1 envelope LIPTON® Recipe Secrets®
  Savory Herb with Garlic or Golden
  Onion Soup Mix
1 cup milk
1 refrigerated pie crust or pastry for
  single-crust pie

*Use 2 cups cut-up cooked chicken or turkey and
eliminate melting butter and cooking chicken.*

Preheat oven to 400°F.

In 10-inch skillet, melt butter over medium-high heat and cook chicken, stirring frequently, 8 minutes or until done. With slotted spoon, remove chicken to 9-inch pie plate. Into skillet, stir celery, carrots and onion; cook 8 minutes. Stir in green beans and savory herb with garlic soup mix blended with milk; bring to a boil over medium-high heat. Turn into pie plate with chicken; top with crust and seal edges tightly. Pierce crust with fork. Bake 25 minutes or until golden. Let stand 10 minutes before serving.

Makes about 4 servings

MENU SUGGESTION: Serve with your favorite LIPTON® Soup and LIPTON® Iced Tea.

14 TORTILLA CHICKEN BAKE

1 can (14½ ounces) DEL MONTE® FRESH CUT™ Diced Tomatoes, undrained
½ cup chopped onion
2 cloves garlic, crushed
½ teaspoon dried oregano, crushed
1 to 2 teaspoons chili powder
½ pound boneless chicken, skinned and cut into strips
4 cups tortilla chips
¾ cup shredded Monterey Jack cheese with jalapeño peppers or Cheddar cheese

1. Preheat oven to 375°F.

2. Drain tomatoes reserving liquid.

3. In large skillet, combine reserved liquid, onion, garlic, oregano and chili powder; boil 5 minutes, stirring occasionally.

4. Stir in tomatoes and chicken; cook over medium heat until chicken is no longer pink, about 3 minutes.

5. In shallow 2-quart baking dish, layer half of chips, chicken mixture and cheese; repeat layers ending with cheese. Cover and bake 15 minutes or until heated through. Serve with sour cream, if desired.

Makes 4 servings

Prep Time: 3 minutes
Cook Time: 25 minutes

15 CHICKEN FIESTA

2½ to 3 pounds chicken pieces
   Salt
   Pepper
   Paprika
 2 tablespoons butter or margarine
¼ pound pork sausage
¾ cup sliced celery
¾ cup sliced green onions with tops
3 cups cooked rice
1 can (12 ounces) whole kernel corn with
   peppers, drained
2 teaspoons lemon juice

Preheat oven to 350°F.

Season chicken with salt, pepper and paprika. In large skillet, melt butter. Add chicken to skillet; brown well. Drain chicken on paper towels; set aside. Cook sausage, celery and onions in same skillet over medium-high heat, stirring frequently, until vegetables are crisp-tender. Add rice, corn and lemon juice; mix well. Pour into prepared shallow baking dish. Arrange chicken on top of rice mixture, pressing chicken slightly into rice mixture. Cover with foil. Bake 30 to 40 minutes or until chicken is no longer pink in center.

Makes 6 servings

Favorite recipe from **USA Rice Council**

16 HEARTY CHICKEN BAKE

3 cups hot mashed potatoes
1 cup (4 ounces) shredded Cheddar
   cheese
1 can (2.8 ounces) FRENCH'S® French
   Fried Onions
1½ cups (7 ounces) cubed cooked chicken
1 package (10 ounces) frozen mixed
   vegetables, thawed and drained
1 can (10¾ ounces) condensed cream of
   chicken soup
¼ cup milk
½ teaspoon ground mustard
¼ teaspoon garlic powder
¼ teaspoon pepper

Preheat oven to 375°F. In medium bowl, combine mashed potatoes, *½ cup* cheese and *½ can* French Fried Onions; mix thoroughly. Spoon potato mixture into greased 1½-quart casserole. Using back of spoon, spread potatoes across bottom and up sides of dish to form a shell. In large bowl, combine chicken, mixed vegetables, soup, milk and seasonings; pour into potato shell. Bake, uncovered, at 375°F for 30 minutes or until heated through. Top with remaining cheese and onions; bake, uncovered, 3 minutes or until onions are golden brown. Let stand 5 minutes before serving.
Makes 4 to 6 servings

Chicken Fiesta

Chicken and Zucchini Casserole

17 CURRIED CHICKEN POT PIE

2 cups (10 ounces) cubed cooked chicken
1 bag (16 ounces) frozen vegetable combination (cauliflower, carrots, broccoli), thawed and drained
1 can (2.8 ounces) FRENCH'S® French Fried Onions
1 cup (4 ounces) shredded Cheddar cheese
1 can (10¾ ounces) condensed cream of chicken soup
⅔ cup milk
½ teaspoon seasoned salt
¼ teaspoon curry powder
1 (9-inch) folded refrigerated unbaked pie crust

Preheat oven to 400°F. In 9-inch pie plate, combine chicken, vegetables, *½ can* French Fried Onions and *½ cup* cheese. In small bowl, combine soup, milk and seasonings; pour over chicken mixture and stir to combine. Place pie crust over chicken mixture; seal edges and cut 4 steam vents. Bake, uncovered, at 400°F for 40 minutes or until crust is golden brown. Top with remaining cheese and onions; bake, uncovered, 1 to 3 minutes or until onions are golden brown. *Makes 4 to 6 servings*

18 CHICKEN AND ZUCCHINI CASSEROLE

1¼ cups hot water
3 tablespoons margarine or butter, divided
3 cups STOVE TOP® Chicken Flavor or Cornbread Stuffing Mix in the Canister
¾ pound boneless skinless chicken breasts, cubed
2 medium zucchini, cut into ½-inch pieces
1½ cups (6 ounces) shredded Cheddar cheese
1 can (8 ounces) water chestnuts, drained, halved (optional)
½ teaspoon dried basil leaves
¼ teaspoon pepper

MIX water and 2 tablespoons of the margarine in large bowl until margarine is melted. Stir in stuffing mix just to moisten.

PLACE chicken, zucchini and remaining 1 tablespoon margarine in 3-quart microwavable casserole. Cover loosely with wax paper.

MICROWAVE on HIGH 4 minutes, stirring halfway through cooking time. Stir in prepared stuffing, cheese, water chestnuts, basil and pepper until well mixed. Cover.

MICROWAVE 10 minutes, stirring halfway through cooking time. Let stand 5 minutes.
Makes 6 servings

Prep Time: 10 minutes
Cook Time: 20 minutes

19 CHICKEN BREASTS FLORENTINE

2 pounds boneless skinless chicken breasts
¼ cup all-purpose flour
2 eggs, well beaten
⅔ cup seasoned dry bread crumbs
1 envelope LIPTON® Recipe Secrets® Golden Onion Soup Mix
1½ cups water
¼ cup dry white wine
1 clove garlic, finely chopped
2 tablespoons finely chopped fresh parsley
⅛ teaspoon pepper
Hot cooked rice pilaf or white rice
Hot cooked spinach

To Microwave: Dip chicken in flour, then eggs, then bread crumbs. In 3-quart microwave-safe casserole, microwave chicken, uncovered, at HIGH (100% power) 4 minutes, rearranging chicken once. Combine golden onion soup mix, water, wine and garlic in small bowl; add to chicken. Microwave, uncovered, at HIGH 5 minutes or until boiling, stirring once. Microwave, uncovered, at MEDIUM (50% power), stirring occasionally, 7 minutes or until chicken is no longer pink in center and sauce is slightly thickened. Stir in parsley and pepper. Let stand, covered, 5 minutes. To serve, arrange chicken over hot rice and spinach; garnish as desired.
Makes about 6 servings

CHICKEN & TURKEY FAVORITES

20 DOWN–HOME CORN AND CHICKEN CASSEROLE

> 2 chickens (2 to 3 pounds *each*), each cut into 10 pieces
> 3 tablespoons Chef Paul Prudhomme's POULTRY MAGIC®, in all
> 1/3 cup vegetable oil
> 8 cups fresh corn, cut off cob (about twelve 8-inch ears), in all
> 3 1/2 cups finely chopped onions
> 1 1/2 cups finely chopped green bell peppers
> 1 pound tomatoes, peeled, chopped
> 3 1/2 cups chicken stock or water
> 2 cups uncooked rice, preferably converted

Remove excess fat from chickens; season chicken pieces with 2 tablespoons of the Poultry Magic® and place in plastic bag. Seal and refrigerate overnight.

Remove chicken from refrigerator. Heat oil in an 8-quart roasting pan over high heat until it just starts to smoke, about 6 minutes. Add the 10 largest pieces of chicken (skin side down first) and brown, cooking 5 minutes on each side. Remove chicken and reheat oil about 1 minute or until oil stops sizzling. Brown remaining chicken 5 minutes on each side. Remove and keep warm.

Add half of corn to pan. Scrape browned bits from bottom of pan. Let corn cook, without stirring, about 6 minutes. (You want it to brown and to start breaking down starch.) Stir in 1 1/2 teaspoons Poultry Magic®. Let mixture cook, without stirring, about 7 minutes to continue browning process. Stir in onions, bell peppers and remaining 1 1/2 teaspoons Poultry Magic®. Cover with tight-fitting lid; cook about 5 minutes. Stir in remaining corn and tomatoes; cover and cook 10 minutes. Transfer corn mixture to another pan; keep warm.

Preheat oven to 400°F. Add water and rice to roasting pan. Bring to a boil, stirring occasionally. Layer chicken pieces on top of rice and cover chicken layer with corn mixture. Cover and bake 25 minutes. Remove casserole from oven. Let stand 10 minutes, covered, then serve.

Makes 8 servings

21 CHICKEN MEXICANA CASSEROLE

> 2 1/2 pounds boned chicken breasts, skinned and cut into 1-inch cubes
> 2 packages (1.25 ounces *each*) LAWRY'S® Taco Spices & Seasonings
> 2 cans (14 1/2 ounces *each*) whole tomatoes, undrained and cut up
> 3 cups (12 ounces) shredded sharp Cheddar cheese, divided
> 1 can (7 ounces) diced green chiles, undrained
> 1 can (12 ounces) whole kernel corn, drained
> 1 package (8 1/4 ounces) corn muffin mix
> 2 eggs
> 1/4 cup dairy sour cream

In large bowl, toss chicken cubes with Taco Spices & Seasonings and tomatoes; blend well. Add 1 cup cheese. Spread mixture evenly into 13×9-inch baking dish. Spoon chiles over chicken mixture; sprinkle with remaining cheese. Set aside. In medium bowl, combine remaining ingredients; blend well. Drop by rounded spoonfuls on top of casserole, spacing evenly. Bake in 350°F oven 50 to 60 minutes or until top is lightly browned and sauce is bubbly. Remove from oven and let stand about 20 minutes before serving. *Makes 10 to 12 servings*

Down-Home Corn and Chicken Casserole

22 CHICKEN BISCUIT BAKE

BASE
- 1 tablespoon CRISCO® Vegetable Oil
- 1 cup chopped onion
- ¼ cup all-purpose flour
- ½ teaspoon salt
- ¼ teaspoon pepper
- ¼ teaspoon dried basil leaves
- ¼ teaspoon dried thyme leaves
- 2½ cups skim milk
- 1 tablespoon Worcestershire sauce
- 1 chicken flavor bouillon cube *or*
    - 1 teaspoon chicken flavor bouillon granules
- 2 cups chopped cooked chicken
- 1 bag (16 ounces) frozen mixed vegetables
- 2 tablespoons grated Parmesan cheese

BISCUITS
- 1 cup all-purpose flour
- 1 tablespoon sugar
- 1½ teaspoons baking powder
- 1 tablespoon chopped fresh parsley
- ⅛ teaspoon salt
- ⅓ cup skim milk
- 3 tablespoons CRISCO® Vegetable Oil

1. Heat oven to 375°F.

2. For base, heat Crisco® Oil in large saucepan on medium-high heat. Add onion. Cook and stir until tender. Remove from heat. Stir in flour, salt, pepper, basil and thyme. Add milk, Worcestershire sauce and bouillon cube. Return to medium-high heat. Cook and stir until mixture comes to a boil and is thickened. Stir in chicken, vegetables and cheese. Heat thoroughly, stirring occasionally. Pour into 2-quart casserole.

3. For biscuits, combine flour, sugar, baking powder, parsley and salt in medium bowl. Add milk and Crisco® Oil. Stir with fork until dry ingredients are just moistened.

4. Drop dough by well-rounded measuring tablespoonfuls onto hot chicken mixture to form 8 biscuits.

5. Bake at 375°F for 35 to 45 minutes or until chicken mixture is bubbly and biscuits are golden brown.   *Makes 8 servings*

23 "WILDLY" DELICIOUS CASSEROLE

- 1 package (14 ounces) ground chicken
- 1 package (14 ounces) frozen broccoli with red peppers
- 1½ cups cooked wild rice
- 1 can (10¾ ounces) condensed cream of chicken soup
- ½ cup mayonnaise
- ½ cup plain yogurt
- 1 teaspoon lemon juice
- ½ teaspoon curry powder
- ¼ cup dry bread crumbs
- 3 to 4 slices process American cheese, cut in half diagonally

Preheat oven to 375°F. Grease 8-inch square baking dish; set aside. In large skillet, cook chicken until no longer pink, stirring occasionally. Drain; set aside. Cook broccoli and peppers according to package directions; set aside. In large bowl, combine wild rice, soup, mayonnaise, yogurt, lemon juice and curry. Stir in chicken and broccoli and peppers. Pour into prepared baking dish; sprinkle with bread crumbs. Bake 45 to 55 minutes or until heated through, arranging cheese slices on top of casserole during last 5 minutes of baking. Remove from oven; let stand 5 minutes.

Makes 6 to 8 servings

Favorite recipe from **Minnesota Cultivated Wild Rice Council**

24 HOME–STYLE CHICKEN CASSEROLE

2 bags SUCCESS® Rice
Vegetable cooking spray
2 tablespoons olive oil
1 pound skinless, boneless chicken breasts, cut into strips
3 cloves garlic, minced
¾ cup spaghetti sauce
¾ cup prepared brown gravy
½ cup plain nonfat yogurt
¼ cup (1 ounce) grated Parmesan cheese
1 teaspoon dried oregano leaves, crushed
½ teaspoon dried rosemary leaves, crushed
1 teaspoon pepper
1 cup (4 ounces) shredded Mozzarella cheese

Prepare rice according to package directions.

Preheat oven to 350°F.

Spray 1½-quart baking dish with cooking spray; set aside. Heat oil in large skillet. Add chicken and garlic; cook and stir until chicken is no longer pink in center. Add all remaining ingredients *except* rice and Mozzarella cheese; mix lightly. Place rice in bottom of prepared baking dish; cover with chicken mixture. Sprinkle with Mozzarella cheese. Bake until mixture is thoroughly heated and cheese is melted, about 15 minutes. *Makes 8 servings*

Chicken Biscuit Bake

CHICKEN & TURKEY FAVORITES

25 POLYNESIAN CHICKEN AND RICE

1 can (20 ounces) DOLE® Pineapple
    Tidbits or Pineapple Chunks
$\frac{1}{2}$ cup DOLE® Seedless or Golden Raisins
$\frac{1}{2}$ cup sliced DOLE® Green Onions
2 teaspoons finely chopped fresh ginger *or*
    $\frac{1}{2}$ teaspoon ground ginger
1 garlic clove, finely chopped
3 cups cooked white or brown rice
2 cups chopped cooked chicken breast or
    turkey breast
2 tablespoons low-sodium soy sauce

• **Drain** pineapple; reserve 4 tablespoons juice.

• **Heat** 2 tablespoons reserved juice over medium heat in large, nonstick skillet. Add raisins, green onions, ginger and garlic; cook and stir 3 minutes.

• **Stir** in pineapple, rice, chicken, soy sauce and remaining 2 tablespoons juice. Cover; reduce heat to low and cook 5 minutes more or until heated through. Garnish with cherry tomatoes and green onions, if desired.

Makes 4 servings

Prep Time: 20 minutes
Cook Time: 10 minutes

26 FESTIVE CHICKEN AND STUFFING

3 tablespoons margarine or butter, divided
$1\frac{1}{4}$ pounds boneless skinless chicken
    breasts, cut into 1-inch pieces
$1\frac{1}{2}$ cups sliced mushrooms
$1\frac{1}{2}$ cups water
1 medium carrot, shredded
1 small zucchini, shredded
1 tablespoon lemon juice
1 teaspoon dill weed
$\frac{1}{4}$ teaspoon pepper
3 cups STOVE TOP® Chicken Flavor
    Stuffing Mix in the Canister

MELT 1 tablespoon of the margarine in large skillet on medium-high heat. Add chicken and mushrooms; cook and stir until chicken is browned.

STIR in water and remaining 2 tablespoons margarine. Bring to boil. Reduce heat to low; cover and simmer 5 minutes.

STIR in carrot, zucchini, lemon juice, dill and pepper. Stir in stuffing mix just to moisten; cover. Remove from heat. Let stand 5 minutes. *Makes 6 servings*

Prep Time: 15 minutes
Cook Time: 15 minutes

Polynesian Chicken and Rice

27 CHICKEN CACCIATORE

1 pound boneless chicken breasts, cut into strips
1 bag (16 ounces) BIRDS EYE® frozen Farm Fresh Mixtures Broccoli, Cauliflower and Carrots
1 jar (14 ounces) prepared spaghetti sauce
½ cup sliced black olives
¼ cup water
¼ cup grated Parmesan cheese

• Spray large skillet with nonstick cooking spray; cook chicken over medium heat 7 to 10 minutes or until browned, stirring occasionally.

• Add vegetables, spaghetti sauce, olives and water. Cover and cook 10 to 15 minutes or until vegetables are heated through.

• Sprinkle cheese over top before serving. Add salt, pepper and/or garlic powder to taste.   *Makes 4 to 6 servings*

Prep Time: 5 to 10 minutes
Cook Time: 20 to 25 minutes

Paella à la Española

28 PAELLA À LA ESPAÑOLA

2 tablespoons margarine or butter
1¼ to 1½ pounds chicken thighs, skinned
1 package (7.2 ounces) RICE-A-RONI® Rice Pilaf
1 can (14½ or 16 ounces) tomatoes or stewed tomatoes, undrained
½ teaspoon turmeric (optional)
⅛ teaspoon hot pepper sauce or black pepper
8 ounces cooked medium shelled, deveined shrimp
1 cup frozen peas
Lemon wedges

1. In large skillet, melt margarine over medium heat. Add chicken; cook 2 minutes on each side or until browned. Remove from skillet; set aside, reserving drippings. Keep warm.

2. In same skillet, sauté rice-pasta mix in reserved drippings over medium heat until rice is lightly browned. Stir in 1½ cups water, tomatoes, turmeric, hot pepper sauce and contents of seasoning packet. Bring to a boil over high heat; stir in chicken.

3. Cover; reduce heat. Simmer 20 minutes. Stir in shrimp and frozen peas.

4. Cover; continue to simmer 5 to 10 minutes or until liquid is absorbed and rice is tender. Serve with lemon wedges.

Makes 4 servings

29 CHICKEN VEGETABLE SKILLET

8 broiler-fryer chicken thighs, skinned, fat trimmed
¾ teaspoon salt, divided
1 tablespoon vegetable oil
3 medium red-skinned potatoes, cut into ¼-inch slices
1 medium onion, sliced
½ pound fresh mushrooms, sliced
1 large tomato, coarsely chopped
¼ cup chicken broth
¼ cup dry white wine
½ teaspoon dried oregano leaves
¼ teaspoon pepper
1 tablespoon chopped fresh parsley

Sprinkle chicken with ¼ teaspoon salt. Heat oil in large nonstick skillet over medium-high heat. Add chicken and cook, turning once, about 8 minutes or until browned on both sides. Remove chicken from skillet; set aside. In same pan, layer potatoes, onion, chicken, mushrooms and tomato.

In 1-cup measure, mix together broth and wine; pour over chicken and vegetables. Sprinkle oregano, remaining ½ teaspoon salt and pepper over chicken. Heat to boiling; cover. Reduce heat to medium-low; cook about 20 minutes or until chicken and vegetables are fork-tender. Sprinkle with parsley before serving.

Makes 4 servings

30 ORANGE GINGER CHICKEN & RICE

1 package (6.9 ounces) RICE-A-RONI® With ⅓ Less Salt Chicken Flavor
1 tablespoon margarine or butter
1 cup orange juice
¾ pound skinless, boneless chicken breasts, cut into thin strips
2 cloves garlic, minced
¼ teaspoon ground ginger
    Dash crushed red pepper flakes (optional)
3 cups broccoli flowerets *or* 1½ cups short, thin carrot strips

1. In large skillet, sauté rice-vermicelli mix and margarine over medium heat, stirring frequently, until vermicelli is golden brown.

2. Stir in 1½ cups water, orange juice, chicken, garlic, ginger, red pepper flakes and contents of seasoning packet; bring to a boil over high heat.

3. Cover; reduce heat. Simmer 10 minutes.

4. Stir in broccoli.

5. Cover; continue to simmer 5 to 10 minutes or until liquid is absorbed and rice is tender.   *Makes 4 servings*

31 PAELLA

1 tablespoon olive oil
½ pound chicken breast cubes
1 cup uncooked rice*
1 medium onion, chopped
1 clove garlic, minced
1½ cups chicken broth
1 can (8 ounces) stewed tomatoes, chopped, reserving liquid
½ teaspoon paprika
⅛ to ¼ teaspoon ground red pepper
⅛ teaspoon ground saffron
½ pound medium shrimp, peeled and deveined
1 small red pepper, cut into strips
1 small green pepper, cut into strips
½ cup frozen green peas

If using medium-grain rice, use 1¼ cups of broth; if using parboiled rice, use 1¾ cups of broth.

Heat oil in Dutch oven over medium-high heat until hot. Add chicken; cook, stirring ocasionally, until browned. Add rice, onion, and garlic. Cook, stirring occasionally, until onion is tender and rice is lightly browned. Add broth, tomatoes, tomato liquid, paprika, ground red pepper, and saffron. Bring to a boil; stir. Reduce heat; cover and simmer 10 minutes. Add shrimp, pepper strips, and peas. Cover and simmer 10 minutes or until rice is tender and liquid is absorbed.

Makes 6 servings

*Favorite Recipe from **USA Rice Council***

Orange Ginger Chicken & Rice

32 CHICKEN PARMESAN

¼ cup seasoned dry bread crumbs
2 tablespoons grated Parmesan cheese
4 boneless skinless chicken breast halves
1 egg, beaten
2 tablespoons oil
1 can (14½ ounces) stewed tomatoes
1 can (8 ounces) tomato sauce
¼ teaspoon dried oregano leaves
1½ cups MINUTE® Original Rice, uncooked
½ cup (2 ounces) shredded mozzarella
     cheese

MIX bread crumbs and Parmesan cheese. Dip chicken in egg, shaking off excess. Coat with crumb mixture.

HEAT oil in large skillet on medium-high heat. Add chicken; brown on both sides until cooked through. Remove from skillet. Drain on paper towels.

STIR tomatoes, tomato sauce and oregano into skillet. Bring to boil.

STIR in rice. Top with chicken. Sprinkle with mozzarella cheese; cover. Remove from heat. Let stand 5 minutes.

Makes 4 servings

Prep Time: 10 minutes
Cook Time: 20 minutes

33 CHICKEN SKILLET SUPPER

1 teaspoon salt
¼ teaspoon pepper
¼ teaspoon ground paprika
⅛ teaspoon garlic powder
1 broiler-fryer chicken (about 3 pounds),
     cut into serving pieces
1 tablespoon vegetable oil
2 tablespoons water
1 medium onion, chopped
1 medium potato, peeled, cut into
     2¼-inch strips
1 tablespoon slivered almonds (optional)
1 can (8 ounces) tomato sauce
1 cup chicken broth
1 teaspoon sugar
1 package (10 ounces) frozen French-cut
     green beans or mixed vegetables

Mix salt, pepper, paprika and garlic powder in small bowl; rub over chicken. Heat oil in large skillet over medium heat; add chicken, skin-side down. Cover and cook 10 minutes. Add water to chicken; cover and cook 30 minutes, turning chicken over every 10 minutes. Remove chicken from skillet; set aside.

Add onion, potato and almonds to pan juices; cook until onion is tender, about 3 minutes. Add tomato sauce, broth and sugar; cook until liquid comes to a boil. Add beans and chicken pieces; cover and cook until beans are tender, about 10 minutes.

Makes 4 to 6 servings

Chicken Skillet Supper

34 SKILLET CHICKEN DIVAN

1 tablespoon oil
1 pound boneless skinless chicken breasts, cut into strips
1 can (10¾ ounces) condensed cream of chicken soup
1 package (10 ounces) frozen broccoli spears, thawed
1 cup water
1 tablespoon dry sherry
1½ cups MINUTE® Original Rice, uncooked
½ cup (2 ounces) shredded Cheddar cheese

HEAT oil in large skillet on medium-high heat. Add chicken; cook and stir until browned.

STIR in soup, broccoli, water and sherry. Bring to boil.

STIR in rice; cover. Remove from heat. Let stand 5 minutes. Stir. Sprinkle with cheese; cover. Let stand 3 minutes or until cheese is melted. *Makes 4 servings*

Prep Time: 5 minutes
Cook Time: 15 minutes

35 ARROZ CON POLLO

1 (3-pound) broiler-fryer chicken, cut up
½ teaspoon ground cumin
1 tablespoon vegetable oil
1 can (14½ ounces) DEL MONTE® FRESH CUT™ Diced Tomatoes, undrained
1 cup uncooked long grain white rice
1 can (14 ounces) chicken broth
1 large onion, thinly sliced
2 cloves garlic, minced
1 to 1½ teaspoons minced jalapeño chile

1. Sprinkle chicken with cumin. Season with salt and pepper, if desired.

2. In 4-quart heavy saucepan, brown chicken in oil over medium-high heat; drain.

3. Drain tomatoes, reserving ⅓ cup liquid. Add reserved liquid, tomatoes and remaining ingredients to saucepan. Cover and cook over low heat about 30 minutes or until chicken is no longer pink in center and rice is tender. *Makes 6 servings*

Prep & Cook Time: 45 minutes

36 LEMON–GARLIC CHICKEN & RICE

4 skinless, boneless chicken breast halves
1 teaspoon paprika
 Salt and pepper (optional)
2 tablespoons margarine or butter
2 cloves garlic, minced
1 package (6.9 ounces) RICE-A-RONI® Chicken Flavor
2 tablespoons lemon juice
1 cup chopped red or green bell pepper
½ teaspoon grated lemon peel

1. Sprinkle chicken with paprika, salt and pepper.

2. In large skillet, melt margarine over medium-high heat. Add chicken and garlic; cook chicken 2 minutes on each side or until browned. Remove chicken from skillet; set aside, reserving drippings. Keep warm.

3. In same skillet, sauté rice-vermicelli mix in reserved drippings over medium heat until vermicelli is golden brown. Stir in 2¼ cups water, lemon juice and contents of seasoning packet. Top rice with chicken; bring to a boil over high heat.

4. Cover; reduce heat. Simmer 10 minutes. Stir in red pepper and lemon peel.

5. Cover; continue to simmer 10 minutes or until liquid is absorbed, rice is tender and chicken is no longer pink inside. *Makes 4 servings*

Arroz con Pollo

37 CHICKEN WALNUT STIR–FRY

SAUCE

⅔ cup chicken broth
1½ tablespoons LA CHOY® Soy Sauce
1 tablespoon *each:* cornstarch and dry sherry
½ teaspoon sugar
¼ teaspoon *each:* pepper and Oriental sesame oil

CHICKEN AND VEGETABLES

2 tablespoons cornstarch
2 teaspoons LA CHOY® Soy Sauce
2 teaspoons dry sherry
1 pound boneless skinless chicken breasts, cut into thin 2-inch strips
4 tablespoons WESSON® Oil, divided
2½ cups fresh broccoli flowerettes
1½ teaspoons minced fresh garlic
1 teaspoon minced ginger root
1 (8-ounce) can LA CHOY® Bamboo Shoots, drained
1 cup toasted chopped walnuts
1 (6-ounce) package frozen LA CHOY® Pea Pods, thawed and drained

In small bowl, combine *sauce* ingredients; set aside. In separate small bowl, combine cornstarch, soy sauce and sherry; mix well. Add chicken; toss gently to coat. In large nonstick skillet or wok, heat *3 tablespoons* Wesson® Oil. Add half of chicken mixture; stir-fry until chicken is no longer pink in center. Remove chicken from skillet; set aside. Repeat with remaining chicken mixture. Heat *remaining 1 tablespoon* Wesson® Oil in same skillet. Add broccoli, garlic and ginger; stir-fry until broccoli is crisp-tender. Return chicken mixture to skillet with remaining ingredients; heat through; stir occasionally. Stir sauce; add to skillet. Cook, stirring constantly, until sauce is thick and bubbly. Garnish, if desired.

Makes 4 to 6 servings

38 CHICKEN THIGHS WITH PEAS

8 boneless skinless chicken thighs
2 tablespoons vegetable oil
2 tablespoons low sodium soy sauce
2 tablespoons dry sherry
1 teaspoon ground ginger
1 teaspoon sugar
¼ teaspoon garlic powder
½ small head iceberg lettuce
1 cup ⅓-less-salt chicken broth
2 tablespoons cornstarch
1 package (10 ounces) frozen green peas, partially thawed
Hot cooked rice

• Rinse chicken and pat dry with paper towels. Cut chicken into 1-inch pieces.

• Heat wok over high heat about 1 minute or until hot. Drizzle oil into wok and heat 30 seconds. Add chicken; stir-fry about 4 minutes or until chicken is well browned and no longer pink in center. Reduce heat to low. Stir in soy sauce, sherry, ginger, sugar and garlic powder. Cover and cook 5 minutes.

• Meanwhile, cut lettuce into ½-inch-wide slices. Rinse, drain and pat dry. Stir broth into cornstarch in cup until smooth. Set aside.

• Increase heat to high. Stir peas into chicken mixture. Cover and cook about 2 minutes or until heated through. Stir broth mixture into chicken mixture. Heat until sauce boils and thickens. Add lettuce; stir-fry until wilted. Transfer to serving dish. Serve with rice. Garnish, if desired.

Makes 4 to 6 servings

Chicken Walnut Stir-Fry

39 ASPARAGUS CHICKEN

1 pound chicken breast tenders
1 egg white
2 tablespoons cornstarch, divided
5 teaspoons soy sauce, divided
2 teaspoons dry sherry
2 large carrots, peeled
1 green onion with tops
1 package (10 ounces) frozen asparagus, partially thawed
½ cup ⅓-less-salt chicken broth
1 teaspoon sesame oil
3 tablespoons vegetable oil, divided
Hot cooked rice

• Rinse chicken and pat dry with paper towels. Cut each chicken tender crosswise in half. Combine egg white, 1 tablespoon cornstarch, 2 teaspoons soy sauce and sherry in large bowl; stir until smooth. Add chicken and toss to coat; set aside.

• Slice carrots crosswise into 2-inch lengths. Slice carrot pieces lengthwise; stack slices and cut lengthwise into julienne strips. Cut onion diagonally into ½-inch slices. Cut asparagus spears diagonally into 1½-inch lengths.

• Stir broth, remaining 3 teaspoons soy sauce and sesame oil into remaining 1 tablespoon cornstarch in cup until smooth. Set aside.

• Heat wok over high heat about 1 minute or until hot. Drizzle 2 tablespoons vegetable oil into wok and heat 30 seconds. Add chicken; stir-fry about 4 minutes or until chicken is no longer pink in center. Remove to medium bowl. Reduce heat to medium.

• Drizzle remaining 1 tablespoon vegetable oil into wok and heat 30 seconds. Add carrots to wok; stir-fry about 3 minutes or until crisp-tender. Add asparagus; stir-fry 1 minute. Stir broth mixture; add to wok. Cook until sauce boils and thickens. Stir in onion, chicken and any accumulated juices to wok; cook until heated through. Serve over rice. *Makes 4 servings*

40 CHICKEN AND VEGETABLES WITH MUSTARD SAUCE

1 pound boneless skinless chicken breasts
1 tablespoon sugar
2 teaspoons cornstarch
2 teaspoons dry mustard
3 tablespoons low-sodium soy sauce
2 tablespoons water
2 tablespoons rice vinegar
2 tablespoons vegetable oil, divided
2 cloves garlic, minced
1 small red bell pepper, cut into strips
½ cup thinly sliced celery
1 small onion, cut into thin wedges
Chinese egg noodles

• Rinse chicken and pat dry with paper towels. Cut chicken into 1-inch pieces; set aside.

CHICKEN & TURKEY FAVORITES

• Combine sugar, cornstarch and mustard in small bowl. Stir soy sauce, water and vinegar into cornstarch mixture until smooth; set aside.

• Heat wok over medium heat 2 minutes or until hot. Drizzle 1 tablespoon oil into wok and heat 30 seconds. Add chicken and garlic; stir-fry 5 to 6 minutes or until chicken is no longer pink in center. Remove chicken to large bowl.

• Drizzle remaining 1 tablespoon oil into wok and heat 30 seconds. Add bell pepper, celery and onion; stir-fry 3 minutes or until vegetables are crisp-tender.

• Stir soy sauce mixture; add to wok. Stir-fry 30 seconds or until sauce boils and thickens.

• Return chicken and any accumulated juices to wok; cook until heated through. Serve with noodles. Garnish, if desired.

Makes 4 servings

Chicken and Vegetables with Mustard Sauce

41 MANDARIN CASHEW CHICKEN

SAUCE
 ½ cup syrup, reserved from mandarin
   oranges (see below)
 ¼ cup chicken broth
 2 tablespoons sugar
1½ tablespoons LA CHOY® Soy Sauce
1½ tablespoons cornstarch
 1 teaspoon rice vinegar

CHICKEN AND VEGETABLES
 1 tablespoon LA CHOY® Soy Sauce
 1 tablespoon cornstarch
1½ pounds boneless skinless chicken
   breasts, cut into thin 2-inch strips
 4 tablespoons WESSON® Oil, divided
 2 cups fresh broccoli flowerettes
 1 teaspoon *each:* minced fresh garlic and
   ginger root
 1 (8-ounce) can LA CHOY® Sliced Water
   Chestnuts, drained
 4 green onions, diagonally sliced
 1 (11-ounce) can mandarin orange slices,
   syrup drained and reserved for sauce
 1 cup roasted cashews

In small bowl, combine *sauce* ingredients;
set aside. In medium bowl, combine soy
sauce and cornstarch; mix well. Add
chicken; toss gently to coat. In large
nonstick skillet or wok, heat *3 tablespoons*
oil. Add half of chicken mixture; stir-fry until
chicken is no longer pink in center. Remove
chicken from skillet; set aside. Repeat with
remaining chicken mixture. Heat *remaining
1 tablespoon* oil in same skillet. Add
broccoli, garlic and ginger; stir-fry 2 minutes.
Stir sauce; add to skillet with water
chestnuts and green onions. Cook, stirring
constantly, until sauce is thick and bubbly.
Return chicken to skillet with orange slices
and cashews; heat thoroughly, stirring
occasionally.   *Makes 6 servings*

42 COUNTRY CHICKEN STEW

 2 tablespoons butter or margarine
 1 pound boneless skinless chicken breasts,
   cut into 1-inch cubes
 ½ pound small red potatoes, cut into
   ½-inch cubes
 2 tablespoons cooking sherry
 2 jars (12 ounces *each*) golden chicken
   gravy
 1 bag (16 ounces) BIRDS EYE® frozen
   Farm Fresh Mixtures Broccoli, Green
   Beans, Pearl Onions and Red Peppers
 ½ cup water

• Melt butter in large saucepan over high
heat. Add chicken and potatoes; cook about
8 minutes or until browned, stirring
frequently.

• Add sherry; cook until evaporated. Add
gravy, vegetables and water.

• Bring to boil; reduce heat to medium-low.
Cover and cook 5 minutes.
          Makes 4 to 6 servings

Prep Time: 5 minutes
Cook Time: 20 minutes

Country Chicken Stew

43 TEX–MEX CHICKEN & RICE CHILI

1 package (6.8 ounces) RICE-A-RONI® Spanish Rice
2 cups chopped cooked chicken or turkey
1 can (15 or 16 ounces) kidney beans or pinto beans, rinsed and drained
1 can (14½ or 16 ounces) tomatoes or stewed tomatoes, undrained
1 medium green bell pepper, cut into ½-inch pieces
1½ teaspoons chili powder
1 teaspoon ground cumin
½ cup (2 ounces) shredded Cheddar or Monterey Jack cheese (optional)
Sour cream (optional)
Chopped cilantro (optional)

1. In 3-quart saucepan, combine rice-vermicelli mix, contents of seasoning packet, 2¾ cups water, chicken, beans, tomatoes, green pepper, chili powder and cumin. Bring to a boil over high heat.

2. Reduce heat to low; simmer, uncovered, about 20 minutes or until rice is tender, stirring occasionally.

3. Top with cheese, sour cream and cilantro, if desired. *Makes 4 servings*

Tex-Mex Chicken & Rice Chili

CHICKEN & TURKEY FAVORITES

44 DIJON ROASTED VEGETABLE SOUP

2 plum tomatoes, halved
1 medium zucchini, split lengthwise and halved
1 large onion, quartered
1 red bell pepper, sliced
1 cup sliced carrots
2 to 3 cloves garlic
5 cups COLLEGE INN® Chicken Broth or Lower Sodium Chicken Broth
¼ teaspoon ground cumin
¼ teaspoon crushed red pepper flakes
2 cups diced cooked chicken (about 10 ounces)
½ cup GREY POUPON® Dijon Mustard
¼ cup chopped fresh parsley

On large baking sheet, arrange tomatoes, zucchini, onion, bell pepper, carrots and garlic. Bake at 325°F for 30 to 45 minutes or until golden and tender. Remove from oven and cool. Chop vegetables.

In 3-quart pot, over high heat, heat chicken broth, chopped vegetables, cumin and red pepper flakes to a boil; reduce heat. Simmer for 5 minutes. Stir in chicken and mustard; cook for 5 minutes more. Stir in parsley and serve warm.   *Makes 8 servings*

45 CAJUN CHILI

6 ounces spicy sausage links, sliced
4 boneless chicken thighs, skinned and cut into cubes
1 medium onion, chopped
⅛ teaspoon cayenne pepper
1 can (15 ounces) black-eyed peas or kidney beans, drained
1 can (14½ ounces) DEL MONTE® FRESH CUT™ Diced Tomatoes with Garlic & Onion, undrained
1 medium green pepper, chopped

1. In large skillet, lightly brown sausage over medium-high heat. Add chicken, onion and cayenne pepper; cook until browned. Drain.

2. Stir in remaining ingredients. Cook 5 minutes, stirring occasionally.
Makes 4 servings

Prep & Cook Time: 20 minutes

CHICKEN & TURKEY FAVORITES

46 RICE LASAGNA

1 bag SUCCESS® Rice
  Vegetable cooking spray
2 tablespoons margarine
1 pound ground turkey
1 cup chopped onion
1 cup sliced fresh mushrooms
1 clove garlic, minced
2 cans (8 ounces *each*) tomato sauce
1 can (6 ounces) tomato paste
1 teaspoon dried oregano leaves, crushed
1 carton (15 ounces) lowfat cottage
  cheese
1/2 cup (2 ounces) grated Parmesan cheese
2 cups (8 ounces) shredded Mozzarella
  cheese
1 tablespoon dried parsley flakes

Prepare rice according to package directions.

Preheat oven to 350°F.

Spray 13×9-inch baking dish with cooking spray; set aside. Melt margarine in large skillet over medium heat. Add ground turkey, onion, mushrooms and garlic; cook until turkey is no longer pink and vegetables are tender, stirring occasionally to separate turkey. Drain. Stir in tomato sauce, tomato paste and oregano; simmer 15 minutes, stirring occasionally. Layer half *each* of rice, turkey mixture, cottage cheese, Parmesan cheese and Mozzarella cheese in prepared baking dish; repeat layers. Sprinkle with parsley; cover. Bake 30 minutes. Uncover; continue baking 15 minutes.

Makes 8 servings

47 MEXICAN TURKEY LASAGNA

1 pound GROUND TURKEY
1 cup onion, chopped
1/2 cup green pepper, chopped
2 cloves garlic, minced
1 can (15 ounces) tomato sauce
1 jar (12 ounces) salsa
1 teaspoon ground cumin
6 flour tortillas
1 cup sliced green onions
2 cups (8 ounces) shredded reduced-fat
  Monterey Jack cheese with jalapeño
  peppers
1 can (4 ounces) ripe olives, sliced

1. In large skillet over medium-high heat, cook turkey, onion, green pepper and garlic 5 minutes or until turkey is no longer pink. Add tomato sauce, salsa and cumin. Bring to boil. Reduce heat to low; cover and simmer 10 minutes.

2. Spray 13×9-inch baking dish with vegetable cooking spray. Spoon 1 cup sauce onto bottom of prepared dish; top with 2 tortillas. Cut additional 2 tortillas into quarters; place in corners of dish. Cover with 1/2 of remaining sauce; sprinkle with 1/2 *each* of the green onions, cheese and olives. Top with remaining tortillas, sauce, onions and olives. Cover with foil.

3. Bake at 350°F for 30 minutes. Remove foil. Sprinkle lasagna with remaining 1 cup cheese. Continue baking 15 minutes or until lasagna is bubbly and cheese is melted.

Makes 8 servings

Favorite recipe from **National Turkey Federation**

Rice Lasagna

Turkey Parmesan

48   TURKEY PARMESAN

⅔ **cup milk**
2 **tablespoons margarine or butter**
2 **cups zucchini slices, halved**
1 **package (5.1 ounces) PASTA RONI®**
    Parmesan Sauce with Angel Hair Pasta
2 **cups cooked turkey strips**
1 **jar (2 ounces) chopped pimento, drained**
2 **tablespoons grated Parmesan cheese**

1. In round 3-quart microwavable glass casserole, combine 1½ cups water, milk, margarine and zucchini. Microwave, uncovered, on HIGH 6 minutes.

2. Stir in pasta, contents of seasoning packet and turkey. Separate pasta with a fork, if needed.

3. Microwave, uncovered, on HIGH 7 to 8 minutes, stirring after 2 minutes. Separate pasta with a fork, if needed. Sauce will be very thin, but will thicken upon standing.

4. Stir in pimento and cheese. Let stand 3 to 4 minutes or until desired consistency. Stir before serving.   *Makes 4 servings*

49 TURKEY FLORENTINE SPAGHETTI PIE

8 ounces spaghetti
1 tablespoon low-fat margarine
½ cup plus 2 tablespoons grated Parmesan
    or Romano cheese, divided
1 egg, beaten slightly
    Vegetable cooking spray
1 pound ground turkey
1 tablespoon olive oil
½ cup chopped onion
1 clove garlic, chopped
1 (29-ounce) can tomatoes, undrained,
    coarsely chopped
1 (6-ounce) can tomato paste
1 tablespoon dried Italian seasoning
1 cup fat-free ricotta cheese
1½ teaspoons dried basil leaves *or*
    3 tablespoons fresh basil, chopped
    finely
    Dash of pepper
1 teaspoon dried parsley flakes *or*
    3 tablespoons chopped fresh parsley
1 (10-ounce) package frozen chopped
    spinach, cooked and drained well
¾ cup (3 ounces) shredded low-fat
    mozzarella cheese
1 large or 2 medium fresh tomatoes

Break spaghetti in half; cook according to package directions. Drain well. Stir in margarine, ½ cup Parmesan cheese and egg. Cool about 5 minutes. Place spaghetti mixture in deep-dish 10-inch pie plate that has been coated with cooking spray; press onto bottom and sides of pie plate to form crust. Set aside.

Brown turkey in olive oil in large skillet with onion and garlic, stirring to break meat into small pieces. Add canned tomatoes, tomato paste and Italian seasoning; bring to simmer and cook about 5 minutes, stirring frequently.

Mix ricotta cheese, basil, pepper and parsley flakes in small bowl; spoon into spaghetti crust. Cover with layers of spinach and mozzarella cheese.

Slice fresh tomatoes into ½-inch-thick slices and arrange on top of turkey mixture. Sprinkle with remaining 2 tablespoons Parmesan cheese.

Bake uncovered 350°F 25 minutes or until heated through. *Makes 6 servings*

NOTE: Baked pie can be frozen and reheated in microwave oven or refrigerated up to 3 days.

Favorite recipe from **North Dakota Wheat Commission**

50 TURKEY COTTAGE PIE

¼ cup butter or margarine
¼ cup all-purpose flour
1 envelope LIPTON® Recipe Secrets®
 Golden Onion Soup Mix
2 cups water
2 cups cut-up cooked turkey or chicken
1 package (10 ounces) frozen mixed
 vegetables, thawed
1¼ cups shredded Swiss cheese (about
 5 ounces), divided
⅛ teaspoon pepper
5 cups hot mashed potatoes

Preheat oven to 375°F.

In large saucepan, melt butter and add flour; cook, stirring constantly, 5 minutes or until golden. Stir in golden onion soup mix thoroughly blended with water. Bring to a boil, then simmer 15 minutes or until thickened. Stir in turkey, vegetables, 1 cup cheese and pepper. Turn into lightly greased 2-quart casserole; top with hot potatoes, then remaining ¼ cup cheese. Bake 30 minutes or until bubbling.

Makes about 8 servings

MICROWAVE DIRECTIONS: In 2-quart casserole, heat butter at HIGH (100% power) 1 minute. Stir in flour and heat uncovered, stirring frequently, 2 minutes. Stir in golden onion soup mix thoroughly blended with water. Heat uncovered, stirring occasionally, 4 minutes or until thickened. Stir in turkey, vegetables, 1 cup cheese and pepper. Top with hot potatoes, then remaining ¼ cup cheese. Heat uncovered, turning casserole occasionally, 5 minutes or until bubbling. Let stand uncovered 5 minutes. For additional color, sprinkle, if desired, with paprika.

51 SOUTHWESTERN PUMPKIN STEW

1 cup (1 medium) chopped onion
½ cup (1 large) sliced carrot
1 pound (about 4) boneless, skinless
 chicken breasts, cut into 1-inch pieces
1 tablespoon vegetable oil
1 cup (3 stalks) sliced celery
½ cup (1 small) red bell pepper, cut into
 1-inch pieces
1¾ cups (15 or 16-ounce can) LIBBY'S®
 Solid Pack Pumpkin
1¾ cups (14.5-ounce can) chicken broth
1¼ cups (15-ounce can) hominy
½ cup sour cream
3 tablespoons chopped cilantro
½ teaspoon salt
½ teaspoon ground black pepper
½ teaspoon dried oregano leaves
½ teaspoon ground cumin
⅛ teaspoon ground nutmeg

SAUTÉ onion, carrot and chicken in oil in 3-quart, heavy-duty saucepan over medium-high heat; cook until chicken is no longer pink. Add celery and red pepper; sauté for 3 to 4 minutes or until vegetables are crisp-tender.

STIR in pumpkin, chicken broth, hominy, sour cream, cilantro, salt, black pepper, oregano, cumin and nutmeg; simmer over low heat for 10 to 15 minutes.

Makes 6 to 8 servings

Turkey Cottage Pie

52 HOMESPUN TURKEY 'N' VEGETABLES

1 can (14 ounces) sliced carrots, drained
1 package (9 ounces) frozen cut green
    beans, thawed and drained
1 can (2.8 ounces) FRENCH'S® French
    Fried Onions, divided
1 can (16 ounces) whole potatoes, drained
1 can (10¾ ounces) condensed cream of
    celery soup
¼ cup milk
1 tablespoon FRENCH'S® CLASSIC
    YELLOW® Mustard
¼ teaspoon garlic powder
1 pound uncooked turkey breast slices

Preheat oven to 375°F. In 12×8-inch baking dish, combine carrots, green beans and *½ can* French Fried Onions. Slice potatoes in half; arrange as many halves as will fit, cut-side down, around edges of baking dish. Combine any remaining potatoes with vegetables in dish. In medium bowl, combine soup, milk, mustard and garlic powder; pour half of soup mixture over vegetables. Overlap turkey slices on vegetables. Pour remaining soup mixture over turkey and potatoes. Bake, covered, at 375°F for 40 minutes or until turkey is done. Top turkey with remaining onions; bake, uncovered, 3 minutes or until onions are golden.   *Makes 4 servings*

53 TURKEY WILD RICE SUPREME

2 pounds ground turkey
½ cup butter
1 can (8 ounces) mushrooms, drained
1 cup chopped onions
½ cup chopped celery
½ cup shredded carrots
2 cups sour cream
¼ cup soy sauce
1 teaspoon salt
¼ teaspoon pepper
6 cups cooked wild rice
    (1½ cups uncooked)
½ cup slivered almonds

Preheat oven to 350°F. Grease 3-quart casserole. Set aside.

Cook turkey in large skillet over medium heat, stirring occasionally. Remove turkey from skillet and set aside. Melt butter in same skillet. Add mushrooms, onions, celery and carrots; cook and stir 5 to 10 minutes or until crisp-tender. Combine sour cream, soy sauce, salt and pepper. Add wild rice, turkey, mushroom mixture and almonds. Toss lightly. Place mixture in prepared casserole. Bake 1 hour or until lightly browned, stirring several times during baking and adding more water, if needed. Season with salt and pepper to taste.

Makes 10 to 12 servings

*Favorite recipe from **Minnesota Cultivated Wild Rice Council***

Homespun Turkey 'n' Vegetables

CHICKEN & TURKEY FAVORITES

54 MEXICAN RICE AND TURKEY BAKE

1 bag SUCCESS® Rice
  Vegetable cooking spray
3 cups chopped cooked turkey
1 can (10 ounces) tomatoes with chilies, undrained*
1 can (12 ounces) Mexican-style corn with sweet peppers, drained
1 cup fat-free sour cream
½ cup (2 ounces) shredded low-fat Cheddar cheese

*Or, use 1 can (14½ ounces) stewed tomatoes. Add 1 can (4 ounces) drained chopped mild green chilies.

Prepare rice according to package directions.

Spray 1½-quart microwavesafe casserole with cooking spray; set aside. Combine rice, turkey, tomatoes and corn in large bowl; mix well. Spoon into prepared casserole. Microwave on HIGH until hot and bubbly, 8 to 10 minutes, stirring after 5 minutes. Top with sour cream and cheese.

Makes 6 servings

CONVENTIONAL: Assemble casserole as directed. Spoon into ovenproof 1½-quart casserole sprayed with vegetable cooking spray. Bake at 350°F until thoroughly heated, 15 to 20 minutes. Top with sour cream and cheese.

55 TURKEY–OLIVE RAGOÛT EN CROÛTE

½ pound boneless white or dark TURKEY MEAT, cut into 1-inch cubes
1 clove garlic, minced
1 teaspoon vegetable oil
¼ cup (about 10) small whole frozen onions
½ cup reduced-sodium chicken bouillon or turkey broth
½ teaspoon dried parsley flakes
⅛ teaspoon dried thyme leaves, crumbled
1 small bay leaf
1 medium red potato, skin on, cut into ½-inch cubes
10 frozen snow peas
8 whole small pitted ripe olives
1 can (4 ounces) refrigerated crescent rolls
½ teaspoon dried dill weed, crumbled

1. Preheat oven to 375°F.

2. In medium skillet over medium heat, cook and stir turkey in garlic and oil 3 to 4 minutes or until no longer pink; remove and set aside. Add onions to skillet; cook and stir until lightly browned. Add bouillon, parsley, thyme, bay leaf and potato. Bring mixture to a boil. Reduce heat; cover and simmer 10 minutes or until potato is tender. Remove and discard bay leaf.

3. Combine turkey mixture with potato mixture. Stir in snow peas and olives. Divide mixture between 2 (1¾-cup) individual ovenproof casseroles.

4. Divide crescent rolls into 2 rectangles; press perforations together to seal. If necessary, roll out each rectangle to make dough large enough to cover top of each casserole. Sprinkle dough with dill weed; press lightly into dough.

Turkey-Olive Ragoût en Croûte

5. Cut small decorative shape from each dough piece; discard cutouts or place on baking sheet and bake in oven with casseroles. Place dough over turkey-vegetable mixture in casseroles. Trim dough to fit; press dough to edge of each casserole to seal. Bake 7 to 8 minutes or until pastry is golden brown.

Makes 2 individual deep-dish pies

LATTICE–CRUST VARIATION: With pastry wheel or knife, cut each rectangle lengthwise into 6 strips. Arrange strips, lattice-fashion, over turkey-vegetable mixture; trim dough to fit. Press ends of dough to edge of each casserole to seal.

NOTE: For more golden crust, brush top of dough with beaten egg yolk before baking.

*Favorite recipe from **National Turkey Federation***

56 TURKEY 'N STUFFING PIE

1¼ cups water
¼ cup butter or margarine
3½ cups seasoned stuffing crumbs*
1 can (2.8 ounces) FRENCH'S® French Fried Onions
1 can (10¾ ounces) condensed cream of celery soup
¾ cup milk
1½ cups (7 ounces) cubed cooked turkey
1 package (10 ounces) frozen peas, thawed and drained

*3 cups leftover stuffing may be substituted for butter, water and stuffing crumbs. If stuffing is dry, stir in water, 1 tablespoon at a time, until moist but not wet.

Preheat oven to 350°F. In medium saucepan, heat water and butter; stir until butter melts. Remove from heat. Stir in seasoned stuffing crumbs and ½ can French Fried Onions. Spoon stuffing mixture into 9-inch round or fluted baking dish. Press stuffing evenly across bottom and up sides of dish to form a shell. In medium bowl, combine soup, milk, turkey and peas; pour into stuffing shell. Bake, covered, at 350°F for 30 minutes or until heated through. Top with remaining onions; bake, uncovered, 5 minutes or until onions are golden brown.

Makes 4 to 6 servings

MICROWAVE DIRECTIONS: In 9-inch round or fluted microwave-safe dish, place water and butter. Cook, covered, on HIGH 3 minutes or until butter melts. Stir in stuffing crumbs and ½ can onions. Press stuffing mixture into dish as directed. Reduce milk to ½ cup. In large microwave-safe bowl, combine soup, milk, turkey and peas; cook, covered, 8 minutes. Stir turkey mixture halfway through cooking time. Pour turkey mixture into stuffing shell. Cook, uncovered, 4 to 6 minutes or until heated through, rotating dish halfway through cooking time. Top with remaining onions; cook, uncovered, 1 minute. Let stand 5 minutes.

57 TASTY TURKEY POT PIE

½ cup MIRACLE WHIP® Salad Dressing
2 tablespoons flour
1 teaspoon instant chicken bouillon
⅛ teaspoon pepper
¾ cup milk
1½ cups chopped cooked turkey or chicken
1 (10-ounce) package frozen mixed vegetables, thawed, drained
1 (4-ounce) can refrigerated crescent rolls

• Combine salad dressing, flour, bouillon and pepper in medium saucepan. Gradually add milk.

• Cook, stirring constantly, over low heat until thickened. Add turkey and vegetables; heat thoroughly, stirring occasionally.

• Spoon into 8-inch square baking dish. Unroll dough into two rectangles. Press perforations together to seal. Place rectangles side-by-side to form square; press edges together to form seam. Cover turkey mixture with dough.

• Bake at 375°F 15 to 20 minutes or until browned. *Makes 4 to 6 servings*

Preparation Time: 15 minutes
Baking Time: 20 minutes

Tasty Turkey Pot Pie

CHICKEN & TURKEY FAVORITES

58 ONE–DISH MEAL

2 bags SUCCESS® Rice
   Vegetable cooking spray
1 cup cubed cooked turkey-ham*
1 cup (4 ounces) shredded low-fat
   Cheddar cheese
1 cup peas

*Or, use cooked turkey, ham or turkey franks.

Prepare rice according to package directions.

Spray 1-quart microwavesafe dish with cooking spray; set aside. Place rice in medium bowl. Add ham, cheese and peas; mix lightly. Spoon into prepared dish; smooth into even layer with spoon. Microwave on HIGH 1 minute; stir. Microwave 30 seconds or until thoroughly heated.   *Makes 4 servings*

CONVENTIONAL: Assemble casserole as directed. Spoon into ovenproof 1-quart baking dish sprayed with vegetable cooking spray. Bake at 350°F until thoroughly heated, about 15 to 20 minutes.

One-Dish Meal

CHICKEN & TURKEY FAVORITES

59 CREAMY TURKEY & BROCCOLI

1 package (6 ounces) stuffing mix, plus ingredients to prepare mix*
1 can (2.8 ounces) FRENCH'S® French Fried Onions
1 package (10 ounces) frozen broccoli spears, thawed and drained
1 package (about 1⅛ ounces) cheese sauce mix
1¼ cups milk
½ cup sour cream
2 cups (10 ounces) cubed cooked turkey or chicken

*3 cups leftover stuffing may be substituted for stuffing mix. If stuffing is dry, stir in water, 1 tablespoon at a time, until moist but not wet.

Preheat oven to 350°F. In medium saucepan, prepare stuffing mix according to package directions; stir in ½ can French Fried Onions. Spread stuffing over bottom of greased 9-inch round baking dish. Arrange broccoli spears over stuffing with flowerets around edge of dish. In medium saucepan, prepare cheese sauce mix according to package directions using 1¼ cups milk. Remove from heat; stir in sour cream and turkey. Pour turkey mixture over broccoli, covering stalks only. Bake, covered, at 350°F for 30 minutes or until heated through. Sprinkle remaining onions over turkey; bake, uncovered, 5 minutes or until onions are golden brown.

Makes 4 to 6 servings

MICROWAVE DIRECTIONS: In 9-inch round microwave-safe dish, prepare stuffing mix according to package microwave directions; stir in ½ can onions. Arrange stuffing and broccoli spears in dish as directed; set aside. In medium microwave-safe bowl, prepare cheese sauce mix according to package microwave directions using 1¼ cups milk. Add turkey and cook, covered, 5 to 6 minutes, stirring turkey halfway through cooking time. Stir in sour cream. Pour turkey mixture over broccoli, covering stalks only. Cook, covered, 8 to 10 minutes or until heated through, rotating dish halfway through cooking time. Top turkey with remaining onions; cook, uncovered, 1 minute. Let stand 5 minutes.

60 EASY TURKEY AND RICE

1 bag SUCCESS® Rice
Vegetable cooking spray
1 tablespoon olive oil
½ pound fresh mushrooms, sliced
¾ cup sliced celery
¼ cup chopped green onion
¼ cup chopped red bell pepper
2 cups chopped cooked turkey
1 can (10¾ ounces) condensed cream of chicken soup
½ cup fat-free mayonnaise
½ cup peanuts (optional)

Prepare rice according to package directions.

Preheat oven to 350°F.

Spray 1½-quart casserole with cooking spray; set aside. Heat oil in large skillet over medium heat. Add vegetables; cook and stir until crisp-tender. Add rice and all remaining ingredients *except* peanuts; mix lightly. Spoon into prepared casserole. Bake until thoroughly heated, about 25 minutes. Sprinkle with peanuts. Garnish, if desired.

Makes 4 servings

61 20–MINUTE WHITE BEAN CHILI

1 cup chopped onions
1 clove garlic, minced
1 tablespoon vegetable oil
1 pound ground turkey
1 cup COLLEGE INN® Chicken Broth or Lower Sodium Chicken Broth
1 (14½-ounce) can stewed tomatoes
⅓ cup GREY POUPON® Dijon Mustard
1 tablespoon chili powder
⅛ to ¼ teaspoon ground red pepper
1 (15-ounce) can cannellini beans, drained and rinsed
1 (8-ounce) can corn, drained
Tortilla chips, shredded Cheddar cheese and cilantro, optional

In 3-quart saucepan, over medium-high heat, sauté onions and garlic in oil until tender. Add turkey; cook until done, stirring occasionally to break up meat. Drain. Stir in chicken broth, tomatoes, mustard, chili powder and pepper. Heat to a boil; reduce heat. Simmer for 10 minutes. Stir in beans and corn; cook for 5 minutes. Top with tortilla chips, shredded cheese and cilantro if desired.   *Makes 6 servings*

62 MEXICAN TURKEY RICE

½ cup chopped onion
⅓ cup long-grain rice
1 clove garlic, minced
1 tablespoon olive oil
1 can (16 ounces) low-salt stewed tomatoes, coarsely chopped
½ cup reduced-sodium chicken bouillon
1 teaspoon chili powder
½ teaspoon dried oregano leaves
⅛ teaspoon crushed red pepper
⅓ cup chopped green bell pepper
1 pound Fully-Cooked Oven-Roasted TURKEY BREAST, cut into ¼-inch cubes

1. In large nonstick skillet over medium-high heat, cook and stir onion, rice and garlic in oil 3 to 4 minutes or until rice is lightly browned. Stir in tomatoes, bouillon, chili powder, oregano and crushed red pepper. Bring to a boil. Reduce heat to low; cover and simmer 15 minutes, stiring occasionally.

2. Stir in bell pepper and turkey. Cover; cook 3 to 4 minutes or until mixture is heated through.   *Makes 6 servings*

*Favorite recipe from **National Turkey Federation***

20-Minute White Bean Chili

63 ARIZONA TURKEY STEW

5 medium carrots, cut into thick slices
1 large onion, cut into ½-inch pieces
3 tablespoons olive oil or vegetable oil
1 pound sliced turkey breast, cut into 1-inch strips
1 teaspoon LAWRY'S® Garlic Powder with Parsley
3 tablespoons all-purpose flour
8 small red potatoes, cut into ½-inch cubes
1 package (10 ounces) frozen peas, thawed
8 ounces sliced fresh mushrooms
1 cup beef broth
1 can (8 ounces) tomato sauce
1 package (1.62 ounces) LAWRY'S® Spices & Seasonings for Chili

Preheat oven to 450°F. In large skillet over medium heat, cook and stir carrots and onion in oil until tender. Stir in turkey strips and Garlic Powder with Parsley; cook 3 minutes or until turkey is just browned. Stir in flour. Pour mixture into 3-quart casserole dish. Stir in remaining ingredients. Bake, covered, 40 to 45 minutes or until potatoes are tender and turkey is no longer pink in center. Let stand 5 minutes before serving. *Makes 8 to 10 servings*

STOVETOP DIRECTIONS: Prepare recipe as directed, substituting Dutch oven for skillet and casserole dish. Bring mixture to a boil. Reduce heat; cover and simmer 40 to 45 minutes or until potatoes are tender and turkey is no longer pink in center. Let stand 5 minutes before serving.

HINT: Spoon dollops of prepared dumpling mix on top of casserole during last 15 minutes of baking.

64 TURKEY OLÉ

½ cup minced onions
2 tablespoons butter or margarine
1 tablespoon all-purpose flour
1½ cups cubed cooked turkey
1½ cups prepared HIDDEN VALLEY RANCH® Original Ranch® Salad Dressing
3 ounces rotini (spiral macaroni), plain or spinach
½ (10-ounce) package frozen peas, thawed
⅓ cup canned diced green chiles, drained
⅛ to ¼ teaspoon black pepper (optional)
1 teaspoon dried oregano, crushed
3 tablespoons dry bread crumbs
1 tablespoon butter or margarine, melted
Tomato wedges

Preheat oven to 350°F. In skillet, sauté onions in 2 tablespoons butter until tender. Stir in flour and cook until smooth and bubbly; remove from heat. In 1½-quart casserole, combine turkey, salad dressing, noodles, peas, chiles, pepper and oregano; stir in onion mixture. In small bowl, combine bread crumbs with melted butter; sprinkle over casserole. Bake until heated through and bread crumbs are browned, 15 to 20 minutes. Garnish with tomato wedges. *Makes 6 servings*

Arizona Turkey Stew

Prime-Time Meats

65 COUNTDOWN CASSEROLE

1 jar (8 ounces) pasteurized process cheese spread
¾ cup milk
2 cups (12 ounces) cubed cooked roast beef
1 bag (16 ounces) frozen vegetable combination (broccoli, corn, red pepper), thawed and drained
4 cups frozen hash brown potatoes, thawed
1 can (2.8 ounces) FRENCH'S® French Fried Onions
½ teaspoon seasoned salt
¼ teaspoon freshly ground black pepper
½ cup (2 ounces) shredded Cheddar cheese

Preheat oven to 375°F. Spoon cheese spread into 12×8-inch baking dish; place in oven just until cheese melts, about 5 minutes. Using fork, stir milk into melted cheese until well blended. Stir in beef, vegetables, potatoes, ½ can French Fried Onions and seasonings. Bake, covered, at 375°F 30 minutes or until heated through. Top with Cheddar cheese; sprinkle remaining onions down center. Bake, uncovered, 3 minutes or until onions are golden brown.

Makes 4 to 6 servings

MICROWAVE DIRECTIONS: In 12×8-inch microwave-safe dish, combine cheese spread and milk. Cook, covered, on HIGH 3 minutes; stir. Add ingredients as directed. Cook, covered, 14 minutes or until heated through, stirring beef mixture halfway through cooking time. Top with Cheddar cheese and remaining onions as directed. Cook, uncovered, 1 minute or until cheese melts. Let stand 5 minutes.

Countdown Casserole

66 PATCHWORK CASSEROLE

2 pounds ground beef
2 cups chopped green bell pepper
1 cup chopped onion
2 pounds frozen Southern-style hash-
  brown potatoes, thawed
2 cans (8 ounces *each*) tomato sauce
1 cup water
1 can (6 ounces) tomato paste
1 teaspoon salt
½ teaspoon dried basil, crumbled
¼ teaspoon ground black pepper
1 pound pasteurized process American
  cheese, thinly sliced

Preheat oven to 350°F.

Cook and stir beef in large skillet over medium heat until crumbled and brown, about 10 minutes; drain off fat.

Add green pepper and onion; cook and stir until tender, about 4 minutes. Stir in potatoes, tomato sauce, water, tomato paste, salt, basil and black pepper.

Spoon ½ of mixture into 13×9-inch baking pan or 3-quart baking dish; top with ½ of cheese. Spoon remaining meat mixture evenly on top of cheese. Cover pan with foil. Bake 45 minutes.

Cut remaining cheese into decorative shapes; place on top of casserole. Let stand loosely covered until cheese melts, about 5 minutes.   *Makes 8 to 10 servings*

67 HEARTLAND SHEPHERD'S PIE

¾ pound ground beef
1 medium onion, chopped
1 can (14½ ounces) DEL MONTE®
  Original Recipe Stewed Tomatoes
1 can (8 ounces) DEL MONTE® Tomato
  Sauce
1 can (16 ounces) DEL MONTE® Mixed
  Vegetables, drained
  Instant mashed potato flakes plus
  ingredients to prepare (enough for
  6 servings)
3 cloves garlic, minced

Preheat oven to 375°F. In large skillet, brown meat and onion over medium-high heat; drain. Add tomatoes and tomato sauce; cook over high heat until thickened, stirring frequently. Stir in mixed vegetables. Season with salt and pepper, if desired. Spoon into 2-quart baking dish; set aside. Prepare 6 servings mashed potatoes according to package directions, first cooking garlic in specified amount of butter. Top meat mixture with potatoes. Bake 20 minutes or until heated through. Garnish with chopped parsley, if desired.   *Makes 4 to 6 servings*

Prep Time: 5 minutes
Cook Time: 30 minutes

Patchwork Casserole

68 TEXAS–STYLE DEEP–DISH CHILI PIE

1 pound beef stew meat, cut into ½-inch cubes
1 tablespoon vegetable oil
2 cans (14½ ounces *each*) Mexican-style stewed tomatoes, undrained
1 medium green bell pepper, diced
1 package (1.25 ounces) LAWRY'S® Taco Spices & Seasonings
1 tablespoon yellow cornmeal
1 can (15¼ ounces) kidney beans, drained
1 package (15 ounces) flat refrigerated pie crusts
½ cup (2 ounces) shredded Cheddar cheese, divided

In Dutch oven, brown beef in oil; drain fat. Add stewed tomatoes, bell pepper, Taco Spices & Seasonings and cornmeal. Bring to a boil; reduce heat and simmer, uncovered, 20 minutes. Add kidney beans.

In 10-inch pie plate, unfold 1 crust and fill with chili mixture and ¼ cup cheese. Top with remaining crust, fluting edges. Bake, uncovered, in 350°F oven 30 minutes. Sprinkle remaining cheese over crust; return to oven and bake 10 minutes longer.

Makes 6 servings

69 CHOP SUEY CASSEROLE

2 cups (12 ounces) cooked roast beef strips
1 can (10¾ ounces) condensed cream of mushroom soup
½ cup milk
1 package (10 ounces) frozen French-style green beans, thawed and drained
1 can (8 ounces) sliced water chestnuts, drained
½ cup diagonally sliced celery
2 tablespoons soy sauce
1 can (2.8 ounces) FRENCH'S® French Fried Onions
1 medium tomato, cut into wedges

Preheat oven to 350°F. In large bowl, combine beef, soup, milk, beans, water chestnuts, celery, soy sauce and ½ *can* French Fried Onions. Spoon beef mixture into 1½-quart casserole. Bake, covered, at 350°F for 30 minutes or until heated through. Arrange tomato wedges around edge of casserole and top with remaining onions. Bake, uncovered, 5 minutes or until onions are golden brown. *Makes 4 servings*

MICROWAVE DIRECTIONS: Prepare beef mixture as directed; spoon into 1½-quart microwave-safe casserole. Cook, covered, on HIGH 10 to 12 minutes or until heated through, stirring beef mixture halfway through cooking time. Top with tomato wedges and remaining onions as directed; cook, uncovered, 1 minute. Let stand 5 minutes.

Texas-Style Deep-Dish Chili Pie

Speedy Stuffed Peppers

70 SPEEDY STUFFED PEPPERS

 4 red, green or yellow bell peppers
³/₄ pound lean ground beef (80% lean)
¹/₃ cup chopped onion
 1 clove garlic, minced
 1 package (6.8 ounces) RICE-A-RONI®
    Beef Flavor
¹/₄ cup tomato paste
¹/₄ cup water
 1 tablespoon brown sugar
 3 tablespoons grated Parmesan cheese
    (optional)

1. Cut peppers in half lengthwise; remove seeds and membranes. Cook in boiling water 5 minutes; drain well. (Or, microwave in 13×9-inch glass baking dish, covered with plastic wrap, 5 minutes on HIGH.)

2. In large skillet, brown ground beef, onion and garlic; drain. Remove from skillet; set aside.

3. In same skillet, prepare Rice-A-Roni® mix as package directs.

4. Heat oven to 375°F. Place cooked peppers cut-side up in 13×9-inch glass baking dish. Combine rice and meat mixture; spoon into pepper halves. Combine tomato paste, water and brown sugar; spoon over rice mixture.

5. Tent peppers with foil; bake 25 to 30 minutes or until heated through. Sprinkle with cheese, if desired.

Makes 4 servings

71 CHUNKY CHILI CASSEROLE

2 cups STOVE TOP® Chicken Flavor or
   Cornbread Stuffing Mix in the
   Canister
½ cup hot water
½ pound ground beef
1 small onion, chopped
1 can (15 ounces) chili with beans
1½ cups (6 ounces) shredded cheddar
   cheese, divided
½ cup frozen sweet corn, thawed
¼ cup sliced pitted ripe olives

MIX stuffing mix and hot water in 2-quart microwavable casserole. Spread evenly in casserole.

MIX meat and onion in large microwavable bowl. Cover loosely with wax paper.

MICROWAVE on HIGH 4 minutes or until meat is no longer pink. Drain. Stir in chili, 1 cup of the cheese, corn and olives. Spoon over stuffing. Cover loosely with wax paper.

MICROWAVE 10 minutes, rotating casserole halfway through cooking time. Let stand 5 minutes. Sprinkle with remaining ½ cup cheese. Serve with BREAKSTONE'S® or KNUDSEN® Sour Cream.

Makes 4 servings

Prep Time: 5 minutes
Cook Time: 20 minutes

NOTE: Recipe can also be prepared in 4 individual 1½-cup microwavable dishes. Microwave each dish on HIGH 3 minutes or until heated through.

72 FAMILY FAVORITE HAMBURGER CASSEROLE

1 tablespoon CRISCO® Vegetable Oil
1 cup chopped onion
1 pound ground beef round
1 package (9 ounces) frozen cut green
   beans
3 cups frozen southern-style hash brown
   potatoes
1 can (10¾ ounces) zesty tomato soup
½ cup water
1 teaspoon dried basil leaves
¾ teaspoon salt
¼ teaspoon pepper
¼ cup plain dry bread crumbs

1. Heat oven to 350°F. Oil 11¾×7½×2-inch baking dish lightly.

2. Heat one tablespoon Crisco® Oil in large skillet on medium-high heat. Add onion. Cook and stir until tender. Add meat. Cook until browned, stirring occasionally. Add beans. Cook and stir 5 minutes or until thawed. Add potatoes.

3. Combine tomato soup and water in small bowl. Stir until well blended. Stir into skillet. Stir in basil, salt and pepper. Spoon into baking dish. Sprinkle with bread crumbs.

4. Bake at 350°F for 30 minutes or until potatoes are tender. Let stand 5 minutes before serving. *Makes 4 servings*

PRIME-TIME MEATS

73 TEX–MEX LASAGNA

1 pound ground beef
1 can (16 ounces) whole tomatoes, undrained and cut up
1 package (about 1⅛ ounces) taco seasoning mix
1 can (2.8 ounces) FRENCH'S® French Fried Onions
1½ cups (12 ounces) cream-style cottage cheese
2 cups (8 ounces) shredded Cheddar cheese
2 eggs, slightly beaten
12 (6-inch) flour or corn tortillas
1 medium tomato, chopped
1 cup shredded lettuce

Preheat oven to 350°F. In large skillet, brown ground beef; drain. Stir in canned tomatoes and taco seasoning. Reduce heat and simmer, uncovered, 5 minutes. Remove from heat and stir in *½ can* French Fried Onions. In medium bowl, combine cottage cheese, *1 cup* Cheddar cheese and the eggs; set aside. Overlap 3 tortillas in bottom of greased 12×8-inch baking dish. Overlap 6 tortillas around sides of dish. Spoon beef mixture over tortillas; top with remaining 3 tortillas. Spoon cheese mixture over beef and tortillas. Bake, covered, at 350°F for 45 minutes or until cheese mixture is set. Top with remaining Cheddar cheese. Sprinkle remaining onions down center of casserole. Bake, uncovered, 5 minutes or until onions are golden brown. Just before serving, arrange tomato and lettuce around edges of casserole. Let stand 5 minutes before serving.   *Makes 6 servings*

74 SPANISH STYLE BEEF AND RICE CASSEROLE

1¼ pounds boneless beef chuck shoulder steak, cut ¾ inch thick
1½ tablespoons olive oil
½ cup chopped green bell pepper
⅓ cup chopped onion
1 clove garlic, crushed
¾ cup uncooked long-grain white rice
2 teaspoons chili powder
¾ teaspoon salt
⅛ teaspoon pepper
1 can (14½ ounces) tomatoes, undrained, broken up
¾ cup frozen peas, thawed

Cut steak into ¼-inch-wide strips; cut strips into 2-inch pieces.

Heat oven to 350°F. Heat oil in large skillet over medium-high heat 5 minutes. Cook and stir beef, bell pepper, onion and garlic 2 to 3 minutes or until beef is no longer pink; place in 2-quart casserole. Stir in rice, chili powder, salt and pepper. Add enough water to tomatoes to measure 2 cups; add to casserole. Cover tightly and bake 50 minutes or until rice is tender. Remove from oven; stir in peas.   *Makes 4 servings*

Favorite recipe from **National Cattlemen's Beef Association**

Tex-Mex Lasagna

75 TACO BAKE

TACO MEAT FILLING
- 1 pound ground beef
- ½ cup chopped onion
- 1 package (about 1⅛ ounces) taco seasoning mix

TACO CRUST
- 1¾ to 2 cups all-purpose flour, divided
- 1 package RED STAR® Active Dry Yeast or QUICK-RISE™ Yeast
- 1 tablespoon sugar
- 2 teaspoons finely chopped onion
- ¾ teaspoon salt
- ⅔ cup warm water
- 2 tablespoons oil
- ½ cup crushed corn chips

TOPPINGS
- 1 cup shredded Cheddar cheese
- 1 cup shredded lettuce
- 1½ cups chopped tomatoes

Brown ground beef with onion; drain. Add taco seasoning. Prepare taco filling according to seasoning packet directions.

Preheat oven to 375°F. In medium mixing bowl, combine 1 cup flour, yeast, sugar, onion and salt; mix well. Add warm water (120° to 130°F) and oil to flour mixture. Mix by hand until almost smooth. Stir in corn chips and enough remaining flour to make a stiff batter. Spread into well-greased 10-inch pie pan, forming a rim around edge. Cover; let rise in warm place about 20 minutes (10 minutes for QUICK-RISE™ Yeast). Spread meat filling over dough. Bake at 375°F 30 to 35 minutes or until edge is crisp and light golden brown. Sprinkle with cheese, lettuce and tomatoes. Serve immediately. *Makes 4 to 6 servings*

76 OLD–FASHIONED BEEF POT PIE

- 1 pound ground beef
- 1 can (11 ounces) condensed beef with vegetables and barley soup
- ½ cup water
- 1 package (10 ounces) frozen peas and carrots, thawed and drained
- ½ teaspoon seasoned salt
- ⅛ teaspoon garlic powder
- ⅛ teaspoon ground black pepper
- 1 cup (4 ounces) shredded Cheddar cheese
- 1 can (2.8 ounces) FRENCH'S® French Fried Onions
- 1 package (7.5 ounces) refrigerated biscuits

Preheat oven to 350°F. In large skillet, brown ground beef in large chunks; drain. Stir in soup, water, vegetables and seasonings; bring to a boil. Reduce heat and simmer, uncovered, 5 minutes. Remove from heat; stir in *½ cup* cheese and *½ can* French Fried Onions.

Pour mixture into 12×8-inch baking dish. Cut each biscuit in half; place, cut side down, around edge of casserole. Bake, uncovered, 15 to 20 minutes or until biscuits are done. Top with remaining cheese and onions; bake, uncovered, 5 minutes or until onions are golden brown.

Makes 4 to 6 servings

PRIME-TIME MEATS

77 OVEN–EASY BEEF & POTATO DINNER

4 cups frozen hash brown potatoes, thawed
3 tablespoons vegetable oil
1/8 teaspoon pepper
1 pound ground beef
1 cup water
1 package (about 3/4 ounce) brown gravy mix
1/2 teaspoon garlic salt
1 package (10 ounces) frozen mixed vegetables, thawed and drained
1 cup (4 ounces) shredded Cheddar cheese
1 can (2.8 ounces) FRENCH'S® French Fried Onions

Preheat oven to 400°F. In 12×8-inch baking dish, combine potatoes, oil and pepper. Firmly press potato mixture evenly across bottom and up sides of dish to form a shell. Bake, uncovered, at 400°F for 15 minutes. Meanwhile, in large skillet, brown ground beef; drain. Stir in water, gravy mix and garlic salt; bring to a boil. Add mixed vegetables; reduce heat to medium and cook, uncovered, 5 minutes. Remove from heat and stir in *1/2 cup* cheese and *1/2 can* French Fried Onions; spoon into hot potato shell. Reduce oven temperature to 350°F. Bake, uncovered, at 350°F for 15 minutes or until heated through. Top with remaining cheese and onions; bake, uncovered, 5 minutes or until onions are golden brown.

Makes 4 to 6 servings

Oven-Easy Beef & Potato Dinner

78 MEXICAN LASAGNA

1½ pounds lean ground beef
1 package (1.25 ounces) LAWRY'S® Taco
   Seasoning Mix
1 teaspoon LAWRY'S® Seasoned Salt
1 cup diced tomatoes, fresh or canned
2 cans (8 ounces *each*) tomato sauce
1 can (4 ounces) diced green chiles
1 cup ricotta cheese
2 eggs, beaten
10 corn tortillas
2½ cups (10 ounces) grated Monterey Jack
   cheese

In large skillet, brown ground beef, stirring
until cooked through; drain fat. Add Taco
Seasoning Mix, Seasoned Salt, tomatoes,
tomato sauce and chiles; blend well. Bring to
a boil. Reduce heat; simmer, uncovered,
10 minutes. In small bowl, combine ricotta
cheese and eggs. In bottom of 13×9×2-inch
baking dish, spread ½ of meat mixture. Top
with ½ of tortillas; spread ½ of ricotta
cheese mixture over tortillas and top with
½ of grated Monterey Jack cheese. Repeat
layering, ending with grated cheese. Bake,
uncovered, in 350°F oven 20 to 30 minutes
or until hot and bubbly. Let stand 10 minutes
before cutting into squares.

Makes 8 servings

HINTS: You may assemble the lasagna early
in the day and refrigerate it, covered, until
ready to bake. Add 10 to 15 minutes to
baking time. Mexican Lasagna also freezes
well; defrost completely before baking.

79 FRENCH VEAL CASSEROLE

1 pound veal steaks
2 tablespoons salad oil
1 cup rice
1 tablespoon chopped onion
2¼ cups water
2 teaspoons salt
2 tablespoons chopped pimiento
½ cup BLUE DIAMOND® Slivered
   Almonds, toasted

Cut meat into ½-inch cubes. Brown lightly in
oil in large skillet. Remove meat from skillet.
Combine rice and onion in same pan; cook,
stirring, until rice is golden brown. Add
water and salt; bring to boil. Stir in veal.
Spoon into casserole dish; cover. Bake at
300°F 50 to 60 minutes or until rice and veal
are tender. Just before serving, add pimiento
and almonds; fluff with fork.

Makes 6 servings

Mexican Lasagna

PRIME-TIME MEATS

80 REUBEN CASSEROLE

1 bag SUCCESS® Rice
   Vegetable cooking spray
$\frac{1}{2}$ cup fat-free mayonnaise
3 tablespoons sweet pickle relish
1 teaspoon prepared mustard
$\frac{1}{4}$ teaspoon pepper
1 can sauerkraut, rinsed and drained
1 can (12 ounces) corned beef, chopped
1 cup (4 ounces) shredded Swiss cheese,
   divided
1 medium tomato, peeled and sliced
$\frac{1}{2}$ cup fresh rye bread crumbs
   (about 1 slice bread)

Prepare rice according to package directions.

Preheat oven to 350°F. Spray shallow 2-quart casserole with cooking spray; set aside. Combine mayonnaise, relish, mustard and pepper in large bowl; mix well. Add rice, sauerkraut, corned beef and $\frac{1}{2}$ cup cheese; mix lightly to coat. Spoon into prepared casserole. Top with tomatoes; sprinkle with remaining $\frac{1}{2}$ cup cheese and bread crumbs. Bake until hot and bubbly, about 30 minutes.

Makes 4 servings

81 CORNED BEEF, POTATO AND PEPPER HASH

1 teaspoon salt
1 pound Russet potatoes, cut into $\frac{1}{2}$-inch
   cubes
2 tablespoons butter, divided
1 medium onion, coarsely chopped
$\frac{1}{3}$ cup *each* chopped red, yellow and green
   bell peppers
12 ounces cooked corned beef, cut into
   $\frac{1}{2}$-inch cubes
3 tablespoons chopped parsley
$\frac{1}{4}$ cup half-and-half
3 tablespoons dry white wine
$\frac{1}{2}$ teaspoon dry mustard
$\frac{1}{8}$ teaspoon black pepper

Bring water to a boil in large saucepan; add salt and potatoes. Return to a boil. Cook 5 minutes; drain well. Melt 1 tablespoon butter in cast-iron or large heavy skillet over medium-high heat; add onion and bell peppers. Cook and stir 2 minutes or until crisp-tender; remove from pan. Add corned beef, potatoes and parsley to onion mixture; mix lightly. Combine half-and-half, wine, mustard and pepper. Add to corned beef mixture; mix well. Wipe out cast-iron skillet with paper towel; place over medium heat until hot. Add remaining butter. Add beef mixture; press down firmly. Cook 15 minutes or until browned; turn with spatula several times.

Makes 4 servings

Favorite recipe from ***National Cattlemen's Beef Association***

Sherried Beef

82 SHERRIED BEEF

¾ **pound boneless beef top round steak**
 1 **cup water**
¼ **cup dry sherry**
 3 **tablespoons soy sauce**
 2 **large carrots, cut into diagonal slices**
 1 **large green pepper, cut into strips**
 1 **medium onion, cut into chunks**
 2 **tablespoons vegetable oil, divided**
 1 **tablespoon cornstarch**
 2 **cups hot cooked rice**

Partially freeze steak; slice across the grain into ⅛-inch strips. Combine water, sherry, and soy sauce. Pour over beef in dish; cover. Marinate 1 hour in refrigerator. Stir-fry vegetables in 1 tablespoon oil in large skillet over medium-high heat. Remove from skillet; set aside. Drain beef, reserving marinade. Brown beef in remaining 1 tablespoon oil. Combine cornstarch with marinade in bowl. Add vegetables and marinade to beef. Cook, stirring, until sauce is thickened; cook 1 minute longer. Serve over rice. *Makes 4 servings*

Favorite recipe from **USA Rice Council**

PRIME-TIME MEATS

83 RANCH STROGANOFF

1½ pounds flank steak or top sirloin steak
2 packages (1 ounce *each*) HIDDEN VALLEY RANCH® Milk Recipe Original Ranch® Salad Dressing mix
¼ cup all-purpose flour
¼ cup vegetable oil
¼ cup minced onion
1 clove garlic, minced
½ pound fresh mushrooms, thinly sliced
1½ cups milk
8 ounces wide egg noodles, cooked and buttered
1 tablespoon poppy seeds

Cut steak diagonally into 2×½-inch strips; set aside. Combine salad dressing mix and flour in plastic bag. Add steak and dredge with flour mixture. Place steak on platter; reserve extra coating mixture. In large skillet, heat oil over medium heat until hot. Add onion and garlic; sauté 1 minute. Add steak and mushrooms and continue cooking until steak is lightly browned, 4 to 5 minutes. Stir in milk and remaining coating mixture and continue cooking over low heat, stirring constantly, until thickened. Serve over noodles tossed with poppy seeds.

Makes 4 servings

Meatball Stroganoff with Rice

84 MEATBALL STROGANOFF WITH RICE

MEATBALLS
  1 egg, lightly beaten
1½ pounds ground beef round
  ⅓ cup plain dry bread crumbs
  1 tablespoon Worcestershire sauce
  1 teaspoon salt
  ¼ teaspoon pepper
  2 tablespoons CRISCO® Vegetable Oil

SAUCE
  1 tablespoon CRISCO® Vegetable Oil
  ½ pound mushrooms, sliced
  2 tablespoons all-purpose flour
  1 teaspoon ketchup
  1 can (10½ ounces) condensed, double
      strength beef broth (bouillon),
      undiluted*
  ½ (1-ounce) envelope dry onion soup mix
      (about 2 tablespoons)
  1 cup sour cream
  4 cups hot cooked rice

*1¼ cups reconstituted beef broth made with double
amount of very low sodium beef broth granules may
be substituted for beef broth (bouillon).

1. For meatballs, combine egg, meat,
bread crumbs, Worcestershire sauce, salt
and pepper in large bowl. Mix until well
blended. Shape into eighteen 2-inch
meatballs.

2. Heat 2 tablespoons Crisco® Oil in large
skillet on medium heat. Add meatballs.
Brown on all sides. Reduce heat to low.
Cook 10 minutes. Remove meatballs from
skillet.

3. For sauce, add one tablespoon Crisco®
Oil to skillet. Add mushrooms. Cook and stir
4 minutes. Remove skillet from heat.

4. Stir in flour and ketchup until blended.
Stir in broth gradually. Add soup mix. Return
to heat. Bring to a boil on medium heat.
Reduce heat to low. Simmer 2 minutes.
Return meatballs to skillet. Heat thoroughly,
stirring occasionally.

5. Stir in sour cream. Heat but do not bring
to a boil. Serve over hot rice. Garnish, if
desired.   *Makes 6 servings*

85 BEEF SONOMA & RICE

  1 pound lean ground beef (80% lean)
  1 clove garlic, minced
  1 package (6.8 ounces) RICE-A-RONI®
      Beef Flavor
  ½ cup chopped green bell pepper *or* 1 can
      (4 ounces) chopped green chiles,
      undrained
  ¼ cup sliced green onions
  1 medium tomato, chopped
  2 tablespoons chopped parsley or cilantro

1. In large skillet, brown ground beef and
garlic; drain. Remove from skillet; set aside.

2. In same skillet, prepare Rice-A-Roni® mix
as package directs, stirring in beef mixture,
green pepper and onions during last
5 minutes of cooking.

3. Sprinkle with tomato and parsley.
                    Makes 4 servings

86 SESAME STEAK

SAUCE

- ¼ cup **LA CHOY® Soy Sauce**
- ¼ cup **chicken broth**
- 1½ tablespoons **cornstarch**
- 1 tablespoon **dry sherry**
- ¼ teaspoon **Oriental sesame oil**

STEAK AND VEGETABLES

- 2 tablespoons **dry sherry**
- 1 tablespoon **LA CHOY® Soy Sauce**
- 1 tablespoon **cornstarch**
- 1 pound **round steak, sliced into thin 2-inch strips**
- 4 tablespoons **WESSON® Oil, divided**
- 1 teaspoon *each:* **minced fresh garlic and gingerroot**
- 1 cup **chopped red bell pepper**
- 1 cup **sliced fresh mushrooms**
- 1 (10-ounce) package **frozen French-cut green beans, thawed and drained**
- 1 (14-ounce) can **LA CHOY® Bean Sprouts, drained**
- 1 (8-ounce) can **LA CHOY® Sliced Water Chestnuts, drained**
- ½ cup **sliced green onions**
- 2 tablespoons **toasted sesame seeds**

In small bowl, combine *sauce* ingredients; set aside. In medium bowl, combine sherry, soy sauce and cornstarch; mix well. Add steak; toss gently to coat. In large nonstick skillet or wok, heat *3 tablespoons* oil. Add half of steak mixture; stir-fry until lightly browned. Remove steak from skillet; set aside. Repeat with remaining steak mixture. Heat *remaining 1 tablespoon* oil in same skillet. Add garlic and ginger; cook and stir

10 seconds. Add bell pepper; stir-fry 1 minute. Add mushrooms and green beans; stir-fry 1 minute. Stir sauce; add to skillet with bean sprouts and water chestnuts. Cook, stirring constantly, until sauce is thick and bubbly. Return steak to skillet; heat thoroughly, stirring occasionally. Sprinkle with green onions and sesame seeds. Garnish, if desired.

Makes 4 to 6 servings

87 QUICK SKILLET SUPPER

- ½ pound **beef sirloin steak**
- 1 tablespoon **vegetable oil**
- 2 cups (about 8 ounces) **sliced fresh mushrooms**
- 1 can (17 ounces) **whole kernel corn, drained**
- 1 can (14½ ounces) **stewed tomatoes, undrained**
- 1 clove **garlic, minced**
- 1 teaspoon **dried oregano leaves**
- ⅛ teaspoon **ground black pepper**
- 3 cups **hot cooked rice**

Partially freeze steak; slice across the grain into ⅛-inch strips. Heat oil in large skillet over medium-high heat until hot. Brown meat quickly in oil, about 2 minutes; remove. Add vegetables, garlic, oregano and pepper; stir. Reduce heat to medium; cover and cook 5 minutes. Add meat and cook until heated. Serve over rice. *Makes 6 servings*

Favorite recipe from **USA Rice Council**

Sesame Steak

88 MANDARIN TOMATO BEEF

1 boneless beef sirloin steak, cut 1 inch
    thick (about 1 pound)
$\frac{1}{2}$ cup low sodium teriyaki sauce
2 teaspoons minced fresh ginger
2 teaspoons cornstarch
2 cups fresh snow peas *or* 1 package
    (6 ounces) frozen snow peas, thawed
2 tablespoons peanut oil or vegetable oil,
    divided
1 medium onion, cut into $\frac{1}{2}$-inch wedges
2 medium tomatoes, cut into $\frac{1}{2}$-inch
    wedges
    Hot cooked rice
    Freshly ground black pepper (optional)

• Trim fat from beef; discard. Cut beef across grain into $\frac{1}{8}$-inch-thick slices; cut each slice into 2-inch pieces. Combine teriyaki sauce and ginger in medium bowl. Add beef; toss to coat. Marinate beef 10 minutes.

• Drain beef, reserving marinade. Stir reserved marinade into cornstarch in small bowl; stir until smooth. Set aside.

• If using fresh snow peas, pinch off stem end from each fresh pea pod, pulling strings down to remove. Rinse pea pods and pat dry. Set aside.

• Heat wok over medium-high heat 2 minutes or until hot. Drizzle 1 tablespoon oil into wok; heat 30 seconds. Add half of beef; stir-fry 2 to 3 minutes or until beef is barely pink in center. Remove beef to large bowl. Repeat with remaining beef.

• Drizzle remaining 1 tablespoon oil into wok; heat 30 seconds. Add onion; cook 3 minutes or until browned, stirring occasionally. Add snow peas; stir-fry 3 minutes for fresh snow peas or 1 minute for frozen.

• Stir marinade mixture until smooth; add to wok. Stir-fry 30 seconds or until sauce boils and thickens.

• Return beef, any accumulated juices and tomatoes to wok; cook until heated through. Serve over rice. Sprinkle with black pepper and garnish, if desired.   *Makes 4 servings*

89 GROUND BEEF CHOW MEIN

SAUCE
$\frac{1}{3}$ cup beef broth
3 tablespoons LA CHOY® Soy Sauce
1 tablespoon cornstarch
1 teaspoon *each:* dry mustard and garlic
    powder
$\frac{1}{2}$ teaspoon *each:* sugar and pepper

MEAT AND VEGETABLES
1 pound lean ground beef
2 tablespoons WESSON® Oil
2 cups sliced fresh mushrooms
1 (14-ounce) can LA CHOY® Bean Sprouts,
    drained
1 (14-ounce) can LA CHOY® Chop Suey
    Vegetables, drained
$\frac{1}{2}$ cup ($\frac{1}{4}$-inch) green onion pieces
1 (5-ounce) can LA CHOY® Chow Mein
    Noodles

In small bowl, combine *sauce* ingredients; set aside. In large nonstick skillet, brown ground beef; remove from skillet. Drain. Heat oil in same skillet. Add mushrooms; cook and stir 1 to 2 minutes or until tender. Stir in bean sprouts and chop suey vegetables; heat thoroughly, stirring occasionally. Return ground beef to skillet. Stir sauce; add to skillet with green onions. Cook, stirring constantly, until sauce is thick and bubbly. Serve over noodles.

Makes 4 to 6 servings

90 TERIYAKI BEEF

¾ **pound sirloin tip steak, cut into thin strips**
½ **cup teriyaki sauce**
¼ **cup water**
1 **tablespoon cornstarch**
1 **teaspoon sugar**
1 **bag (16 ounces) BIRDS EYE® frozen Farm Fresh Mixtures Broccoli, Carrots and Water Chestnuts**

• Spray large skillet with nonstick cooking spray; cook beef strips over medium-high heat 7 to 8 minutes, stirring occasionally.

• Combine teriyaki sauce, water, cornstarch and sugar; mix well.

• Add teriyaki sauce mixture and vegetables to beef. Bring to boil; quickly reduce heat to medium.

• Cook 7 to 10 minutes or until broccoli is heated through, stirring occasionally.

Makes 4 to 6 servings

Prep Time: 5 to 10 minutes
Cook Time: 20 minutes

Teriyaki Beef

91 THREE–PEPPER STEAK

- 1 pound boneless beef top round or flank steak
- 3 tablespoons low sodium soy sauce
- 1 tablespoon cornstarch
- 1 tablespoon brown sugar
- 1½ teaspoons sesame oil
- ¼ teaspoon crushed red pepper
- 1 small green bell pepper
- 1 small red bell pepper
- 1 small yellow bell pepper
- 1 medium onion
- 2 cloves garlic
- 3 tablespoons vegetable oil, divided
  Hot cooked rice

• Cut beef across grain into ¼-inch-thick slices. Combine soy sauce, cornstarch, brown sugar, sesame oil and crushed red pepper in medium bowl; stir until smooth. Add beef and toss to coat; set aside.

• Cut green, red and yellow peppers lengthwise in half. Remove stems and seeds. Rinse, dry and cut into ½-inch strips. Cut onion in half and then into 1-inch pieces. Finely chop garlic. Set aside.

• Heat wok over high heat about 1 minute or until hot. Drizzle 1 tablespoon vegetable oil into wok and heat 30 seconds. Add pepper strips; stir-fry until crisp-tender. Remove to large bowl. Add 1 tablespoon vegetable oil and heat 30 seconds. Add half the beef mixture to wok; stir-fry until well browned. Remove beef to bowl with peppers. Repeat with remaining 1 tablespoon vegetable oil and beef mixture. Reduce heat to medium.

• Add onion; stir-fry about 3 minutes or until softened. Add garlic; stir-fry 30 seconds. Return peppers, beef and any accumulated juices to wok; cook until heated through. Spoon rice into serving dish; top with beef and vegetable mixture. *Makes 4 servings*

92 MOUSSAKA–STYLE BEEF AND ZUCCHINI

- 3 medium zucchini
- 1 tablespoon vegetable oil
- 1 pound lean ground beef
- 1 medium onion, chopped
- 2 cloves garlic, minced
- 1 teaspoon dried basil leaves
- ½ teaspoon ground cinnamon
- 2 cans (8 ounces *each*) tomato sauce
- ½ cup low fat sour cream
- 1 egg yolk
- ¼ cup crumbled feta cheese

• Scrub zucchini; cut off ends. Cut each zucchini crosswise into thirds. Cut pieces lengthwise into slices.

• Heat wok over high heat. Drizzle oil into wok; heat 30 seconds. Add zucchini; cook 8 minutes, stirring often. Remove to medium bowl.

• Add beef to wok; stir-fry until well browned. Add onion and garlic; stir-fry 1 minute. Reduce heat to medium. Add basil and cinnamon; mix well. Stir in tomato sauce; cover and simmer 5 minutes. Mix sour cream and egg yolk in small bowl until well blended.

• Skim fat from beef mixture; discard. Spread beef mixture evenly into wok; top with zucchini. Spoon sour cream mixture in center of zucchini. Cover; cook 5 minutes or until top is set. Sprinkle with cheese. Remove from heat; let stand 1 minute. Serve hot. *Makes 4 servings*

Three-Pepper Steak

Hunan Chili Beef

93 BEEF BENIHANA

1 pound boneless beef sirloin, cut 1 inch
    thick
2 medium zucchini
1 large onion
1 tablespoon sesame seeds
2 tablespoons vegetable oil, divided
½ pound sliced mushrooms
3 tablespoons teriyaki sauce
1 teaspoon sugar
½ teaspoon salt
¼ teaspoon black pepper
    Hot cooked rice

• Trim fat from beef; discard. Slice beef across grain into ¼-inch-thick slices. Scrub zucchini; cut off ends. Cut each zucchini crosswise and lengthwise in half. Cut pieces lengthwise into ½-inch strips. Cut onion lengthwise in half; slice crosswise into ¼-inch slices. Set aside.

• Heat wok over high heat about 1 minute or until hot. Add sesame seeds; cook and stir until lightly browned. Remove to small bowl.

• Drizzle 1 tablespoon oil into wok and heat 30 seconds. Add beef; stir-fry about 2 minutes or until well browned on outside and rare on inside. Remove beef to large bowl. Reduce heat to medium.

• Add remaining 1 tablespoon oil to wok and heat 30 seconds. Add mushrooms, zucchini and onion; stir-fry about 5 minutes or until vegetables are crisp-tender. Stir in teriyaki sauce, sugar, salt and pepper. Return beef and any accumulated juices to wok; cook until heated through. Spoon rice onto serving plate; top with beef mixture. Sprinkle with sesame seeds.

Makes 4 servings

94 HUNAN CHILI BEEF

1 pound beef flank steak
3 tablespoons low sodium soy sauce
3 tablespoons vegetable oil, divided
1 tablespoon rice wine or dry sherry
1 tablespoon cornstarch
2 teaspoons brown sugar
1 jalapeño pepper, halved, stemmed and
    seeded*
3 green onions with tops
¼ small red bell pepper
1 cup drained canned baby corn
1 (1-inch square) piece fresh ginger,
    peeled and minced
2 cloves garlic, minced
1 teaspoon hot chili oil
   Hot cooked rice

Jalapeños can sting and irritate the skin; wear rubber gloves when handling jalapeños and do not touch eyes. Wash hands after handling jalapeños.

• Cut beef across grain into $2 \times \frac{1}{4}$-inch slices. Combine soy sauce, 1 tablespoon vegetable oil, wine, cornstarch and brown sugar in medium bowl. Add beef; toss to coat. Set aside.

• Cut jalapeño lengthwise into strips. Cut onions into 1-inch pieces. Remove seeds from bell pepper. Rinse, dry and cut pepper into ¼-inch strips. Set aside.

• Heat wok over high heat 1 minute or until hot. Drizzle 1 tablespoon vegetable oil into wok; heat 30 seconds. Add half of beef mixture; stir-fry until well browned. Remove to large bowl. Repeat with remaining 1 tablespoon vegetable oil and beef mixture. Reduce heat to medium.

• Add corn, onions, ginger and garlic to wok; stir-fry 1 minute. Add jalapeño and bell pepper; stir-fry 1 minute.

• Return beef and any accumulated juices to wok; add chili oil. Toss to combine; cook until heated through. Serve with rice.

Makes 4 servings

95 TERIYAKI CHOP SUEY

SAUCE
- ⅓ cup beef broth
- 3 tablespoons LA CHOY® Teriyaki Marinade & Sauce
- 1½ tablespoons *each:* cornstarch and packed brown sugar
- 1 teaspoon garlic powder
- ¼ teaspoon pepper

BEEF AND VEGETABLES
- 1 tablespoon LA CHOY® Teriyaki Marinade & Sauce
- 1 tablespoon cornstarch
- 1 pound flank or sirloin steak, sliced across grain into thin 2-inch strips
- 3 tablespoons WESSON® Oil
- 2 cups sliced fresh mushrooms
- 1 (14-ounce) can LA CHOY® Bean Sprouts, drained
- 1 (14-ounce) can LA CHOY® Chop Suey Vegetables, drained
- ½ cup diagonally cut ½-inch green onion pieces
- 1 (5-ounce) can LA CHOY® Chow Mein Noodles

In small bowl, combine *sauce* ingredients; set aside. In medium bowl, combine teriyaki sauce and cornstarch. Add beef; toss gently. In large nonstick skillet or wok, heat oil. Add half of beef mixture; stir-fry until lightly browned. Remove beef from skillet; set aside. Repeat with remaining beef mixture. Add mushrooms to skillet; stir-fry 1 minute. Add bean sprouts and chop suey vegetables; heat thoroughly, stirring occasionally. Stir sauce; add to skillet with beef and green onions. Cook, stirring constantly, until sauce is thick and bubbly. Garnish, if desired. Serve over noodles.

Makes 4 to 6 servings

96 BEEF AND BROCCOLI

SAUCE
- 2 tablespoons oyster sauce
- ¼ cup water
- 1 tablespoon *each:* cornstarch and dry sherry
- ⅛ teaspoon Oriental sesame oil

BEEF AND VEGETABLES
- 3 tablespoons LA CHOY® Soy Sauce
- 1 tablespoon cornstarch
- 1 pound flank steak, sliced across grain into thin 2-inch strips
- 4 tablespoons WESSON® Oil, divided
- 3 cups fresh broccoli flowerettes
- 1 cup julienne-cut carrots
- 1 tablespoon *each:* minced fresh garlic and gingerroot
- 1 (8-ounce) can LA CHOY® Sliced Water Chestnuts, drained
- 1 (5-ounce) can LA CHOY® Chow Mein Noodles

In small bowl, combine sauce ingredients; set aside. In large bowl, combine soy sauce and cornstarch; mix well. Add beef; toss gently to coat. Cover and marinate 30 minutes. In large nonstick skillet or wok, heat *2 tablespoons* oil. Add half of beef mixture; stir-fry until lightly browned. Remove beef from skillet; set aside. Repeat with remaining beef mixture. Heat *remaining 2 tablespoons* oil in same skillet. Add broccoli, carrots, garlic and ginger; stir-fry 1 to 2 minutes or until vegetables are crisp-tender. Return beef to skillet. Stir sauce; add to skillet with water chestnuts. Cook, stirring constantly, until sauce is thick and bubbly. Reserve a few noodles; serve beef mixture over remaining noodles. Garnish with reserved noodles.

Makes 4 to 6 servings

Teriyaki Chop Suey

97 OLD–FASHIONED BEEF STEW

1 tablespoon CRISCO® Vegetable Oil
1¼ pounds boneless beef round steak, trimmed and cut into 1-inch cubes
2¾ cups water, divided
1 teaspoon Worcestershire sauce
2 bay leaves
1 clove garlic, minced
½ teaspoon paprika
¼ teaspoon pepper
8 medium carrots, quartered
8 small potatoes, peeled and quartered
4 small onions, quartered
1 package (9 ounces) frozen cut green beans
1 tablespoon cornstarch
Salt (optional)

1. Heat Crisco® Oil in Dutch oven on medium-high heat. Add beef. Cook and stir until browned. Add 1½ cups water, Worcestershire sauce, bay leaves, garlic, paprika and pepper. Bring to a boil. Reduce heat to low. Cover. Simmer one hour 15 minutes, stirring occasionally. Remove bay leaves.

2. Add carrots, potatoes and onions. Cover. Simmer 30 to 45 minutes or until vegetables are almost tender. Add beans. Simmer 5 minutes or until tender. Remove from heat. Add one cup water to Dutch oven.

3. Combine remaining ¼ cup water and cornstarch in small bowl. Stir well. Stir into ingredients in Dutch oven. Return to low heat. Cook and stir until thickened. Season with salt, if desired.   *Makes 8 servings*

98 EASY BEEF AND RICE STEW

2 tablespoons flour
½ teaspoon salt
¼ teaspoon pepper
1 pound boneless beef top round, cut into ¾-inch chunks
1 tablespoon oil
2 medium carrots, diagonally sliced
1 medium onion, coarsely chopped
1 jar (4½ ounces) sliced mushrooms, drained
1 can (14½ ounces) whole tomatoes, undrained, coarsely chopped
1 can (10¼ ounces) beef gravy
¼ cup burgundy or other dry red wine
1½ cups MINUTE® Original Rice, uncooked

MIX flour, salt and pepper in large bowl. Add meat; toss to coat.

HEAT oil in large skillet on medium-high heat. Add meat; cook and stir until browned. Add carrots, onion and mushrooms; cook and stir 2 minutes.

STIR in tomatoes, gravy and wine. Bring to a boil. Reduce heat to low; cover and simmer 10 minutes.

STIR in rice; cover. Remove from heat. Let stand 5 minutes. Stir.   *Makes 4 servings*

Prep Time: 10 minutes
Cook Time: 20 minutes

Old-Fashioned Beef Stew

99 SOUTHWESTERN BEEF STEW

1 tablespoon plus 1 teaspoon olive or vegetable oil, divided
1½ pounds boneless beef chuck, cut into 1-inch cubes
1 can (4 ounces) chopped green chilies, drained
2 large cloves garlic, finely chopped
1 teaspoon ground cumin (optional)
1 can (14 to 16 ounces) whole or plum tomatoes, undrained and chopped
1 envelope LIPTON® Recipe Secrets® Onion or Beefy Onion Soup Mix
1 cup water
1 package (10 ounces) frozen cut okra or green beans, thawed
1 large red or green bell pepper, cut into 1-inch pieces
4 frozen half-ears corn-on-the-cob, thawed and each cut into 3 round pieces
2 tablespoons chopped fresh cilantro (optional)

In 5-quart Dutch oven or heavy saucepot, heat 1 tablespoon oil over medium-high heat and brown ½ of the beef; remove and set aside. Repeat with remaining beef; remove and set aside. In same Dutch oven, heat remaining 1 teaspoon oil over medium heat and cook chilies, garlic and cumin, stirring constantly, 3 minutes. Return beef to Dutch oven. Stir in tomatoes and onion soup mix blended with water. Bring to a boil over high heat. Reduce heat to low and simmer covered, stirring occasionally, 1 hour. Stir in okra, red pepper and corn. Bring to a boil over high heat. Reduce heat to low and simmer covered, stirring occasionally, 30 minutes or until meat is tender. Sprinkle with cilantro. *Makes about 6 servings*

100 BISTRO BURGUNDY STEW

1 pound boneless beef sirloin, cut into 1½-inch pieces
3 tablespoons all-purpose flour
6 slices bacon, cut into 1-inch pieces (about ¼ pound)
2 cloves garlic, crushed
3 carrots, peeled and cut into 1-inch pieces (about 1½ cups)
¾ cup Burgundy or other dry red wine
½ cup GREY POUPON® Dijon Mustard
½ cup COLLEGE INN® Beef Broth or Lower Sodium Beef Broth
12 small mushrooms
1½ cups green onions, cut into 1½-inch pieces
Tomato rose and parsley, for garnish
Breadsticks, optional

Coat beef with flour, shaking off excess; set aside.

In large skillet, over medium heat, cook bacon just until done; pour off excess fat. Add beef and garlic; cook until browned. Add carrots, wine, mustard and beef broth. Heat to a boil; reduce heat. Cover; simmer for 30 minutes or until carrots are tender, stirring occasionally. Stir in mushrooms and green onions; cook 10 minutes more, stirring occasionally. Garnish with tomato rose and parsley. Serve with breadsticks if desired.
Makes 4 servings

101 HUNGARIAN GOULASH STEW

¾ **pound lean ground beef (8)% lean)**
½ **cup chopped onion**
1 **clove garlic, minced**
1 **package (4.8 ounces) PASTA RONI®**
   Herb Sauce with Angel Hair Pasta
1 **can (14½ ounces) diced tomatoes,**
   undrained
1 **cup frozen corn *or* 1 can (8 ounces)**
   whole kernel corn, drained
1½ **teaspoons paprika**
⅛ **teaspoon black pepper**
   Sour cream (optional)

1. In 3-quart saucepan, brown ground beef, onion and garlic; drain.

2. Add 1⅓ cups water, pasta, contents of seasoning packet, tomatoes, frozen corn and seasonings. Bring just to a boil.

3. Reduce heat to medium.

4. Boil, uncovered, stirring frequently, 5 to 6 minutes or until pasta is tender.

5. Let stand 3 minutes or until desired consistency. Stir before serving. Serve with sour cream, if desired.   *Makes 4 servings*

Bistro Burgundy Stew

102 BEAN AND RICE SOUP

3 ounces thinly sliced pancetta, chopped
    (about ½ cup)*
1 cup chopped onion
2 quarts (four 10½-ounce cans) beef broth
3½ cups (two 14.5-ounce cans)
    CONTADINA® Pasta Ready Chunky
    Tomatoes with Olive Oil, Garlic and
    Spices, undrained
1 tablespoon chopped fresh rosemary *or*
    1 teaspoon dried rosemary leaves,
    crushed
1 cup arborio or long-grain white rice,
    uncooked
¼ teaspoon salt
¼ teaspoon ground black pepper
1¾ cups (15½-ounce can) Great Northern
    white beans, drained
2 tablespoons chopped fresh Italian
    parsley

Substitute 3 bacon slices for 3 ounces pancetta.

In large saucepan, sauté pancetta for
1 minute. Add onion; sauté for 2 to 3 minutes
or just until pancetta is crisp. Add broth,
tomatoes and juice and rosemary. Bring to a
boil. Reduce heat to low; simmer, uncovered,
for 10 minutes. Add rice, salt and pepper;
simmer, covered, for 20 to 25 minutes or
until rice is tender. Add beans; simmer for
5 minutes. Sprinkle with parsley just before
serving.   *Makes 10 cups*

103 SPICY QUICK AND EASY CHILI

1 pound ground beef
1 large clove garlic, minced
1 can (15¼ ounces) DEL MONTE® Whole
    Kernel Golden Sweet Corn, drained
1 can (16 ounces) kidney beans, drained
1½ cups DEL MONTE® Traditional Salsa,
    Mild, Medium or Hot
1 can (4 ounces) diced green chiles,
    undrained

1. In large saucepan, brown meat with
garlic; drain.

2. Add remaining ingredients. Simmer,
uncovered, 10 minutes, stirring occasionally.
Garnish with green onions, if desired.
                    Makes 4 servings

Prep & Cook Time: 15 minutes

Spicy Quick and Easy Chili

104 STUFFED FRANKS 'N TATERS

4 cups frozen hash brown potatoes, thawed
1 can (10¾ ounces) condensed cream of celery soup
1 cup (4 ounces) shredded Cheddar cheese
1 cup sour cream
1 can (2.8 ounces) FRENCH'S® French Fried Onions
½ teaspoon salt
¼ teaspoon pepper
6 frankfurters

Preheat oven to 400°F. In large bowl, combine potatoes, soup, *½ cup* cheese, the sour cream, *½ can* French Fried Onions and the seasonings. Spread potato mixture in 12×8-inch baking dish. Split frankfurters lengthwise almost into halves. Arrange frankfurters, split-side up, along center of casserole. Bake, covered, at 400°F for 30 minutes or until heated through. Fill frankfurters with remaining cheese and onions; bake, uncovered, 1 to 3 minutes or until onions are golden brown.

Makes 6 servings

MICROWAVE DIRECTIONS: Prepare potato mixture as above; spread in 12×8-inch microwave-safe dish. Cook, covered, on HIGH 8 minutes, stirring potato mixture halfway through cooking time. Split frankfurters and arrange on potatoes as directed. Cook, covered, 4 to 6 minutes or until frankfurters are heated through, rotating dish halfway through cooking time. Fill frankfurters with remaining cheese and onions; cook, uncovered, 1 minute or until cheese melts. Let stand 5 minutes.

105 RICE & SAUSAGE CASSEROLE

1 cup uncooked rice
1 pound BOB EVANS FARMS® Zesty Hot or Special Seasonings Roll Sausage
2 tablespoons butter or margarine
1 cup chopped celery
1 large onion, chopped
¼ cup *each:* chopped red and green bell peppers
1 (10½-ounce) can condensed cream of mushroom soup
1 cup milk
Salt and black pepper to taste
½ cup (2 ounces) shredded longhorn or colby cheese

Cook rice according to package directions; transfer to large bowl. Preheat oven to 350°F. Crumble sausage into medium skillet. Cook over medium heat until lightly browned, stirring occasionally. Remove sausage to paper towels; set aside. Drain off any drippings and wipe skillet clean with paper towels. Stir sausage into cooked rice. Melt butter in same skillet over medium-high heat until hot. Add celery, onion and bell peppers; cook and stir until tender. Stir into rice and sausage mixture. Stir in soup, milk, salt and black pepper; mix well. Spoon mixture into lightly greased 2-quart baking dish. Sprinkle with cheese. Bake, uncovered, 40 minutes or until heated through. Serve hot. Refrigerate leftovers.

Makes 6 servings

Stuffed Franks 'n Taters

PRIME-TIME MEATS

106 TOMATO, BACON AND CHEESE SUPPER

1 medium onion, chopped
2 tablespoons margarine or butter
1 cup ricotta cheese
1 cup milk
3 eggs, well beaten
3 cups STOVE TOP® Chicken Flavor or Cornbread Stuffing Mix in the Canister
1 cup (4 ounces) KRAFT® Natural Shredded Swiss Cheese, divided
2 large tomatoes, chopped
8 slices OSCAR MAYER® Bacon, crisply cooked, crumbled
¼ teaspoon pepper

PLACE onion and margarine in 3-quart microwavable casserole. Cover loosely with wax paper.

MICROWAVE on HIGH 3 minutes. Stir in ricotta cheese, milk and eggs. Stir in stuffing mix, ¾ cup of the Swiss cheese, tomatoes, bacon and pepper until well mixed. Cover loosely with wax paper.

MICROWAVE 10 minutes, stirring halfway through cooking time. Sprinkle with remaining ¼ cup Swiss cheese. Let stand 5 minutes.   *Makes 6 servings*

Prep Time: 5 minutes
Cook Time: 20 minutes

Tomato, Bacon and Cheese Supper

107 PRIZE POTLUCK CASSEROLE

1 cup lentils, rinsed and drained
2 cups water
1 can (16 ounces) tomatoes
¼ cup minced onion
¼ cup chopped green pepper
1 teaspoon salt
½ teaspoon dry mustard
¼ teaspoon Worcestershire sauce
¼ teaspoon pepper
⅛ teaspoon dried thyme leaves
1 pound Polish sausage, cut into
    1½-inch-thick slices

Cook lentils in water in medium saucepan until tender, about 30 minutes; drain if necessary. Combine lentils with tomatoes, onion, green pepper and seasonings; spoon into 13×9-inch casserole. Top with sausage; cover. Bake at 350°F for 45 minutes. Remove cover; continue baking 15 minutes longer.

Makes 6 servings

Favorite recipe from **USA Dry Pea & Lentil Council**

108 HAM STARBURST CASSEROLE

1 can (10¾ ounces) condensed cream of potato soup
¾ cup sour cream
1 can (16 ounces) sliced potatoes, drained
1 package (10 ounces) frozen peas, thawed and drained
1 can (2.8 ounces) FRENCH'S® French Fried Onions
2 tablespoons diced pimiento (optional)
8 to 12 ounces cooked ham or turkey ham, unsliced

Preheat oven to 350°F. In medium bowl, combine soup, sour cream, potatoes, peas, ½ *can* French Fried Onions and the pimiento; stir well. Spoon into 10-inch round baking dish. Cut ham into 3 thick slices; cut each slice crosswise into halves. Press ham slices into potato mixture, rounded-side up in spoke-fashion, to form a starburst. Bake, covered, at 350°F for 30 minutes or until heated through. Top with remaining onions; bake, uncovered, 5 minutes or until onions are golden brown. *Makes 4 servings*

109 EASY SPINACH PIE

3 eggs
¾ cup milk
2 cups STOVE TOP® Chicken Flavor Stuffing Mix in the Canister
1 package (10 ounces) frozen chopped spinach, thawed, well drained
1 cup cubed ham
¾ cup cottage cheese
⅓ cup sliced green onions
¼ teaspoon garlic powder
⅓ cup (about 1½ ounces) KRAFT® Natural Shredded Cheddar Cheese

BEAT eggs in large bowl; stir in milk. Stir in stuffing mix, spinach, ham, cottage cheese, onions and garlic powder until well mixed. Spoon into greased 9-inch microwavable pie plate. Cover loosely with wax paper.

MICROWAVE on HIGH 5 minutes. Stir thoroughly to completely mix center and outside edges; smooth top. Cover.

MICROWAVE 5 minutes or until center is no longer wet. Sprinkle with cheddar cheese; cover. Let stand 5 minutes.

Makes 6 servings

Prep Time: 10 minutes
Cook Time: 15 minutes

PRIME-TIME MEATS

110 ITALIAN SAUSAGE SUPPER

1 pound mild Italian sausage, casings removed
1 cup chopped onion
3 medium zucchini, sliced (about 1½ cups)
⅔ cup (6-ounce can) CONTADINA® Tomato Paste
1 cup water
1 teaspoon dried basil leaves, crushed
½ teaspoon salt
3 cups cooked rice
1 cup (4 ounces) shredded mozzarella cheese
¼ cup (1 ounce) grated Romano cheese

In large skillet, brown sausage with onion, stirring to break up sausage; drain, reserving 1 tablespoon drippings. Spoon sausage mixture into greased 2-quart casserole dish. Add zucchini to skillet; sauté for 5 minutes or until crisp-tender. In medium bowl, combine tomato paste, water, basil and salt. Stir in rice. Spoon over sausage mixture. Arrange zucchini slices on top; sprinkle with mozzarella and Romano cheeses. Cover. Bake in preheated 350°F oven for 20 minutes. *Makes 6 servings*

111 FAMILY BAKED BEAN DINNER

1 can (20 ounces) DOLE® Pineapple Chunks in Juice
½ DOLE® Green Bell Pepper, julienne cut
½ cup chopped onion
1 pound Polish sausage or frankfurters, cut into 1-inch chunks
⅓ cup packed brown sugar
1 teaspoon dry mustard
2 cans (16 ounces *each*) baked beans

• **Microwave Directions:** Drain pineapple; reserve juice for beverage. Add green pepper and onion to 13×9-inch microwavable dish.

• Cover; microwave on HIGH (100% power) 3 minutes. Add sausage, arranging around edges of dish. Cover; continue microwaving on HIGH (100% power) 6 minutes.

• In bowl, combine brown sugar and mustard; stir in beans and pineapple. Add to sausage mixture. Stir to combine. Microwave, uncovered, on HIGH (100% power) 8 to 10 minutes, stirring after 4 minutes.
Makes 6 servings

Italian Sausage Supper

112 BEEF SAUSAGE SKILLET DINNER

12 ounces fully cooked smoked beef link
    sausage, cut diagonally into 1-inch
    pieces
2 tablespoons water
1 medium onion
2 small red apples
2 tablespoons butter, divided
12 ounces frozen potato wedges
1/4 cup cider vinegar
3 tablespoons sugar
1/2 teaspoon caraway seeds
2 tablespoons chopped fresh parsley

Place sausage and water in large nonstick
skillet; cover tightly and cook over medium
heat 8 minutes, stirring occasionally.
Meanwhile, cut onion into 12 wedges; core
and cut each apple into 8 wedges. Remove
sausage to warm platter. Pour off drippings.
Cook and stir onion and apples in
1 tablespoon of butter in same skillet
4 minutes or until apples are crisp-tender.
Remove to sausage platter.

Heat remaining 1 tablespoon butter; add
potatoes and cook, covered, over medium-
high heat 5 minutes or until potatoes are
tender and golden brown, stirring
occasionally. Combine vinegar, sugar and
caraway seeds. Reduce heat; return sausage,
apple mixture and vinegar mixture to skillet.
Cook 1 minute or until heated through,
stirring gently. Sprinkle with parsley.

Makes 4 servings

*Favorite recipe from **National Cattlemen's Beef
Association***

113 NEW ORLEANS RICE AND SAUSAGE

1/2 pound smoked sausage, cut into slices*
1 can (14 1/2 ounces) stewed tomatoes,
    Cajun- or Italian-style
3/4 cup water
1 3/4 cups uncooked instant rice
    Dash hot pepper sauce, or to taste
1 bag (16 ounces) BIRDS EYE® frozen
    Farm Fresh Mixtures Broccoli, Corn
    and Red Peppers

*For a spicy dish, use andouille sausage. Any type of
kielbasa or turkey kielbasa can also be used.*

• Heat sausage in large skillet 2 to 3 minutes.

• Add tomatoes, water, rice and hot pepper
sauce; mix well.

• Add vegetables; mix well. Cover and cook
over medium heat 5 to 7 minutes or until
rice is tender and vegetables are heated
through. *Makes 6 servings*

Prep Time: 5 minutes
Cook Time: 10 minutes

New Orleans Rice and Sausage

114 HAM & POTATO SCALLOP

1 package (5 ounces) scalloped potatoes plus ingredients as package directs
1 bag (16 ounces) BIRDS EYE® frozen Broccoli Cuts
½ pound cooked ham, cut into ½-inch cubes
½ cup shredded Cheddar cheese (optional)

• Prepare potatoes according to package directions for stove-top method, adding broccoli and ham when adding milk and butter.

• Stir in cheese just before serving.

Makes 4 servings

Prep Time: 5 minutes
Cook Time: 25 minutes

SERVING SUGGESTION: Spoon mixture into shallow casserole dish. Sprinkle with cheese; broil until lightly browned.

115 MEXICAN SKILLET RICE

¾ pound lean ground pork or lean ground beef
1 medium onion, chopped
1 tablespoon plus 1½ teaspoons chili powder
1 teaspoon ground cumin
½ teaspoon salt
3 cups cooked brown rice
1 can (16 ounces) pinto beans, drained
2 cans (4 ounces *each*) diced green chiles, undrained
1 medium tomato, seeded and chopped (optional)

Brown meat in large skillet over medium-high heat, stirring to crumble; drain. Return meat to skillet. Add onion, chili powder, cumin and salt; cook until onion is soft but not brown. Stir in rice, beans and chiles; heat thoroughly. Top with tomato.

Makes 6 servings

MICROWAVE: Combine meat and onion in 2- to 3-quart microwavable dish; stir well. Cover with waxed paper. Microwave on HIGH 4 to 5 minutes or until meat is no longer pink, stirring after 2 minutes. Drain. Add chili powder, cumin, salt, rice, beans and chiles. Microwave on HIGH 4 to 5 minutes or until thoroughly heated, stirring after 2 minutes. Top with tomato.

*Favorite recipe from **USA Rice Council***

Sausage Ham Jambalaya

116 SAUSAGE HAM JAMBALAYA

6 ounces spicy smoked sausage links, sliced

6 ounces cooked ham, diced

2 cans (14½ ounces *each*) DEL MONTE® Cajun Recipe Stewed Tomatoes

1 cup uncooked long grain white rice

1 large clove garlic, minced

1 tablespoon chopped fresh parsley

1 bay leaf

In heavy 4-quart saucepan, brown sausage and ham. Drain tomatoes, reserving liquid; pour liquid into measuring cup. Add water to measure 1½ cups. Add reserved liquid, tomatoes and remaining ingredients to sausage mixture. Cover and simmer 30 to 35 minutes, stirring occasionally. Remove bay leaf. Garnish with additional chopped parsley, if desired.

Makes 4 to 6 servings

Prep Time: 10 minutes
Cook Time: 40 minutes

117 COUNTRY SKILLET HASH

2 tablespoons butter or margarine
4 pork chops (¾ inch thick), diced
¼ teaspoon black pepper
¼ teaspoon cayenne pepper (optional)
1 medium onion, chopped
2 cloves garlic, minced
1 can (14½ ounces) DEL MONTE® Whole New Potatoes, drained and diced
1 can (14½ ounces) DEL MONTE® FRESH CUT™ Diced Tomatoes, undrained
1 medium green bell pepper, chopped
½ teaspoon thyme, crushed

1. In large skillet, melt butter over medium heat. Add meat; cook, stirring occasionally, until no longer pink in center. Season with black pepper and cayenne pepper, if desired.

2. Add onion and garlic; cook until tender. Stir in potatoes, tomatoes, green pepper and thyme. Cook 5 minutes, stirring frequently. Season with salt, if desired.

Makes 4 servings

Prep Time: 5 minutes
Cook Time: 15 minutes

TIP: The hash may be topped with a poached or fried egg.

118 QUICK CASSOULET

2 slices bacon, cut into ½-inch pieces
¾ pound boneless pork chops, sliced crosswise ¼ inch thick
1 medium onion, chopped
1 clove garlic, minced
1 teaspoon dried thyme, crushed
1 can (14½ ounces) DEL MONTE® Original Recipe Stewed Tomatoes
½ cup dry white wine
1 can (15 ounces) white or pinto beans, drained

In large skillet, cook bacon over medium-high heat until almost crisp. Stir in meat, onion, garlic and thyme. Season with salt and pepper, if desired. Cook 4 minutes. Add tomatoes and wine; bring to boil. Cook, uncovered, over medium-high heat 10 minutes or until thickened, adding beans during last 5 minutes. *Makes 4 servings*

Prep & Cook Time: 30 minutes

Country Skillet Hash

119 PORK CHOPS O'BRIEN

1 tablespoon vegetable oil
6 pork chops, ½ to ¾ inch thick
   Seasoned salt
1 can (10¾ ounces) condensed cream of
   celery soup
½ cup milk
½ cup sour cream
¼ teaspoon pepper
1 bag (24 ounces) frozen O'Brien or
   hash brown potatoes, thawed
1 cup (4 ounces) shredded Cheddar
   cheese
1 can (2.8 ounces) FRENCH'S® French
   Fried Onions

Preheat oven to 350°F. In large skillet, heat oil. Brown pork chops on both sides; drain. Sprinkle chops with seasoned salt; set aside. In large bowl, combine soup, milk, sour cream, pepper and ½ teaspoon seasoned salt. Stir in potatoes, *½ cup* cheese and *½ can* French Fried Onions. Spoon mixture into 13×9-inch baking dish; arrange pork chops on top. Bake, covered, at 350°F for 35 to 40 minutes or until pork chops are done. Top chops with remaining cheese and onions; bake, uncovered, 5 minutes or until onions are golden brown.

Makes 6 servings

Pork Chops O'Brien

PRIME-TIME MEATS

120 SAVORY PORK CHOP SUPPER

6 medium potatoes, thinly sliced (about 5 cups)
1 can (2.8 ounces) FRENCH'S® French Fried Onions
1 jar (2 ounces) sliced mushrooms, drained
2 tablespoons butter or margarine
¼ cup soy sauce
1½ teaspoons ground mustard
½ teaspoon REDHOT® Cayenne Pepper Sauce
⅛ teaspoon garlic powder
1 tablespoon vegetable oil
6 pork chops, ½ to ¾ inch thick

Preheat oven to 350°F. In 12×8-inch baking dish, layer *half* the potatoes and *½ can* French Fried Onions. Top with mushrooms and remaining potatoes. In small saucepan, melt butter; stir in soy sauce, mustard, cayenne pepper sauce and garlic powder. Brush *half* the soy sauce mixture over potatoes. In large skillet, heat oil. Brown pork chops on both sides; drain. Arrange chops over potatoes and brush with remaining soy sauce mixture. Bake, covered, at 350°F for 1 hour. Bake, uncovered, 15 minutes or until pork chops and potatoes are done. Top chops with remaining onions; bake, uncovered, 5 minutes or until onions are golden brown. *Makes 4 to 6 servings*

121 PORK CHOPS WITH APPLES AND STUFFING

4 pork chops, ½ inch thick
Salt and pepper
1 tablespoon oil
2 medium apples, cored, cut into 8 wedges
1 cup apple juice
2 cups STOVE TOP® Cornbread Stuffing Mix in the Canister
¼ cup chopped pecans

SPRINKLE chops with salt and pepper. Heat oil in large skillet on medium-high heat. Add chops and apples; cook until chops are browned on both sides.

STIR in apple juice. Bring to boil. Reduce heat to low; cover and simmer 8 minutes or until chops are cooked through. Remove chops from skillet.

STIR stuffing mix and pecans into skillet. Return chops to skillet; cover. Remove from heat. Let stand 5 minutes.

Makes 4 servings

Prep Time: 10 minutes
Cook Time: 20 minutes

122 QUICK PAELLA

1 tablespoon oil
1 pound hot Italian sausage, cut into
   1-inch pieces
2 cloves garlic, minced
1 tablespoon cornstarch
1 can (13¾ ounces) chicken broth
1 package (10 ounces) frozen peas and
   pearl onions, thawed
½ pound medium shrimp, cleaned
1 can (8 ounces) stewed tomatoes
1½ cups MINUTE® Original Rice, uncooked
⅛ teaspoon saffron *or* ground turmeric
   (optional)

HEAT oil in large skillet on medium-high heat. Add sausage and garlic; cook and stir until sausage is browned.

MIX cornstarch and broth until smooth. Stir into skillet. Add vegetables, shrimp and tomatoes; cook and stir until mixture thickens and comes to boil.

STIR in rice and saffron; cover. Remove from heat. Let stand 5 minutes. Stir.

Makes 6 servings

Prep Time: 10 minutes
Cook Time: 15 minutes

123 HERBED TOMATO PORK CHOPS AND STUFFING

1 tablespoon oil
4 pork chops, ½ inch thick
1 can (8 ounces) stewed tomatoes
1 can (8 ounces) tomato sauce
1 medium green pepper, chopped
½ teaspoon dried oregano leaves
¼ teaspoon ground pepper
2 cups STOVE TOP® Chicken Flavor
   Stuffing Mix in the Canister
1 cup (4 ounces) shredded mozzarella
   cheese, divided

HEAT oil in large skillet on medium-high heat. Add chops; brown on both sides.

STIR in tomatoes, tomato sauce, green pepper, oregano and ground pepper. Bring to boil. Reduce heat to low; cover and simmer 15 minutes or until chops are cooked through. Remove chops from skillet.

STIR stuffing mix and ½ cup of the cheese into skillet. Return chops to skillet. Sprinkle with remaining ½ cup cheese; cover. Remove from heat. Let stand 5 minutes.

Makes 4 servings

Prep Time: 5 minutes
Cook Time: 25 minutes

Quick Paella

124 SWEET & SOUR MUSTARD PORK

1 pound boneless pork, cut into strips
¼ cup GREY POUPON® Dijon Mustard, divided
3 teaspoons soy sauce, divided
1 (3-ounce) package chicken-flavored Ramen noodles
1 (8-ounce) can pineapple chunks, drained, reserving juice
½ cup water
2 tablespoons firmly packed light brown sugar
½ teaspoon grated fresh ginger
1 tablespoon cornstarch
2 cups broccoli flowerettes
½ cup chopped red or green cabbage
½ cup chopped red bell pepper
½ cup coarsely chopped onion
2 tablespoons vegetable oil

In medium bowl, combine pork strips, 2 tablespoons mustard and 1 teaspoon soy sauce. Refrigerate for 1 hour.

In small bowl, combine remaining mustard and soy sauce, chicken flavor packet from noodles, reserved pineapple juice, water, brown sugar, ginger and cornstarch; set aside. Cook Ramen noodles according to package directions; drain and set aside.

In large skillet, over medium-high heat, stir-fry vegetables in oil until tender-crisp; remove from skillet. Add pork mixture; stir-fry for 3 to 4 minutes or until done. Return vegetables to skillet with pineapple chunks and cornstarch mixture; heat until mixture thickens and begins to boil. Add cooked noodles, tossing to coat well. Garnish as desired. Serve immediately.

Makes 4 servings

125 PORK AND CABBAGE RICE

2 teaspoons oil
¾ pound boneless pork, cut into strips
½ cup red cabbage strips
½ teaspoon caraway seed (optional)
½ teaspoon pepper
1½ cups water
½ cup applesauce
2 tablespoons cider vinegar
1½ cups MINUTE® Brown Rice, uncooked
1 tart apple, cored, sliced

HEAT oil in large skillet on medium-high heat. Add meat; cook and stir until lightly browned. Add cabbage, caraway seed and pepper; cook and stir 1 minute.

STIR in water, applesauce and vinegar. Bring to boil.

STIR in rice and apple. Reduce heat to low; cover and simmer 5 minutes. Remove from heat and stir; cover. Let stand 5 minutes. Stir.   *Makes 4 servings*

Prep Time: 10 minutes
Cook Time: 20 minutes

Sweet & Sour Mustard Pork

126 SOUTHWEST PORK AND DRESSING

1 pound boneless pork, cut into 1-inch strips
2 teaspoons chili powder
¼ cup margarine or butter
½ cup diagonally sliced green onions
1½ cups water
1 cup frozen sweet corn, thawed
1 can (4 ounces) chopped green chilies, drained
3 cups STOVE TOP® Cornbread Stuffing Mix in the Canister
1¼ cups (5 ounces) KRAFT® Natural Shredded Monterey Jack Cheese, divided

TOSS meat with chili powder. Melt margarine in large skillet on medium-high heat. Add meat and onions; cook and stir until meat is browned.

STIR in water, corn and chilies. Bring to boil. Stir in stuffing mix and ¾ cup of the cheese. Remove from heat. Sprinkle with remaining ½ cup cheese. Cover. Let stand 5 minutes.   *Makes 4 to 6 servings*

Prep Time: 10 minutes
Cook Time: 15 minutes

Savory Pork & Apple Stir-Fry

127 SAVORY PORK & APPLE STIR–FRY

1 package (7.2 ounces) RICE-A-RONI® Rice Pilaf
1⅓ cups apple juice or apple cider
1 pound boneless pork loin, pork tenderloin or skinless, boneless chicken breast halves
1 teaspoon paprika
1 teaspoon dried thyme leaves
½ teaspoon ground sage or poultry seasoning
½ teaspoon salt (optional)
2 tablespoons margarine or butter
2 medium apples, cored, sliced
1 teaspoon cornstarch
⅓ cup coarsely chopped walnuts

1. Prepare Rice-A-Roni® mix as package directs, substituting 1 cup water and 1 cup apple juice for water in directions.

2. While Rice-A-Roni® is simmering, cut pork into 1½×¼-inch strips. Combine seasonings; toss with meat.

3. In second large skillet, melt margarine over medium heat. Stir-fry meat 3 to 4 minutes or just until pork is no longer pink.

4. Add apples; stir-fry 2 to 3 minutes or until apples are almost tender. Add combined remaining ⅓ cup apple juice and cornstarch. Stir-fry 1 to 2 minutes or until thickened to form glaze.

5. Stir in nuts. Serve rice topped with pork mixture. *Makes 4 servings*

128 SWEET & SOUR PORK

1 egg, well beaten
1 tablespoon *each:* cornstarch and all-purpose flour
1 pound lean boneless pork, cut into 1-inch pieces
3 cups WESSON® Oil
1 teaspoon *each:* minced fresh garlic and gingerroot
1 green bell pepper, cut into 1-inch pieces
1 onion, cut into chunks
1 (8-ounce) can LA CHOY® Bamboo Shoots, drained
1 (8-ounce) can LA CHOY® Sliced Water Chestnuts, drained
2 (10-ounce) jars LA CHOY® Sweet & Sour Sauce
2 teaspoons LA CHOY® Soy Sauce
Hot cooked rice
1 (5-ounce) can LA CHOY® Chow Mein Noodles

In medium bowl, combine egg, cornstarch and flour. Add pork; toss gently. In large saucepan, heat oil to 350°F. Carefully add a few pieces of pork; deep-fry 3 minutes. Remove pork from oil; drain on paper towels. Let stand 5 minutes. Meanwhile, repeat with remaining pieces of pork. Return pork to hot oil; continue deep-frying until golden brown. Remove pork from oil; drain again. Remove all but *2 tablespoons* oil from saucepan. Add garlic and ginger to saucepan; cook and stir 30 seconds. Add green pepper and onion; stir-fry 2 minutes or until crisp-tender. Stir in *all remaining* ingredients *except* rice and noodles; bring to a boil. Return pork to saucepan; heat thoroughly, stirring occasionally. Serve over rice. Sprinkle with noodles.

Makes 4 to 6 servings

129 IVORY, RUBIES AND JADE

¾ pound lean pork, cut into thin 2-inch strips
2 tablespoons LA CHOY® Soy Sauce
1 teaspoon minced fresh garlic
4 tablespoons WESSON® Oil, divided
1½ cups diagonally sliced celery
1 cup chopped red bell pepper
1 (8-ounce) can LA CHOY® Sliced Water Chestnuts, drained
1 (6-ounce) package frozen LA CHOY® Pea Pods, thawed and drained
1 (10-ounce) jar LA CHOY® Sweet & Sour Sauce
3 green onions, diagonally cut into 1-inch pieces
⅛ teaspoon cayenne pepper
1 (5-ounce) can LA CHOY® Chow Mein Noodles

In medium bowl, combine pork, soy sauce and garlic; cover and marinate 30 minutes in refrigerator. Drain. In large nonstick skillet or wok, heat *3 tablespoons* oil. Add pork mixture; stir-fry until pork is no longer pink in center. Remove pork from skillet; set aside. Heat *remaining 1 tablespoon* oil in same skillet. Add celery and bell pepper; stir-fry until crisp-tender. Return pork to skillet with *all remaining* ingredients *except* noodles; heat thoroughly, stirring occasionally. Serve over noodles.

Makes 4 servings

130 SEE THE LITE PORK FRIED RICE

½ pound boneless pork, cut into ½-inch pieces
3 tablespoons LA CHOY® Lite Soy Sauce, divided
1 teaspoon *each:* minced fresh garlic and gingerroot
¼ teaspoon *each:* pepper and Oriental sesame oil
2 tablespoons WESSON® Oil
2 eggs, well beaten
½ cup *each:* julienne-cut carrots and diagonally sliced celery
4 cups cold cooked long-grain rice
1 (14-ounce) can LA CHOY® Chop Suey Vegetables, drained
1 (6-ounce) package frozen LA CHOY® Pea Pods, thawed and cut crosswise in half
⅓ cup diagonally sliced green onions

In small bowl, combine pork, *1 tablespoon* soy sauce, garlic, ginger, pepper and sesame oil; cover and marinate 15 minutes. Drain. In large nonstick skillet or wok, heat Wesson® Oil. Add eggs; cook and stir until softly scrambled. Add pork, carrots and celery to skillet; cook and stir until pork is no longer pink in center. Add *remaining 2 tablespoons* soy sauce and *all remaining* ingredients; heat thoroughly, stirring occasionally. Garnish, if desired.

Makes 6 to 8 servings

Ivory, Rubies and Jade

131 HOT 'N SPICY PORK

SAUCE

- ¼ **cup water**
- 3 **tablespoons LA CHOY® Soy Sauce**
- 2 **tablespoons dry sherry**
- 1 **tablespoon cornstarch**
- 1 **teaspoon sugar**
- ½ **teaspoon crushed red pepper**
- ¼ **teaspoon Oriental sesame oil**

PORK AND VEGETABLES

- 1 **tablespoon LA CHOY® Soy Sauce**
- 1 **tablespoon cornstarch**
- 1 **pound lean boneless pork, cut into thin 2-inch strips**
- 4 **tablespoons WESSON® Oil, divided**
- 1½ **tablespoons minced fresh garlic**
- 1 **tablespoon minced gingerroot**
- 1 **green bell pepper, cut into ½-inch pieces**
- ½ **cup diagonally sliced celery**
- 1 **(8-ounce) can LA CHOY® Sliced Water Chestnuts, drained**
- 1 **(8-ounce) can LA CHOY® Bamboo Shoots, drained**
- ¼ **cup sliced green onions**
- 1 **(5-ounce) can LA CHOY® Chow Mein Noodles**

In small bowl, combine *sauce* ingredients; set aside. In medium bowl, combine soy sauce and cornstarch; mix well. Add pork; toss gently to coat. In large nonstick skillet or wok, heat *3 tablespoons* Wesson® Oil. Add half of pork mixture; stir-fry until pork is no longer pink in center. Remove pork from skillet; drain. Set aside. Repeat with remaining pork mixture. Heat *remaining 1 tablespoon* Wesson® Oil in same skillet. Add garlic and ginger; cook and stir

30 seconds. Add green pepper and celery; stir-fry 1 to 2 minutes or until crisp-tender. Stir sauce; add to skillet with water chestnuts and bamboo shoots. Cook, stirring constantly, until sauce is thick and bubbly. Return pork to skillet with green onions; heat thoroughly, stirring occasionally. Serve over noodles. Garnish, if desired.

Makes 4 to 6 servings

132 MANDARIN PORK STIR–FRY

- 1½ **cups DOLE® Mandarin Tangerine Juice or Pineapple Orange Juice, divided Vegetable cooking spray**
- 12 **ounces lean pork tenderloin or boneless, skinless chicken breast halves, cut into thin strips**
- 1 **tablespoon finely chopped fresh ginger** *or* ½ **teaspoon ground ginger**
- 2 **cups DOLE® Shredded Carrots**
- ½ **cup chopped DOLE® Pitted Prunes**
- 4 **DOLE® Green Onions, diagonally cut into 1-inch pieces**
- 2 **tablespoons low-sodium soy sauce**
- 1 **teaspoon cornstarch Hot cooked rice (optional)**

PRIME-TIME MEATS

• **Heat** 2 tablespoons juice over medium-high heat in large, nonstick skillet sprayed with cooking spray until juice bubbles.

• **Add** pork and ginger. Cook and stir 3 minutes or until pork is no longer pink; remove pork from skillet.

• **Heat** 3 tablespoons juice in skillet. Add carrots, prunes and green onions; cook and stir 3 minutes.

• **Stir** soy sauce and cornstarch into remaining juice; add to carrot mixture in skillet. Return pork to skillet; cover. Cook 2 minutes or until heated through and sauce is slightly thickened. Serve over rice and garnish with green onions and orange peel, if desired. *Makes 4 servings*

Prep Time: 15 minutes
Cook Time: 15 minutes

Mandarin Pork Stir-Fry

133 HAM AND CAULIFLOWER CHOWDER

1 bag (16 ounces) BIRDS EYE® frozen
    Cauliflower
2 cans (10¾ ounces *each*) cream of
    mushroom or cream of celery soup
2½ cups milk or water
  ½ pound ham, cubed
  ⅓ cup shredded colby cheese (optional)

• Cook cauliflower according to package directions.

• Combine cauliflower, soup, milk and ham in saucepan; mix well.

• Cook over medium heat 4 to 6 minutes, stirring occasionally. Top individual servings with cheese.   *Makes 4 to 6 servings*

Prep Time: 2 minutes
Cook Time: 10 to 12 minutes

Ham and Cauliflower Chowder

134 BLACK BEAN & PORK STEW

2 (15-ounce) cans cooked black beans, rinsed and drained
2 cups water
1 pound boneless ham, cut into ¾-inch cubes
¾ pound BOB EVANS FARMS® Italian Dinner Link Sausage, cut into 1-inch pieces
¾ pound BOB EVANS FARMS® Smoked Sausage, cut into 1-inch pieces
1 pint cherry tomatoes, stems removed
1 medium onion, chopped
1 teaspoon red pepper flakes
6 cloves garlic, minced
⅛ teaspoon grated orange peel
Cornbread or rolls (optional)

Preheat oven to 350°F. Combine all ingredients except cornbread in large Dutch oven. Bring to a boil over high heat, skimming foam off if necessary. Cover; transfer to oven. Bake 30 minutes; uncover and bake 30 minutes more, stirring occasionally. Serve hot with cornbread, if desired, or cool slightly, then cover and refrigerate overnight. Remove any fat from surface. Reheat over low heat. Refrigerate leftovers.   *Makes 8 servings*

135 DIJON HAM AND LENTIL SOUP

1 cup finely chopped onion
¾ cup finely chopped green bell pepper
½ cup finely chopped carrot
1 clove garlic, minced
1 bay leaf
2 (13¾-fluid ounce) cans COLLEGE INN® Chicken Broth or Lower Sodium Chicken Broth
1 (14½-ounce) can stewed tomatoes
1¼ cups water
1 cup diced ham
¾ cup dry lentils
½ cup GREY POUPON® COUNTRY DIJON® Mustard

In large saucepan, combine all ingredients except mustard. Heat to a boil over medium-high heat. Reduce heat; simmer, uncovered, for 1 hour. Stir in mustard. Serve hot.

Makes 6 servings

136 MINESTRONE

3 slices bacon, diced
1/2 cup chopped onion
1 large clove garlic, minced
2 1/2 cups (two 10 1/2-ounce cans) beef broth
1 1/2 cups water
1 3/4 cups (15 1/2-ounce can) Great Northern white beans, undrained
2/3 cup (6-ounce can) CONTADINA® Tomato Paste
1 teaspoon Italian herb seasoning
1/4 teaspoon ground black pepper
2 medium zucchini, sliced (about 2 cups)
1 package (10 ounces) frozen mixed vegetables
1/2 cup elbow macaroni, uncooked
1/2 cup (2 ounces) grated Parmesan cheese (optional)

In large saucepan, sauté bacon until crisp. Add onion and garlic; sauté until onion is tender. Add broth, water, beans and liquid, tomato paste, Italian seasoning and pepper. Reduce heat to low; simmer, uncovered, for 10 minutes. Add zucchini, mixed vegetables and macaroni. Return to a boil over high heat, stirring to break up vegetables. Reduce heat to low; simmer for 8 to 10 minutes or until vegetables and macaroni are tender. Sprinkle with Parmesan cheese just before serving, if desired. *Makes 8 cups*

137 CORN, BACON & RICE CHOWDER

1 package (7.2 ounces) RICE-A-RONI® Rice Pilaf
2 tablespoons margarine or butter
1 can (13 3/4 ounces) reduced-sodium or regular chicken broth
1 1/2 cups frozen corn *or* 1 can (16 or 17 ounces) whole kernel corn, drained
1 cup milk
1 cup water
1/2 cup sliced green onions
2 slices crisply cooked bacon, crumbled

1. In 3-quart saucepan, sauté rice-pasta mix and margarine over medium heat, stirring frequently, until pasta is lightly browned.

2. Stir in chicken broth and contents of seasoning packet; bring to a boil over high heat.

3. Cover; reduce heat. Simmer 8 minutes.

4. Stir in frozen corn, milk, water and onions. Simmer, uncovered, 10 to 12 minutes, stirring occasionally. Stir in bacon before serving. *Makes 4 servings*

Minestrone

PRIME-TIME MEATS

138 NAVAJO LAMB STEW WITH CORNMEAL DUMPLINGS

2 pounds lean lamb stew meat with bones, cut into 2-inch pieces, *or* 1½ pounds lean boneless lamb, cut into 1½-inch cubes
1 teaspoon salt
½ teaspoon pepper
2 tablespoons plus 1½ teaspoons vegetable oil, divided
1 large onion, chopped
1 clove garlic, minced
4 cups water
2 tablespoons tomato paste
2 teaspoons chili powder
1 teaspoon ground coriander
3 small potatoes, cut into 1½-inch chunks
2 large carrots, cut into 1-inch pieces
1 package (10 ounces) frozen whole kernel corn
⅓ cup coarsely chopped celery leaves
Cornmeal Dumplings (recipe follows)

Sprinkle meat with salt and pepper. Heat 2 tablespoons oil in 5-quart Dutch oven over medium-high heat. Add meat, a few pieces at a time; cook until browned, stirring occasionally. Transfer meat to medium bowl. Heat remaining 1½ teaspoons oil in Dutch oven over medium heat. Add onion and garlic; cook and stir until onion is tender. Stir in water, tomato paste, chili powder and coriander. Return meat to Dutch oven. Add potatoes, carrots, corn and chopped celery leaves. Bring to a boil. Cover; reduce heat to low. Simmer 1 hour and 15 minutes or until meat is tender. During last 15 minutes of cooking, prepare Cornmeal Dumplings. Drop dough onto stew to make 6 dumplings. Cover and simmer 18 minutes or until dumplings are firm to the touch and wooden pick inserted into centers comes out clean. To serve, spoon stew onto individual plates; serve with dumplings.   *Makes 6 servings*

CORNMEAL DUMPLINGS
½ cup yellow cornmeal
½ cup all-purpose flour
1 teaspoon baking powder
¼ teaspoon salt
2½ tablespoons cold butter or margarine
½ cup milk

Combine cornmeal, flour, baking powder and salt in medium bowl. Cut in butter with fingers, pastry blender or 2 knives until mixture resembles coarse crumbs; make a well in center. Pour in milk all at once; stir with fork until mixture forms dough.
Makes 6 dumplings

Navajo Lamb Stew with Cornmeal Dumplings

Lamb & Pork Cassoulet

139 SHEPHERD'S PIE

2 cups diced cooked leg of American lamb
2 large potatoes, cubed and cooked
3 green onions, sliced
1 cup cooked peas
1 cup cooked carrot slices
1 clove garlic, minced
2 cups prepared brown gravy
1 teaspoon black pepper
2 sheets prepared pie dough*

*Or, use mashed potatoes on top in place of second crust.

In large bowl, combine lamb, potatoes, green onions, peas, carrots, garlic, brown gravy and pepper.

Place 1 sheet pie dough in 9-inch pie plate; fill with lamb mixture. Cover with second sheet of pie dough. Crimp edges; cut slits in top to allow steam to escape.

Bake 30 minutes at 350°F or until pie crust is golden brown.   *Makes 4 to 6 servings*

*Favorite recipe from **American Lamb Council***

PRIME-TIME MEATS

140 LAMB & PORK CASSOULET

1 package (1 pound) dry white navy
    beans, rinsed
1/2 pound salt pork, sliced
1 1/2 pounds boneless lamb shoulder or leg,
    cut into 1-inch cubes
4 large pork chops
1/2 pound pork sausage links
  Salt
  Pepper
2 large onions, chopped
1 can (28 ounces) tomatoes, drained
1/2 cup dry red wine
3 cloves garlic, finely chopped
1/4 cup chopped fresh parsley
1 teaspoon dried thyme, crushed
1 bay leaf

Place beans in large bowl. Cover with cold
water; soak overnight. Drain and rinse
beans. Place beans in Dutch oven; cover
with cold water. Bring to a boil over high
heat, skimming foam as necessary. Reduce
heat to low. Cover and simmer about 1 hour.
Drain beans, reserving liquid.

Cook salt pork in large skillet over medium-
high heat until some of the fat is rendered.
Remove salt pork. In batches, brown lamb,
pork chops and sausage in fat. Remove
meats from skillet; drain on paper towels.
Cut chops and sausage into 1-inch pieces.
Sprinkle meat with salt and pepper. Remove
all but 2 tablespoons of the fat from skillet.
Add onions. Cook and stir over medium-high
heat until onions are tender. Add tomatoes,
wine, garlic, parsley, thyme and bay leaf.

Combine tomato mixture, drained beans and
meats in large bowl. Spoon into large
casserole. Pour reserved bean liquid over
mixture just to cover. Bake at 350°F about
1 1/2 hours or until meat is fork-tender.
Remove bay leaf before serving.

Makes 6 to 8 servings

*Favorite recipe from **American Lamb Council***

141 DIJON LAMB STEW

1/2 pound boneless lamb, cut into small
    pieces*
1/2 medium onion, chopped
1/2 teaspoon dried rosemary
1 tablespoon olive oil
1 can (14 1/2 ounces) DEL MONTE® Italian
    Recipe Stewed Tomatoes
1 carrot, julienne cut
1 tablespoon Dijon mustard
1 can (15 ounces) white beans or pinto
    beans, drained

Top sirloin steak may be substituted for lamb.

In large skillet, brown meat with onion and
rosemary in oil over medium-high heat,
stirring occasionally. Season with salt and
pepper, if desired. Add tomatoes, carrot and
mustard. Cover and cook over medium heat,
10 minutes; add beans. Cook, uncovered,
over medium heat 5 minutes, stirring
occasionally. Garnish with sliced ripe olives
and chopped parsley, if desired.

Makes 4 servings

Prep Time: 10 minutes
Cook Time: 20 minutes

Treasures from the Sea

142 EASY THREE CHEESE TUNA SOUFFLE

4 cups large croutons*
2½ cups milk
4 large eggs
1 can (10¾ ounces) cream of celery soup
3 cups shredded cheese, use a combination of Cheddar, Monterey Jack and Swiss
1 can (12 ounces) STARKIST® Solid White or Chunk Light Tuna, drained and flaked
1 tablespoon butter or margarine
½ cup chopped celery
½ cup finely chopped onion
¼ pound mushrooms, sliced

*Use garlic and herb or ranch-flavored croutons.

In bottom of lightly greased 13×9-inch baking dish, arrange croutons. In medium bowl, beat together milk, eggs and soup; stir in cheeses and tuna. In small skillet, melt butter over medium heat. Add celery, onion and mushrooms; sauté until onion is soft.

Spoon sautéed vegetables over croutons; pour egg-tuna mixture over top. Cover; refrigerate overnight. Remove from refrigerator 1 hour before baking; bake in 325°F oven 45 to 50 minutes or until hot and bubbly.   *Makes 8 servings*

Prep Time: 60 minutes

Easy Three Cheese Tuna Souffle

143 HERB–BAKED FISH & RICE

1½ cups hot chicken bouillon
½ cup uncooked regular rice
¼ teaspoon Italian seasoning
¼ teaspoon garlic powder
1 package (10 ounces) frozen chopped broccoli, thawed and drained
1 can (2.8 ounces) FRENCH'S® French Fried Onions
1 tablespoon grated Parmesan cheese
1 pound unbreaded fish fillets, thawed if frozen
Paprika (optional)
½ cup (2 ounces) shredded Cheddar cheese

Preheat oven to 375°F. In 12×8-inch baking dish, combine hot bouillon, uncooked rice and seasonings. Bake, covered, at 375°F for 10 minutes. Top with broccoli, ½ can French Fried Onions and the Parmesan cheese. Place fish fillets diagonally down center of dish; sprinkle fish lightly with paprika. Bake, covered, at 375°F for 20 to 25 minutes or until fish flakes easily with fork. Stir rice. Top fish with Cheddar cheese and remaining onions; bake, uncovered, 3 minutes or until onions are golden brown.

Makes 3 to 4 servings

MICROWAVE DIRECTIONS: In 12×8-inch microwave-safe dish, prepare rice mixture as above, except reduce bouillon to 1¼ cups. Cook, covered, on HIGH 5 minutes, stirring halfway through cooking time. Stir in broccoli, ½ can onions and the Parmesan cheese. Arrange fish fillets in single layer on top of rice mixture; sprinkle fish lightly with paprika. Cook, covered, on MEDIUM (50-60%) 18 to 20 minutes or until fish flakes easily with fork and rice is done, rotating dish halfway through cooking time. Top fish with Cheddar cheese and remaining onions; cook, uncovered, on HIGH 1 minute or until cheese melts. Let stand 5 minutes.

144 CREAMY SCALLOPED POTATOES AND TUNA

2 cups milk
2 cups whipping cream
2 cloves garlic, minced
2½ pounds (about 6 medium) white or russet potatoes
¾ teaspoon salt
½ teaspoon white pepper
1 tablespoon butter or margarine
1 can (12 ounces) STARKIST® Solid White or Chunk Light Tuna, drained and chunked
1½ cups shredded mozzarella cheese

In 3-quart saucepan over medium heat, heat milk, cream and garlic while preparing potatoes. Peel potatoes; slice about ⅛ to ¼ inch thick. Add potatoes, salt and white pepper to milk mixture; heat to simmering.

Grease 11×7-inch casserole with butter; spoon potato-milk mixture into dish. Bake 25 minutes; remove from oven. Add tuna, stirring gently; top with cheese. Bake 35 more minutes or until potatoes are cooked through and top is golden brown. Let stand, covered, about 15 minutes to thicken.

Makes 6 to 8 servings

Prep Time: 70 minutes

Herb-Baked Fish & Rice

145 BAKED FISH WITH POTATOES AND ONIONS

1 pound baking potatoes, very thinly sliced
1 large onion, very thinly sliced
1 small red or green bell pepper, thinly sliced
Salt
Black pepper
½ teaspoon dried oregano leaves, crushed, divided
1 pound lean fish fillets, cut 1 inch thick
¼ cup butter or margarine
¼ cup all-purpose flour
2 cups milk
¾ cup (3 ounces) shredded Cheddar cheese

Preheat oven to 375°F.

Arrange ½ of the potatoes in buttered 3-quart casserole. Top with ½ *each* of the onion and bell pepper. Season with salt and black pepper. Sprinkle with ¼ teaspoon oregano. Arrange fish in 1 layer over vegetables. Arrange remaining potatoes, onion and bell pepper over fish. Season with salt, black pepper and remaining ¼ teaspoon oregano.

Melt butter in medium saucepan over medium heat. Stir in flour; cook until bubbly, stirring constantly. Gradually stir in milk. Cook until thickened, stirring constantly. Pour white sauce over casserole. Cover and bake at 375°F 40 minutes or until potatoes are tender. Sprinkle with cheese. Bake, uncovered, about 5 minutes more or until cheese is melted.   *Makes 4 servings*

146 SO–EASY FISH DIVAN

1 package (about 1⅛ ounces) cheese sauce mix
1⅓ cups milk
1 bag (16 ounces) frozen vegetable combination (brussels sprouts, carrots, cauliflower), thawed and drained
1 can (2.8 ounces) FRENCH'S® French Fried Onions
1 pound unbreaded fish fillets, thawed if frozen
½ cup (2 ounces) shredded Cheddar cheese

Preheat oven to 375°F. In small saucepan, prepare cheese sauce mix according to package directions using 1⅓ cups milk. In 12×8-inch baking dish, combine vegetables and ½ *can* French Fried Onions; top with fish fillets. Pour cheese sauce over fish and vegetables. Bake, covered, at 375°F for 25 minutes or until fish flakes easily with fork. Top fish with Cheddar cheese and remaining onions; bake, uncovered, 3 minutes or until onions are golden brown.   *Makes 3 to 4 servings*

Baked Fish with Potatoes and Onions

Tuna Tortilla Roll-Ups

147 TUNA TORTILLA ROLL–UPS

1 can (10¾ ounces) condensed cream of celery soup
1 cup milk
1 can (9¼ ounces) tuna, drained and flaked
1 package (10 ounces) frozen broccoli spears, thawed, drained and cut into 1-inch pieces
1 cup (4 ounces) shredded Cheddar cheese
1 can (2.8 ounces) FRENCH'S® French Fried Onions
6 (7-inch) flour or corn tortillas
1 medium tomato, chopped

Preheat oven to 350°F. In small bowl, combine soup and milk; set aside. In medium bowl, combine tuna, broccoli, ½ *cup* cheese and ½ *can* French Fried Onions; stir in ¾ *cup* soup mixture. Divide tuna mixture evenly among tortillas; roll up tortillas. Place, seam-side down, in lightly greased 13×9-inch baking dish. Stir tomato into remaining soup mixture; pour down center of roll-ups. Bake, covered, at 350°F for 35 minutes or until heated through. Top center of roll-ups with remaining cheese and onions; bake, uncovered, 5 minutes or until onions are golden brown.

Makes 6 servings

148 FISH BROCCOLI CASSEROLE

1 package (10 ounces) frozen broccoli
    spears, thawed, drained
1 cup cooked, flaked whitefish
1 can (10¾ ounces) condensed cream of
    mushroom soup
½ cup milk
¼ teaspoon salt
⅛ teaspoon freshly ground black pepper
½ cup crushed potato chips

Preheat oven to 425°F. Grease 1½-quart
casserole. Layer broccoli in prepared
casserole. Combine fish, soup, milk, salt and
pepper in large bowl.

Spread fish mixture over broccoli. Sprinkle
with potato chips. Bake 12 to 15 minutes or
until golden brown.   *Makes 4 servings*

Favorite recipe from **Florida Department of
Agriculture & Consumer Services, Bureau of
Seafood and Aquaculture**

149 TAG–ALONG TUNA BAKE

3 to 4 tablespoons butter or margarine,
    softened
12 slices bread
1 can (12½ ounces) water-packed tuna,
    drained and flaked
1 cup chopped celery
1 can (2.8 ounces) FRENCH'S® French
    Fried Onions
2 cups milk
1 cup mayonnaise
4 eggs, slightly beaten
1 can (10¾ ounces) condensed cream of
    mushroom soup
3 slices (¾ ounce *each*) process American
    cheese, cut diagonally into halves

Butter 1 side of each bread slice; arrange
6 slices, buttered-side down in 13×9-inch
baking dish. Layer tuna, celery and *½ can*
French Fried Onions evenly over bread. Top
with remaining bread slices, buttered-side
down. In medium bowl, combine milk,
mayonnaise, eggs and soup; mix well. Pour
evenly over layers in baking dish; cover and
refrigerate overnight. Bake, covered, at
350°F for 30 minutes. Uncover and bake
15 minutes or until center is set. Arrange
cheese slices down center of casserole,
overlapping slightly, points all in same
direction. Top with remaining onions; bake,
uncovered, 5 minutes or until onions are
golden brown.   *Makes 8 servings*

150 BISCUIT–TOPPED TUNA BAKE

2 tablespoons vegetable oil
$\frac{1}{2}$ cup chopped onion
$\frac{1}{2}$ cup chopped celery
1 can (12 ounces) STARKIST® Solid White
   or Chunk Light Tuna, drained and
   chunked
1 can (10$\frac{3}{4}$ ounces) cream of potato soup
1 package (10 ounces) frozen peas and
   carrots, thawed
$\frac{3}{4}$ cup milk
$\frac{1}{4}$ teaspoon ground black pepper
$\frac{1}{4}$ teaspoon garlic powder
1 can (7$\frac{1}{2}$ ounces) refrigerator flaky
   biscuits

In large skillet, heat oil over medium-high
heat; sauté onion and celery until onion is
soft. Add remaining ingredients except
biscuits; heat thoroughly. Transfer mixture
to 1$\frac{1}{2}$-quart casserole. Arrange biscuits
around top edge of dish; bake in 400°F oven
10 to 15 minutes or until biscuits are golden
brown.   *Makes 4 to 6 servings*

Prep Time: 25 minutes

151 OLD–FASHIONED TUNA NOODLE CASSEROLE

3 tablespoons butter or margarine, melted
   and divided
$\frac{1}{4}$ cup plain dry bread crumbs
1 tablespoon finely chopped parsley
$\frac{1}{2}$ cup chopped onion
$\frac{1}{2}$ cup chopped celery
1 cup water
1 cup milk
1 package LIPTON® Noodles & Sauce-
   Butter
2 cans (6$\frac{1}{2}$ ounces *each*) tuna, drained
   and flaked

Melt 1 tablespoon butter; place in small
bowl. Add bread crumbs and parsley; mix
well. Set aside.

In medium saucepan, melt remaining
2 tablespoons butter. Cook onion and celery
over medium heat, stirring occasionally,
2 minutes or until onion is tender. Add water
and milk; bring to a boil. Stir in Noodles &
Butter Sauce. Continue boiling over medium
heat, stirring occasionally, 8 minutes or until
noodles are tender. Stir in tuna. Turn into
greased 1-quart casserole, then top with
bread crumb mixture. Broil until bread
crumbs are golden.

Makes about 4 servings

Biscuit-Topped Tuna Bake

152 LOUISIANA SEAFOOD BAKE

²/₃ cup uncooked regular rice
1 cup sliced celery
1 cup water
1 can (14½ ounces) whole tomatoes, undrained and cut up
1 can (8 ounces) tomato sauce
1 can (2.8 ounces) FRENCH'S® French Fried Onions
1 teaspoon FRANK'S® Original REDHOT® Cayenne Pepper Sauce
½ teaspoon garlic powder
¼ teaspoon dried oregano, crumbled
¼ teaspoon dried thyme, crumbled
½ pound white fish, thawed if frozen and cut into 1-inch chunks
1 can (4 ounces) shrimp, drained
⅓ cup sliced pitted ripe olives
¼ cup (1 ounce) grated Parmesan cheese

Preheat oven to 375°F. In 1½-quart casserole, combine uncooked rice, celery, water, tomatoes, tomato sauce, ½ can French Fried Onions and the seasonings. Bake, covered, at 375°F for 20 minutes. Stir in fish, shrimp and olives. Bake, covered, 20 minutes or until heated through. Top with cheese and remaining onions; bake, uncovered, 3 minutes or until onions are golden brown. *Makes 4 servings*

MICROWAVE DIRECTIONS: In 2-quart microwave-safe casserole, prepare rice mixture as above. Cook, covered, on HIGH 15 minutes, stirring rice halfway through cooking time. Add fish, shrimp and olives. Cook, covered, 12 to 14 minutes or until rice is cooked, stirring casserole halfway through cooking time. Top with cheese and remaining onions; cook, uncovered, 1 minute. Let stand 5 minutes.

153 HOMESTYLE TUNA POT PIE

1 package (15 ounces) refrigerated pie crusts
1 can (12 ounces) STARKIST® Solid White or Chunk Light Tuna, drained and chunked
1 package (10 ounces) frozen peas and carrots, thawed and drained
½ cup chopped onion
1 can (10¾ ounces) cream of potato or cream of mushroom soup
⅓ cup milk
½ teaspoon poultry seasoning or dried thyme
Salt and pepper to taste

Line 9-inch pie pan with one crust; set aside. Reserve second crust. In medium bowl, combine remaining ingredients; mix well. Pour tuna mixture into pie shell; top with second crust. Crimp edges to seal. Cut slits in top crust to vent. Bake in 375°F oven 45 to 50 minutes or until golden brown.
Makes 6 servings

Prep and Cook Time: 55 to 60 minutes

Homestyle Tuna Pot Pie

154 TUNA–SWISS PIE

2 cups cooked unsalted regular rice
    (²/₃ cup uncooked)
1 tablespoon butter or margarine
¼ teaspoon garlic powder
3 eggs
1 can (2.8 ounces) FRENCH'S® French
    Fried Onions
1 cup (4 ounces) shredded Swiss cheese
1 can (9¼ ounces) water-packed tuna,
    drained and flaked
1 cup milk
¼ teaspoon salt
¼ teaspoon pepper

Preheat oven to 400°F. To hot rice in
saucepan, add butter, garlic powder and
1 slightly beaten egg; mix thoroughly. Spoon
rice mixture into *ungreased* 9-inch pie plate.
Press rice mixture firmly onto bottom and
up side of pie plate to form a crust. Layer
½ can French Fried Onions, *½ cup* cheese
and the tuna evenly over rice crust. In small
bowl, combine milk, remaining eggs and the
seasonings; pour over tuna filling. Bake,
uncovered, at 400°F for 30 to 35 minutes or
until center is set. Top with remaining
cheese and onions; bake, uncovered, 1 to
3 minutes or until onions are golden brown.

Makes 4 to 6 servings

155 SICILIAN FISH AND RICE BAKE

3 tablespoons olive or vegetable oil
¾ cup chopped onion
½ cup chopped celery
1 clove garlic, minced
½ cup uncooked long-grain white rice
3½ cups (two 14.5-ounce cans)
    CONTADINA® Recipe Ready Diced
    Tomatoes, undrained
1 teaspoon salt
1 teaspoon ground black pepper
½ teaspoon granulated sugar
⅛ teaspoon cayenne pepper
1 pound fish fillets (any firm white fish)
¼ cup finely chopped fresh parsley

In large skillet, heat oil. Add onion, celery
and garlic; sauté for 2 to 3 minutes or until
vegetables are tender. Stir in rice; sauté for
5 minutes or until rice browns slightly. Add
tomatoes and juice, salt, black pepper, sugar
and cayenne pepper; mix well. Place fish in
bottom of greased 12×7½-inch baking dish.
Spoon rice mixture over fish; cover with foil.
Bake in preheated 400°F oven for 45 to
50 minutes or until rice is tender. Let stand
for 5 minutes before serving. Sprinkle with
parsley.   *Makes 6 servings*

156 SURFIN' TUNA CASSEROLE

3 eggs
¾ cup milk
2 cups STOVE TOP® Chicken Flavor Stuffing Mix in the Canister
1½ cups (6 ounces) KRAFT® Natural Shredded Colby/Monterey Jack Cheese, divided
1 cup frozen green peas, thawed
1 can (6⅛ ounces) tuna, drained, flaked
½ cup condensed cream of mushroom soup
¼ cup chopped green onions
2 tablespoons chopped pimiento

BEAT eggs in large bowl; stir in milk. Stir in stuffing mix, 1 cup of the cheese, peas, tuna, soup, onions and pimiento until well mixed. Spoon into greased 9-inch microwavable pie plate. Cover loosely with wax paper.

MICROWAVE on HIGH 5 minutes. Stir thoroughly to completely mix center and outside edges; smooth top. Cover.

MICROWAVE 5 minutes or until center is no longer wet. Sprinkle with remaining ½ cup cheese; cover. Let stand 5 minutes.

Makes 6 servings

Prep Time: 10 minutes
Cook Time: 15 minutes

Surfin' Tuna Casserole

157 TUNA AND BROCCOLI BAKE

1 package (16 ounces) frozen broccoli cuts, thawed and well drained
2 slices bread, cut in ½-inch cubes
1 can (12 ounces) STARKIST® Solid White or Chunk Light Tuna, drained and chunked
3 eggs
2 cups cottage cheese
1 cup shredded Cheddar cheese
¼ teaspoon ground black pepper

Place broccoli on bottom of 2-quart baking dish. Top with bread cubes and tuna. In medium bowl, combine eggs, cottage cheese, Cheddar cheese and pepper. Spread evenly over tuna mixture. Bake in 400°F oven 30 minutes or until golden brown and puffed. *Makes 4 servings*

Prep Time: 35 minutes

158 STARKIST® SWISS POTATO PIE

1 cup milk
4 large eggs, beaten
4 cups frozen shredded hash brown potatoes, thawed
2 cups shredded Swiss cheese
½ to 1 cup chopped green onions, including tops
½ cup sour cream
½ cup chopped green bell pepper (optional)
½ teaspoon garlic powder
1 can (6 ounces) STARKIST® Solid White Tuna, drained and flaked

In large bowl, combine all ingredients. Pour into lightly greased deep 10-inch pie plate. Bake in 350°F oven 1 hour and 20 minutes or until golden and crusty. Let stand a few minutes before slicing into serving portions. *Makes 6 servings*

Prep Time: 90 minutes

Tuna and Broccoli Bake

159 SUPERB FILLET OF SOLE & VEGETABLES

1 can (10¾ ounces) condensed cream of
    celery soup
½ cup milk
1 cup (4 ounces) shredded Swiss cheese
½ teaspoon dried basil, crumbled
¼ teaspoon seasoned salt
¼ teaspoon pepper
1 package (10 ounces) frozen baby
    carrots, thawed and drained
1 package (10 ounces) frozen asparagus
    cuts, thawed and drained
1 can (2.8 ounces) FRENCH'S® French
    Fried Onions
1 pound unbreaded sole fillets, thawed if
    frozen

Preheat oven to 375°F. In small bowl, combine soup, milk, ½ *cup* cheese and the seasonings; set aside. In 12×8-inch baking dish, combine carrots, asparagus and ½ *can* French Fried Onions. Roll up fish fillets. (If fillets are wide, fold in half lengthwise before rolling.) Place fish rolls upright along center of vegetable mixture. Pour soup mixture over fish and vegetables. Bake, covered, at 375°F for 30 minutes or until fish flakes easily with fork. Stir vegetables; top fish with remaining cheese and onions. Bake, uncovered, 3 minutes or until onions are golden brown.

Makes 3 to 4 servings

Superb Fillet of Sole & Vegetables

160 TUNA, RICE AND BISCUITS

1 tablespoon margarine or butter
1 cup chopped onions
2½ cups milk
1 can (10¾ ounces) condensed cream of celery soup
1 package (10 ounces) frozen mixed vegetables, thawed
½ teaspoon dill weed
⅛ teaspoon pepper
1½ cups MINUTE® Original Rice, uncooked
1 can (12½ ounces) tuna, drained, flaked
1 package (7½ ounces) refrigerated buttermilk biscuits

HEAT oven to 450°F.

MELT margarine in large skillet on medium-high heat. Add onion; cook and stir until tender. Stir in milk, soup, vegetables, dill and pepper. Bring to boil.

STIR in rice and tuna. Pour into greased 2-quart casserole. Top with biscuits.

BAKE 8 to 10 minutes or until biscuits are golden brown.   *Makes 6 servings*

Prep Time: 5 minutes
Cook Time: 20 minutes

CHICKEN, RICE AND BISCUITS: Prepare as directed above, substituting 2 cups chopped cooked chicken for tuna.

161 CRUNCHY TUNA SQUARES

1 can (12 ounces) STARKIST® Solid White or Chunk Light Tuna, drained and chunked
1 cup chopped celery
1 cup chopped roasted cashews
½ cup drained sliced water chestnuts
½ cup chopped green onions, including tops
⅓ cup chopped drained roasted red peppers
1½ cups shredded Cheddar cheese, divided
½ cup mayonnaise or light mayonnaise
½ cup sour cream or light sour cream
2 tablespoons lemon juice
¾ teaspoon seasoned salt
1 cup cheese crackers, crushed into coarse crumbs

In medium bowl, place tuna, celery, cashews, water chestnuts, onions, peppers and 1 cup cheese; mix lightly with fork. In small bowl, whisk together mayonnaise, sour cream, lemon juice and seasoned salt. Add to tuna mixture; mix gently.

Spoon into greased 11×7-inch baking pan. Sprinkle with crushed cracker crumbs; top with remaining ½ cup cheese. Bake in 450°F oven 12 to 15 minutes or until mixture bubbles and begins to brown. Let stand several minutes before cutting into 6 squares.   *Makes 6 servings*

Prep Time: 20 minutes

162 MUSHROOM AND TUNA BAKE

- 1 can (10¾ ounces) cream of celery soup
- 1 cup milk
- 1 jar (4 ounces) sliced mushrooms, drained
- ½ cup grated Parmesan cheese, divided
- 1 teaspoon dried Italian herb blend
- ½ teaspoon seasoned salt
- ⅛ to ¼ teaspoon garlic powder
- 1 can (12 ounces) STARKIST® Solid White or Chunk Light Tuna, drained and chunked
- 3 cups cooked egg noodles
- 1 cup crispy rice cereal

In medium saucepan, combine soup and milk; blend well. Add mushrooms, ¼ cup cheese, Italian herb blend, seasoned salt, garlic powder and tuna; cook over low heat until heated through. Remove from heat; stir in egg noodles. Transfer mixture to lightly greased 11×7-inch baking dish. Top with remaining ¼ cup Parmesan cheese and cereal. Bake in 350°F oven 30 minutes.

Makes 6 servings

Prep Time: 40 minutes

163 SOLE ALMONDINE

- 1 package (6.5 ounces) RICE-A-RONI® Broccoli Au Gratin
- 1 medium zucchini
- 4 sole, scrod or orange roughy fillets
- 1 tablespoon lemon juice
- ¼ cup grated Parmesan cheese
  Salt and pepper (optional)
- ¼ cup sliced almonds
- 2 tablespoons margarine or butter, melted

1. Prepare Rice-A-Roni® mix as package directs.

2. While Rice-A-Roni® is simmering, cut zucchini lengthwise into 12 thin slices. Heat oven to 350°F.

3. In 11×7-inch glass baking dish, spread prepared rice evenly. Set aside. Sprinkle fish with lemon juice, 2 tablespoons cheese, salt and pepper, if desired. Place zucchini strips over fish; roll up. Place fish seam-side down on rice.

4. Combine almonds and margarine; sprinkle evenly over fish. Top with remaining 2 tablespoons cheese. Bake 20 to 25 minutes or until fish flakes easily with fork.

Makes 4 servings

164 QUICK AND EASY TUNA RICE WITH PEAS

1 package (10 ounces) frozen green peas, thawed
1¼ cups water
1 can (11 ounces) condensed Cheddar cheese soup
1 can (12½ ounces) tuna, drained and flaked
1 chicken bouillon cube
1½ cups MINUTE® Rice

• Bring peas, water, soup, tuna and bouillon cube to a full boil in medium saucepan. Stir in rice. Cover; remove from heat. Let stand 5 minutes. Fluff with fork.

Makes 4 servings

165 TUNA AND RICE SKILLET DINNER

1 package (6½ ounces) chicken flavored rice mix
½ cup chopped onion
Water
1½ cups frozen peas and carrots, thawed
1 can (10¾ ounces) cream of mushroom soup
⅛ teaspoon ground black pepper
1 can (12 ounces) STARKIST® Solid White or Chunk Light Tuna, drained and chunked
⅓ cup toasted slivered almonds (optional)

In medium saucepan, combine rice mix and onion. Add water and prepare rice according to package directions. Stir in vegetables, soup and pepper; blend well. Simmer, covered, 5 to 7 minutes, stirring occasionally. Stir in tuna; top with almonds, if desired. *Makes 4 to 6 servings*

Prep Time: 30 minutes

166 TUNA AND PASTA FRITTATA

1 tablespoon olive oil
2 cups cooked spaghetti
4 large eggs
2 tablespoons milk
¼ cup prepared pesto sauce
1 can (6 ounces) STARKIST® Solid White or Chunk Light Tuna, drained and flaked
½ cup shredded mozzarella cheese

Preheat broiler. In medium ovenproof skillet, heat oil over medium-high heat; sauté spaghetti. In bowl, combine eggs, milk and pesto sauce; blend well. Add tuna; pour mixture over hot spaghetti. Cook over medium-low heat, stirring occasionally, until eggs are almost completely set. Sprinkle cheese over cooked eggs; place under broiler until cheese is bubbly and golden. Serve hot or at room temperature.

Makes 2 to 4 servings

Prep Time: 8 minutes

TREASURES FROM THE SEA

167 ALBACORE VEGETABLE PILAF

1 cup long grain white rice
1 can (14½ ounces) chicken broth
¼ cup water
2 to 3 tablespoons lemon juice
1 teaspoon dried dill weed
½ teaspoon salt
¼ teaspoon ground black pepper
¼ teaspoon garlic powder
½ cup chopped red bell pepper
½ cup chopped green bell pepper
½ cup chopped zucchini
½ cup corn
1 cup sour cream
1 can (12 ounces) STARKIST® Solid White Tuna, drained and chunked

In medium saucepan with tight-fitting lid, combine rice, chicken broth, water, lemon juice, dill, salt, black pepper and garlic powder. Bring to a boil; cover. Reduce heat; simmer 15 minutes. Stir in vegetables; cover and continue cooking 5 to 7 more minutes or until all liquid is absorbed. Stir in sour cream and tuna. Serve hot or cold.

Makes 6 servings

Prep Time: 30 minutes

168 NEW ENGLAND FISHERMAN'S SKILLET

4 small red potatoes, diced
1 medium onion, chopped
1 tablespoon olive oil
2 stalks celery, chopped
2 cloves garlic, minced
½ teaspoon dried thyme, crushed
1 can (14½ ounces) DEL MONTE® Original Recipe Stewed Tomatoes
1 pound firm white fish (such as halibut, snapper or cod)

In large skillet, brown potatoes and onion in oil over medium-high heat, stirring occasionally. Season with herb seasoning mix, if desired. Stir in celery, garlic and thyme; cook 4 minutes. Add tomatoes; bring to boil. Cook 4 minutes or until thickened. Add fish; cover and cook over medium heat 5 to 8 minutes or until fish flakes easily with fork. Garnish with lemon wedges and chopped parsley, if desired.

Makes 4 servings

Prep Time: 10 minutes
Cook Time: 25 minutes

Albacore Vegetable Pilaf

TREASURES FROM THE SEA

169 RAINBOW STIR-FRIED FISH

SAUCE
- ½ cup chicken broth
- 2 tablespoons LA CHOY® Soy Sauce
- 1 tablespoon cornstarch
- 1 teaspoon sugar
- ¼ teaspoon crushed red pepper (optional)

FISH AND VEGETABLES
- 1 pound orange roughy filets,* cut into 1-inch chunks
- 1 tablespoon LA CHOY® Soy Sauce
- 3 tablespoons WESSON® Oil
- ½ cup julienne-cut carrots
- 1 teaspoon *each:* minced fresh garlic and gingerroot
- 2 cups fresh broccoli flowerettes
- 1 (8-ounce) can LA CHOY® Sliced Water Chestnuts, drained
- 1 (6-ounce) package frozen LA CHOY® Pea Pods, thawed and drained
- ½ cup diagonally sliced green onions

Any firm-fleshed white fish may be substituted.

In small bowl, combine *sauce* ingredients; set aside. In medium bowl, combine fish and soy sauce; toss lightly to coat. In large nonstick skillet or wok, heat oil. Add fish mixture; stir-fry 2 to 3 minutes or until fish flakes easily with fork. Remove fish from skillet; drain. Set aside. Add carrots, garlic and ginger to same skillet; stir-fry 30 seconds. Add broccoli; stir-fry 1 minute. Add water chestnuts and pea pods; heat thoroughly, stirring occasionally. Return fish to skillet. Stir sauce; add to skillet. Heat, stirring gently, until sauce is thick and bubbly. Sprinkle with green onions. Garnish, if desired.   *Makes 4 servings*

170 SAUCY STIR-FRIED FISH

SAUCE
- ½ cup chicken broth
- 3 tablespoons dry sherry
- 1 tablespoon LA CHOY® Soy Sauce
- 1½ teaspoons cornstarch

FISH AND VEGETABLES
- 1 tablespoon cornstarch
- 1 tablespoon vodka *or* chicken broth
- 1 teaspoon LA CHOY® Soy Sauce
- 1 pound firm-fleshed white fish, cut into 1-inch chunks
- 2 tablespoons WESSON® Oil
- ½ teaspoon minced fresh garlic
- ¼ teaspoon minced gingerroot
- 1 (8-ounce) can LA CHOY® Bamboo Shoots, drained
- ½ cup chopped carrots
- 1 (5-ounce) can LA CHOY® Chow Mein Noodles

In small bowl, combine *sauce* ingredients; set aside. In medium glass or plastic bowl, combine cornstarch, vodka and soy sauce; mix well. Add fish; toss gently to coat. Cover and marinate 10 to 15 minutes. In large nonstick skillet or wok, heat oil. Add garlic and ginger; cook and stir 30 seconds. Add fish; gently stir-fry until fish flakes easily with fork, about 3 to 4 minutes. Remove fish from skillet; set aside. Add bamboo shoots and carrots to same skillet; stir-fry 1 to 2 minutes or until carrots are crisp-tender. Stir sauce; add to skillet. Cook, stirring constantly, until sauce is thick and bubbly. Return fish to skillet; heat thoroughly, stirring occasionally. Serve over noodles.
Makes 4 to 6 servings

Rainbow Stir-Fried Fish

171 SAVORY RICE PILAF WITH TUNA

2 tablespoons butter or margarine
1 cup long grain white rice
$\frac{1}{2}$ cup finely chopped onion
$\frac{1}{4}$ teaspoon ground black pepper
$1\frac{1}{2}$ teaspoons dried basil
$2\frac{1}{4}$ cups chicken or vegetable broth
$1\frac{1}{2}$ cups assorted fresh or frozen and
    thawed vegetables*
1 can (12 ounces) STARKIST® Solid White
    or Chunk Light Tuna, drained and
    chunked
$\frac{3}{4}$ cup shredded Cheddar cheese, divided

Suggested vegetables include peas, corn, sliced carrots, broccoli flowerets, sliced zucchini and sliced mushrooms.

In medium saucepan with tight-fitting lid, melt butter over medium-high heat; sauté rice and onion until rice is golden and onion is soft. Stir in pepper, basil, chicken broth and vegetables. Bring to a boil; cover. Reduce heat; simmer about 20 minutes or until rice is tender *(not all liquid will be absorbed)*. Add tuna and $\frac{1}{2}$ cup cheese, stirring to blend; transfer to serving dish. Sprinkle with remaining $\frac{1}{4}$ cup cheese.

Makes 4 servings

Prep Time: 30 minutes

172 LEMON–GARLIC SHRIMP

1 package (6.2 ounces) RICE-A-RONI®
    With $\frac{1}{3}$ Less Salt Broccoli Au Gratin
1 tablespoon margarine or butter
1 pound raw medium shrimp, shelled,
    deveined or large scallops, halved
1 medium red or green bell pepper, cut
    into short thin strips
2 cloves garlic, minced
$\frac{1}{2}$ teaspoon Italian seasoning
$\frac{1}{2}$ cup reduced-sodium or regular chicken
    broth
1 tablespoon lemon juice
1 tablespoon cornstarch
3 medium green onions, cut into $\frac{1}{2}$-inch
    pieces
1 teaspoon grated lemon peel

1. Prepare Rice-A-Roni® mix as package directs.

2. While Rice-A-Roni® is simmering, heat margarine in second large skillet or wok over medium-high heat. Add shrimp, red pepper, garlic and Italian seasoning. Stir-fry 3 to 4 minutes or until seafood is opaque.

3. Combine chicken broth, lemon juice and cornstarch, mixing until smooth. Add broth mixture and onions to skillet. Stir-fry 2 to 3 minutes or until sauce thickens.

4. Stir $\frac{1}{2}$ teaspoon lemon peel into rice. Serve rice topped with shrimp mixture; sprinkle with remaining $\frac{1}{2}$ teaspoon lemon peel.

Makes 4 servings

Lemon-Garlic Shrimp

Garlic Shrimp with Wilted Spinach

173 GARLIC SHRIMP WITH WILTED SPINACH

2 teaspoons olive or vegetable oil

¼ cup diagonally sliced green onions

2 tablespoons sherry or dry white wine (optional)

1 envelope LIPTON® Recipe Secrets® Savory Herb with Garlic Soup Mix

1 cup water

1 pound uncooked medium shrimp, peeled and deveined

1 large tomato, diced

2 cups fresh trimmed spinach leaves (about 4 ounces)

¼ cup chopped unsalted cashews (optional)

In 12-inch skillet, heat oil over medium heat and cook green onions 2 minutes or until slightly soft, stirring occasionally. Add sherry and bring to a boil over high heat, stirring frequently. Stir in savory herb with garlic soup mix blended with water. Bring to a boil over high heat. Reduce heat to low and simmer 2 minutes or until sauce is thickened. Stir in shrimp, tomato, spinach and cashews. Simmer, stirring occasionally, 2 minutes or until shrimp turn pink.

Makes about 4 servings

NOTE: Also terrific with LIPTON® Recipe Secrets® Golden Herb with Lemon or Golden Onion Soup Mix.

174 SEAFOOD GUMBO

1 bag SUCCESS® Rice
1 tablespoon reduced-calorie margarine
¼ cup chopped onion
¼ cup chopped green bell pepper
2 cloves garlic, minced
1 can (28 ounces) whole tomatoes, cut up, undrained
2 cups chicken broth
½ teaspoon ground red pepper
½ teaspoon dried thyme leaves, crushed
½ teaspoon dried basil leaves, crushed
¾ pound white fish, cut into 1-inch pieces
1 package (10 ounces) frozen cut okra, thawed and drained
½ pound shrimp, peeled and deveined

Prepare rice according to package directions.

Melt margarine in large saucepan over medium-high heat. Add onion, green pepper and garlic; cook and stir until crisp-tender. Stir in tomatoes, broth, red pepper, thyme and basil. Bring to a boil. Reduce heat to low; simmer, uncovered, until thoroughly heated, 10 to 15 minutes. Stir in fish, okra and shrimp; simmer until fish flakes easily with fork and shrimp curl and turn pink. Add rice; heat thoroughly, stirring occasionally, 5 to 8 minutes. *Makes 4 servings*

175 SHRIMP À LA LOUISIANA

1 tablespoon margarine
1½ cups uncooked long-grain white rice
1 medium onion, chopped
1 green pepper, chopped
2¾ cups beef broth
¼ teaspoon salt
¼ teaspoon ground black pepper
¼ teaspoon hot pepper sauce
1 pound medium shrimp, peeled and deveined
1 can (4 ounces) sliced mushrooms, drained
3 tablespoons snipped parsley
¼ cup sliced green onions for garnish (optional)

Melt margarine in 3-quart saucepan. Add rice, onion and green pepper. Cook 2 to 3 minutes. Add broth, salt, black pepper and pepper sauce; bring to a boil. Cover and simmer 15 minutes. Add shrimp, mushrooms and parsley. Cook 5 minutes longer or until shrimp turn pink. Garnish with green onions. *Makes 8 servings*

Favorite recipe from **USA Rice Council**

176 STIR–FRIED CORKSCREW SHRIMP WITH VEGETABLES

SAUCE
- ¼ cup LA CHOY® Soy Sauce
- ¼ cup chicken broth
- 3 tablespoons dry sherry
- 1 tablespoon cornstarch
- 1 teaspoon sugar
- ¼ teaspoon *each:* pepper and Oriental sesame oil

SHRIMP AND VEGETABLES
- 1 egg white
- 1 tablespoon cornstarch
- 1 pound shrimp, peeled, deveined and cut in half lengthwise
- 3 tablespoons WESSON® Oil, divided
- 1 cup sliced onion
- 1 tablespoon minced fresh garlic
- 1½ teaspoons minced gingerroot
- 1 cup sliced fresh mushrooms
- ½ cup thinly sliced carrots
- 1 (14-ounce) can LA CHOY® Bean Sprouts, well drained
- 1 (8-ounce) can LA CHOY® Sliced Water Chestnuts, drained
- 1 (6-ounce) package frozen LA CHOY® Pea Pods, thawed

In small bowl, combine *sauce* ingredients; set aside. In medium bowl, beat together egg white and cornstarch until well blended. Add shrimp; toss gently to coat. In large nonstick skillet or wok, heat *2 tablespoons* oil. Add shrimp mixture; stir-fry until shrimp curl and turn pink. Remove shrimp from skillet; drain. Heat *remaining 1 tablespoon* oil in same skillet. Add onion, garlic and ginger; stir-fry 30 seconds. Add mushrooms and carrots; stir-fry 1 to 2 minutes or until carrots are crisp-tender. Stir sauce; add to skillet. Cook, stirring constantly, until sauce

is thick and bubbly. Return shrimp to skillet with bean sprouts, water chestnuts and pea pods; heat thoroughly, stirring occasionally. Garnish, if desired.

Makes 4 to 6 servings

177 SHRIMP CLASSICO

- ⅔ cup milk
- 2 tablespoons margarine or butter
- 1 package (4.8 ounces) PASTA RONI® Herb Sauce with Angel Hair Pasta
- 1 clove garlic, minced
- 1 package (10 ounces) frozen chopped spinach, thawed, well drained
- 1 package (10 ounces) frozen precooked shrimp, thawed, well drained
- 1 jar (2 ounces) chopped pimento, drained

1. In 3-quart round microwaveable glass casserole, combine 1⅔ cups water, milk and margarine. Microwave, uncovered, on HIGH 4 to 5 minutes or until boiling.

2. Gradually add pasta while stirring. Separate pasta with a fork, if needed. Stir in contents of seasoning packet and garlic.

3. Microwave, uncovered, on HIGH 4 minutes, stirring gently after 2 minutes. Separate pasta with a fork, if needed. Stir in spinach, shrimp and pimento. Microwave on HIGH 1 to 2 minutes. Sauce will be very thin, but will thicken upon standing.

4. Let stand, uncovered, 2 minutes or until desired consistency. Stir before serving.

Makes 4 servings

Stir-Fried Corkscrew Shrimp with Vegetables

178 CHESAPEAKE CRAB STRATA

4 tablespoons butter or margarine
4 cups unseasoned croutons
2 cups (8 ounces) shredded Cheddar
   cheese
2 cups milk
8 eggs, beaten
½ teaspoon dry mustard
½ teaspoon seafood seasoning
   Salt and black pepper to taste
1 pound crabmeat, picked over to remove
   any shells

Preheat oven to 325°F. Place butter in
11×7-inch baking dish. Heat in oven until
melted; tilt to coat dish. Remove dish from
oven; spread croutons over melted butter.
Top with cheese; set aside.

Combine milk, eggs, dry mustard, seafood
seasoning, salt and black pepper; mix well.
Pour egg mixture over cheese in dish;
sprinkle with crabmeat. Bake for 50 minutes
or until mixture is set. Remove from oven.
Let stand for about 10 minutes. Garnish, if
desired.   *Makes 6 to 8 servings*

Chesapeake Crab Strata

179 COMPANY CRAB

1 pound blue crabmeat, fresh, frozen or
   pasteurized
1 can (15 ounces) artichoke hearts,
   drained
1 can (4 ounces) sliced mushrooms,
   drained
2 tablespoons butter or margarine
2½ tablespoons all-purpose flour
½ teaspoon salt
⅛ teaspoon ground red pepper
1 cup half-and-half
2 tablespoons dry sherry
2 tablespoons crushed corn flakes
1 tablespoon grated Parmesan cheese
   Paprika

Preheat oven to 450°F. Thaw crabmeat if
frozen. Remove any pieces of shell or
cartilage. Cut artichoke hearts in half; place
artichokes in well-greased, shallow 1½-quart
casserole. Add crabmeat and mushrooms;
cover and set aside.

Melt butter in small saucepan over medium
heat. Stir in flour, salt and ground red
pepper. Gradually stir in half-and-half.
Continue cooking until sauce thickens,
stirring constantly. Stir in sherry. Pour sauce
over crabmeat. Combine corn flakes and
cheese in small bowl; sprinkle over
casserole. Sprinkle with paprika. Bake 12 to
15 minutes or until bubbly.

Makes 6 servings

Favorite recipe from **Florida Department of
Agriculture and Consumer Services, Bureau of
Seafood and Aquaculture**

180 CRAB AND BROWN RICE CASSEROLE

1 pound blue crabmeat, fresh or frozen,
   thawed
3 eggs, slightly beaten
1 cup mayonnaise
1 cup cooked brown rice
¾ cup evaporated milk
¾ cup (3 ounces) shredded Cheddar
   cheese
¼ teaspoon hot pepper sauce

Preheat oven to 350°F. Grease 1½-quart
casserole; set aside. Remove any pieces of
cartilage from crabmeat. Set aside.

Combine eggs, mayonnaise, brown rice,
milk, cheese and hot pepper sauce in large
bowl. Stir in crabmeat. Bake 30 to
35 minutes or until knife inserted 1 inch
from center comes out clean.

Makes 6 servings

Favorite recipe from **Florida Department of
Agriculture & Consumer Services, Bureau of
Seafood and Aquaculture**

181 STIR–FRIED SCALLOPS WITH VEGETABLES

1 pound sea scallops
¼ teaspoon salt
⅛ teaspoon black pepper
½ cup vegetable broth
1 tablespoon cornstarch
3 tablespoons butter or margarine, divided
1 package (6 ounces) red radishes, quartered
¼ cup dry white wine
1 package (6 ounces) frozen snow peas, partially thawed
½ cup sliced bamboo shoots
  Hot cooked couscous

• Rinse scallops and pat dry with paper towels. Sprinkle with salt and black pepper.

• Stir broth into cornstarch in cup until smooth; set aside.

• Heat wok over high heat about 1 minute or until hot. Add 1½ tablespoons butter; swirl to coat bottom and heat 30 seconds. Arrange half the scallops in single layer in wok, leaving ½ inch between. (Scallops should not touch.) Cook scallops until browned on both sides. Remove scallops to large bowl. Repeat with remaining 1½ tablespoons butter and scallops. Reduce heat to medium-high.

• Add radishes to wok; stir-fry about 1 minute or until crisp-tender. Remove radishes to bowl with scallops.

• Add wine to wok. Stir broth mixture; add to wok. Add snow peas and bamboo shoots; stir-fry until heated through.

• Return scallops and radishes to wok; stir-fry until heated through. Serve over couscous. Garnish, if desired.

Makes 4 servings

182 SOUTHERN ITALIAN CLAM CHOWDER

2 slices bacon, diced
1 cup chopped onion
½ cup chopped peeled carrots
½ cup chopped celery
3½ cups (two 14.5-ounce cans) CONTADINA® Recipe Ready Diced Tomatoes, undrained
1 cup (8-ounce can) CONTADINA® Tomato Sauce
1 cup (8-ounce bottle) clam juice
½ teaspoon chopped fresh rosemary *or* ¼ teaspoon dried rosemary leaves, crushed
⅛ teaspoon ground black pepper
1½ cups (two 6½-ounce cans) chopped clams, undrained

In large saucepan, sauté bacon until crisp. Add onion, carrots and celery; sauté for 2 to 3 minutes or until vegetables are tender. Stir in tomatoes and juice, tomato sauce, clam juice, rosemary and pepper. Bring to a boil. Reduce heat to low; simmer, uncovered, for 15 minutes. Stir in clams and juice. Simmer for 5 minutes or until heated through.

Makes 8 cups

Stir-Fried Scallops with Vegetables

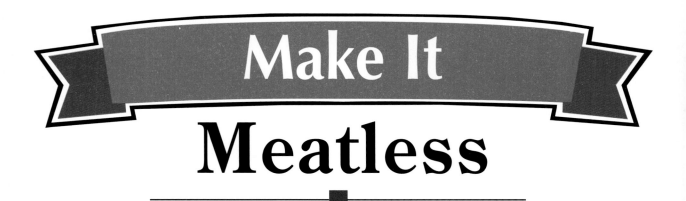

Make It Meatless

183 BROCCOLI LASAGNA BIANCA

1 (15- to 16-ounce) container fat-free
    ricotta cheese
1 cup EGG BEATERS® Healthy Real Egg
    Product
1 tablespoon minced basil *or* 1 teaspoon
    dried basil leaves
½ cup chopped onion
1 clove garlic, minced
2 tablespoons FLEISCHMANN'S®
    Margarine
¼ cup all-purpose flour
2 cups skim milk
2 (10-ounce) packages frozen chopped
    broccoli, thawed and well drained
1 cup (4 ounces) shredded part-skim
    mozzarella cheese
9 lasagna noodles, cooked and drained
1 small tomato, chopped
2 tablespoons grated Parmesan cheese
    Fresh basil leaves, for garnish

In medium bowl, combine ricotta cheese, Egg Beaters® and minced basil; set aside.

In large saucepan, over medium heat, sauté onion and garlic in margarine until tender-crisp. Stir in flour; cook for 1 minute. Gradually stir in milk; cook, stirring until mixture thickens and begins to boil. Remove from heat; stir in broccoli and mozzarella cheese.

In lightly greased 13×9×2-inch baking dish, place 3 lasagna noodles; top with ⅓ *each* ricotta and broccoli mixtures. Repeat layers 2 more times. Top with tomato; sprinkle with Parmesan cheese. Bake at 350°F for 1 hour or until set. Let stand 10 minutes before serving. Garnish with basil leaves.

Makes 8 servings

Prep Time: 20 minutes
Cook Time: 90 minutes

Broccoli Lasagna Bianca

Valley Eggplant Parmigiano

184 VALLEY EGGPLANT PARMIGIANO

2 eggplants (about 1 pound *each*)
⅓ cup olive or vegetable oil
1 container (15 ounces) ricotta cheese
2 packages (1 ounce *each*) HIDDEN
    VALLEY RANCH® Milk Recipe
    Original Ranch® Salad Dressing Mix
2 eggs
2 teaspoons dry bread crumbs
1 cup tomato sauce
½ cup shredded mozzarella cheese
1 tablespoon grated Parmesan cheese
    Chopped parsley

Preheat oven to 350°F. Cut eggplants into ½-inch slices. Brush some of the oil onto two large baking sheets. Arrange eggplant slices in single layer on sheets and brush tops with additional oil. Bake until eggplant is fork-tender, about 20 minutes.

In large bowl, whisk together ricotta cheese and salad dressing mix; whisk in eggs. In 13×9-inch baking dish, layer half the eggplant. Sprinkle 1 teaspoon of the bread crumbs over eggplant; spread all the ricotta mixture on top. Arrange remaining eggplant in another layer. Sprinkle with remaining 1 teaspoon bread crumbs; top with tomato sauce. Sprinkle cheeses on top. Bake until cheeses begin to brown, about 30 minutes. Sprinkle with parsley.

Makes 6 to 8 servings

MAKE IT MEATLESS

185 VEGETARIAN LASAGNA

2 (14.5-ounce) cans FRANK'S or SNOWFLOSS Italian Style Diced Tomatoes

2 (14-ounce) cans FRANK'S or SNOWFLOSS Bavarian Style Kraut, well drained

1 (16-ounce) package lasagna noodles

3 pounds fresh spinach or 4 (10-ounce) packages frozen chopped spinach

1 tablespoon vegetable oil

1 small onion, chopped

1 (8-ounce) can tomato sauce

1 (6-ounce) can tomato paste

2 teaspoons dried basil or oregano leaves

¼ teaspoon dried thyme leaves

¼ teaspoon ground nutmeg

2 eggs, beaten

1 (15-ounce) container ricotta cheese

8 ounces fresh Parmesan cheese, grated

3 cups (12 ounces) shredded Swiss cheese

1. Preheat oven to 350°F.

2. Cook noodles and drain. Set aside.

3. Cook fresh spinach or thaw and squeeze dry frozen spinach; set aside.

4. Heat oil in large skillet. Add onion; cook and stir until tender. Add tomatoes, tomato sauce, tomato paste and herbs; simmer, uncovered, 15 minutes, stirring often.

5. Mix eggs and ricotta cheese; set aside.

6. Spread thin layer of tomato sauce onto bottom of 13×9-inch baking dish; top with layers of ⅓ of the lasagna noodles, ½ of the spinach, the ricotta mixture and Parmesan cheese. Cover with layers of ½ of the remaining noodles, a thin layer of tomato sauce, the kraut and ½ of the Swiss cheese. Top with layers of the remaining noodles, tomato sauce, spinach and Swiss cheese.

7. Bake 30 minutes or until bubbly and lightly browned. Let stand 20 minutes before cutting to serve.

Makes 8 to 10 servings

Prep Time: 45 minutes
Bake Time: 30 minutes

LASAGNA ROLL–UPS: Combine ricotta cheese, eggs, Parmesan cheese and Swiss cheese; mix well. Spread thin layers of spinach and kraut onto individual lasagna noodles. Top each with 3 to 4 tablespoons ricotta cheese mixture. Roll up, jelly-roll fashion; place in baking dish. Cover with tomato sauce mixture. Bake as directed.

MAKE IT MEATLESS

186 BROCCOLI & CHEDDAR NOODLE CASSEROLE

3 tablespoons margarine or butter, divided
2 cups chopped onions
4 cups broccoli flowerets
1¾ cups (14½-ounce can) CONTADINA® Stewed Tomatoes and juice
⅔ cup (6-ounce can) CONTADINA® Tomato Paste
1 package (1.5 ounces) spaghetti sauce seasoning mix
2 cups water
1 teaspoon garlic salt
6 cups (12-ounce package) dry wide egg noodles, cooked, drained
1½ cups (6 ounces) shredded Cheddar cheese
½ cup CONTADINA® Seasoned Bread Crumbs

In 5-quart saucepan, melt 2 tablespoons margarine; sauté onions until tender. Stir in broccoli, tomatoes and juice, tomato paste, seasoning mix, water and garlic salt. Bring to a boil. Reduce heat; simmer, uncovered, for 10 minutes, stirring occasionally. Stir in cooked noodles. In 13×9×2-inch baking dish, layer half of the noodle mixture. Sprinkle with cheese. Layer with remaining noodle mixture. Melt remaining 1 tablespoon margarine; stir in crumbs. Sprinkle over casserole; cover and bake in preheated 350°F oven 20 minutes. Uncover; bake 5 minutes. *Makes 6 servings*

187 WISCONSIN SWISS LINGUINE TART

½ cup butter, divided
2 garlic cloves, minced
30 thin French bread slices
3 tablespoons flour
1 teaspoon salt
¼ teaspoon white pepper
Dash nutmeg
2½ cups milk
¼ cup grated Wisconsin Parmesan cheese
2 eggs, beaten
2 cups (8 ounces) shredded Wisconsin Baby Swiss cheese, divided
8 ounces fresh linguine, cooked, drained
⅓ cup green onion slices
2 teaspoons dried basil, crushed
2 plum tomatoes

Melt ¼ cup butter. Add garlic; cook 1 minute. Brush 10-inch pie plate with butter mixture; line bottom and sides with bread, allowing bread to come 1 inch over sides. Brush bread with remaining butter mixture. Bake at 350°F for 5 minutes or until lightly browned. Set aside.

Melt remaining butter in saucepan over low heat. Blend in flour and seasonings. Gradually add milk; cook, stirring constantly, until thickened. Remove from heat; add Parmesan cheese. Stir small amount of sauce into eggs; mix well. Stir in remaining sauce.

Toss 1¼ cups Swiss cheese with linguine, green onion and basil. Pour sauce over linguine mixture; mix well. Pour into crust. Cut each tomato lengthwise into eight slices; place on tart. Sprinkle with remaining ¾ cup cheese. Bake at 350°F for 25 minutes or until warm. Let stand 5 minutes.

Makes 8 servings

Favorite recipe from **Wisconsin Milk Marketing Board**

Wisconsin Swiss Linguine Tart

MAKE IT MEATLESS

188 BROCCOLI LASAGNA

1 tablespoon **CRISCO® Vegetable Oil**
1 cup chopped onion
3 cloves garlic, minced
1 can (14½ ounces) tomatoes, undrained and chopped
1 can (8 ounces) tomato sauce
1 can (6 ounces) tomato paste
1 cup thinly sliced fresh mushrooms
¼ cup chopped fresh parsley
1 tablespoon red wine vinegar
1 teaspoon dried oregano leaves
1 teaspoon dried basil leaves
1 bay leaf
½ teaspoon salt
¼ teaspoon crushed red pepper
1½ cups lowfat cottage cheese
1 cup (4 ounces) shredded low moisture part-skim mozzarella cheese, divided
6 lasagna noodles, cooked and well drained
3 cups chopped broccoli, cooked and well drained
1 tablespoon grated Parmesan cheese

1. Heat oven to 350°F. Oil 11¾×7½×2-inch baking dish lightly.

2. Heat 1 tablespoon Crisco® Oil in large saucepan on medium heat. Add onion and garlic. Cook and stir until tender. Stir in tomatoes, tomato sauce, tomato paste, mushrooms, parsley, vinegar, oregano, basil, bay leaf, salt and crushed red pepper. Bring to a boil. Reduce heat to low. Cover. Simmer 30 minutes, stirring occasionally. Remove bay leaf.

3. Combine cottage cheese and ½ cup mozzarella cheese in small bowl. Stir well.

4. Place 2 lasagna noodles in bottom of baking dish. Layer with 1 cup broccoli, ⅓ of tomato sauce and ⅓ of cottage cheese mixture. Repeat layers two times. Cover with foil.

5. Bake at 350°F for 25 minutes. Uncover. Sprinkle with remaining ½ cup mozzarella cheese and Parmesan cheese. Bake, uncovered, 10 minutes or until cheese melts. Let stand 10 minutes before serving.

Makes 8 servings

Broccoli Lasagna

MAKE IT MEATLESS

189 RIGATONI WITH FOUR CHEESES

3 cups milk
1 tablespoon chopped carrot
1 tablespoon chopped celery
1 tablespoon chopped onion
1 tablespoon fresh parsley sprigs
¼ teaspoon black peppercorns
¼ teaspoon hot pepper sauce
½ bay leaf
   Dash nutmeg
¼ cup Wisconsin butter
¼ cup flour
½ cup (2 ounces) grated Wisconsin
      Parmesan cheese
¼ cup (1 ounce) grated Wisconsin Romano
      cheese
12 ounces rigatoni, cooked, drained
1½ cups (6 ounces) shredded Wisconsin
      Cheddar cheese
1½ cups (6 ounces) shredded Wisconsin
      Mozzarella cheese
¼ teaspoon chili powder

In a 2-quart saucepan, combine milk, carrot, celery, onion, parsley, peppercorns, hot pepper sauce, bay leaf and nutmeg. Bring to a boil. Reduce heat to low; simmer 10 minutes. Strain, reserving liquid. Melt butter in 2-quart saucepan over low heat. Blend in flour. Gradually add reserved liquid; cook, stirring constantly, until thickened. Remove from heat. Add Parmesan and Romano cheeses; stir until blended. Pour over pasta; toss well. Combine Cheddar and Mozzarella cheeses. In buttered 2-quart casserole, layer ½ of pasta mixture, Cheddar cheese mixture and remaining pasta mixture. Sprinkle with chili powder. Bake at 350°F for 25 minutes or until hot.

Makes 6 servings

Favorite recipe from **Wisconsin Milk Marketing Board**

190 SPINACH ZITI CASSEROLE

1 pound ziti or other pasta
2 teaspoons vegetable oil
1 medium onion, chopped
1 (16-ounce) can tomato sauce
2 teaspoons sugar
2 tablespoons dried oregano leaves
½ teaspoon black pepper
½ teaspoon chili powder
1 (10-ounce) package frozen spinach,
      thawed and squeezed dry
1 (16-ounce) container non-fat cottage
      cheese
1 (15-ounce) can kidney beans, drained
      and rinsed

In large saucepan, cook pasta according to directions. When done, drain pasta and return to saucepan.

Meanwhile, heat oil in a medium saucepan over medium-high heat. Add onion; cook and stir 5 minutes. Add tomato sauce, sugar, oregano, pepper, chili powder and spinach. Reduce heat to low; cook 15 minutes. Add sauce to pasta along with cottage cheese and beans; mix well. Pour into 2-quart baking dish; cover. Bake in 350°F oven 20 minutes.   *Makes 6 servings*

NOTE: If desired, recipe can be finished on the stovetop. Do not remove pasta mixture from saucepan; heat thoroughly over medium heat, stirring occasionally.

Favorite recipe from **The Sugar Association**

Rigatoni with Four Cheeses

MAKE IT MEATLESS

191 CHILAQUILES

1 medium onion, chopped
2 tablespoons vegetable oil
1 can (1 pound 12 ounces) whole
    tomatoes, cut up
1 package (1.25 ounces) LAWRY'S® Taco
    Spices & Seasonings
1 can (4 ounces) diced green chiles
    (optional)
6 ounces tortilla chips
4 cups (16 ounces) grated Monterey Jack
    cheese
1 cup dairy sour cream
½ cup (2 ounces) grated Cheddar cheese

In large skillet, sauté onion in oil. Add tomatoes, Taco Spices & Seasonings and chiles; blend well. Simmer, uncovered, 10 to 15 minutes. In lightly greased 2-quart casserole, layer ½ of tortilla chips, sauce and Monterey Jack cheese. Repeat layers; top with sour cream. Bake in 350°F oven 30 minutes. Sprinkle with Cheddar cheese and bake 10 minutes longer. Let stand 15 minutes before cutting into squares.

MICROWAVE DIRECTIONS: In 2-quart microwave-safe bowl, combine onion and oil; microwave on HIGH (100% power) 2 to 2½ minutes until tender. Add tomatoes, Taco Spices & Seasonings and green chiles; blend well. Cover with waxed paper and microwave on HIGH (100% power) 5 to 7 minutes. In 2-quart microwave-safe casserole, layer ½ of tortilla chips, sauce and Monterey Jack cheese. Repeat layers. Cover with waxed paper and microwave on HIGH (100% power) 12 minutes rotating after 6 minutes. Top with sour cream and sprinkle with Cheddar cheese. Microwave, uncovered, on HIGH 2 minutes or until cheese is melted. Let stand 3 minutes before cutting into squares.

Makes 6 to 8 servings

192 SPINACH–CHEESE LASAGNA ROLLS

½ cup chopped onion
1 clove garlic, minced
1 tablespoon olive or vegetable oil
1 can (15 ounces) whole leaf spinach, well
    drained, finely chopped
1 cup low-fat ricotta cheese
½ cup grated Parmesan cheese
1 egg
1 teaspoon sugar
⅛ teaspoon pepper
6 lasagna noodles, cooked
2 cans (8 ounces *each*) no-salt-added
    tomato sauce
1 teaspoon dried basil leaves
½ teaspoon dried oregano leaves
1 can (4 ounces) no-salt-added mushroom
    pieces and stems, drained
2 thinly sliced green onions with tops *or*
    2 tablespoons minced fresh parsley

Sauté onion and garlic in oil in medium skillet over medium heat until tender. Add spinach; cook until mixture is very dry, stirring occasionally. Mix spinach mixture, cheeses, egg, sugar and pepper. Spread scant ½ cup mixture onto each lasagna noodle; roll up. Place lasagna rolls in greased baking pan; cover. Bake in preheated 350°F oven until hot, about 20 minutes.

Meanwhile, heat tomato sauce, herbs and mushrooms in small saucepan. Spoon sauce onto serving plates. Cut lasagna rolls into thirds; place cut sides up on sauce. Sprinkle with green onions. *Makes 6 servings*

Favorite recipe from Canned Food Information Council

Spinach-Cheese Lasagna Rolls

193 HARVEST CASSEROLE

2 cups USA lentils, rinsed and cooked
2 cups fresh or frozen broccoli, chopped
1½ cups cooked rice
1¼ cups (6 ounces) shredded Cheddar cheese
1 tablespoon soy sauce
½ teaspoon salt (optional)
¼ teaspoon dried thyme leaves
¼ teaspoon marjoram
¼ teaspoon dried rosemary
4 eggs
1 cup milk

Preheat oven to 350°F.

Combine lentils, broccoli, rice, cheese, soy sauce, salt, thyme, marjoram and rosemary in large bowl; mix well. Place mixture in greased 9-inch casserole dish.

Stir together eggs and milk in medium bowl. Pour egg mixture over lentil mixture. Bake 45 minutes or until lightly browned. Top with additional shredded Cheddar cheese, if desired.   *Makes 8 servings*

Favorite recipe from **USA Dry Pea & Lentil Council**

MAKE IT MEATLESS

194 BROCCOLI STUFFED SHELLS

1 tablespoon butter or margarine
¼ cup chopped onion
1 cup ricotta cheese
1 egg
2 cups chopped cooked broccoli *or*
    1 package (10 ounces) frozen
    chopped broccoli, thawed and well
    drained
1 cup (4 ounces) shredded Monterey Jack
    cheese
20 jumbo pasta shells
1 can (28 ounces) crushed tomatoes with
    added purée
1 package (1 ounce) HIDDEN VALLEY
    RANCH® Milk Recipe Original Ranch®
    salad dressing mix
¼ cup grated Parmesan cheese

Preheat oven to 350°F. In small skillet, melt butter over medium heat. Add onion; cook until onion is tender but not browned. Remove from heat; cool. In large bowl, stir ricotta cheese and egg until well blended. Add broccoli and Monterey Jack cheese; mix well. In large pot of boiling water, cook pasta shells 8 to 10 minutes or just until tender; drain. Rinse under cold running water; drain again. Stuff each shell with about 2 tablespoons broccoli-cheese mixture.

In medium bowl, combine tomatoes, sautéed onion and salad dressing mix; mix well. Pour one third of the tomato mixture into 13×9-inch baking dish. Arrange filled shells in dish. Spoon remaining tomato mixture over top. Sprinkle with Parmesan cheese. Bake, covered, until hot and bubbly, about 30 minutes.   *Makes 4 servings*

195 VEGETARIAN PAELLA

1 tablespoon olive oil
1 medium onion, chopped
1 serrano pepper, finely chopped
1 red bell pepper, diced
1 green bell pepper, diced
3 cloves garlic, minced
½ teaspoon saffron threads, crushed
½ teaspoon paprika
1 cup uncooked long-grain white rice
3 cups water
1 can (15 ounces) chick-peas (garbanzo
    beans), rinsed and drained
14 ounces artichoke hearts in water,
    drained, cut into halves
1 cup frozen green peas
1½ teaspoons grated lemon peel

1. Preheat oven to 375°F. Heat oil in large paella pan or heavy, ovenproof skillet over medium-high heat. Add onion, serrano pepper and bell peppers; cook and stir about 7 minutes.

2. Add garlic, saffron and paprika; cook 3 minutes. Add rice; cook and stir 1 minute. Add water, chick-peas, artichoke hearts, green peas and lemon peel; mix well.

3. Cover and bake 25 minutes or until rice is tender. Garnish, if desired.
                                   Makes 6 servings

Vegetarian Paella

MAKE IT MEATLESS

196 SPICY RAVIOLI AND CHEESE

1 medium red bell pepper, thinly sliced
1 medium green bell pepper, thinly sliced
1 medium yellow bell pepper, thinly sliced
1 tablespoon olive or vegetable oil
½ teaspoon LAWRY'S® Seasoned Salt
¼ teaspoon LAWRY'S® Garlic Powder with Parsley
¼ teaspoon sugar
1 package (8 or 9 ounces) fresh or frozen ravioli
1½ cups chunky salsa, divided
4 ounces mozzarella cheese, thinly sliced
2 green onions, sliced

Place bell peppers in broilerproof baking dish; sprinkle with oil, Seasoned Salt, Garlic Powder with Parsley and sugar. Broil 15 minutes or until tender and browned, turning once. Prepare ravioli according to package directions. Pour ¾ cup salsa in bottom of 8-inch square baking dish. Alternate layers of bell peppers, ravioli, cheese and green onions. Pour remaining ¾ cup salsa over layers. Cover with foil; bake in 350°F oven 15 to 20 minutes or until heated through and cheese melts.

Makes 4 to 6 servings

197 HEARTY MANICOTTI

1 package (10 ounces) frozen chopped spinach, thawed, squeezed dry
2 cups (15-ounce container) ricotta cheese
1 egg, lightly beaten
½ cup (2 ounces) grated Parmesan cheese
⅛ teaspoon ground black pepper
8 to 10 dry manicotti shells, cooked, drained
1⅓ cups (two 6-ounce cans) CONTADINA® Italian-Style Tomato Paste
1⅓ cups water
½ cup (2 ounces) shredded mozzarella cheese

In medium bowl, combine spinach, ricotta cheese, egg, Parmesan cheese and pepper; mix well. Spoon into manicotti shells. Place in ungreased 12×7½-inch baking dish. In small bowl, combine tomato paste and water; pour over manicotti. Sprinkle with mozzarella cheese. Bake in preheated 350°F oven for 30 to 40 minutes or until heated through.

Makes 4 to 5 servings

Hearty Manicotti

MAKE IT MEATLESS

198 ROASTED VEGETABLES WITH FETTUCCINE

2 pounds assorted fresh vegetables*
1 envelope LIPTON® Recipe Secrets®
    Golden Herb with Lemon Soup Mix
3 tablespoons olive or vegetable oil
½ cup light cream, whipping or heavy
    cream *or* half-and-half
¼ cup grated Parmesan cheese
8 ounces fettuccine *or* linguine, cooked
    and drained

*Use any of the following, cut into 1-inch chunks:
red, green or yellow bell peppers, zucchini, yellow
squash, red onion or eggplant.*

Preheat oven to 450°F.

In large plastic bag or bowl, combine
vegetables, golden herb with lemon soup
mix and oil. Close bag and shake, or toss in
bowl, until vegetables are evenly coated. In
13×9-inch baking or roasting pan, arrange
vegetables; discard bag.

Bake uncovered, stirring once, 20 minutes or
until vegetables are tender. Stir in light
cream and cheese until evenly coated. Toss
with hot fettuccine. Serve, if desired, with
additional grated Parmesan cheese and
freshly ground black pepper.

Makes about 2 servings

NOTE: Also terrific with LIPTON® Recipe
Secrets® Savory Herb with Garlic, Fiesta
Herb with Red Pepper or Golden Onion
Soup Mix.

199 VEGETABLE & CHEESE PLATTER

1 cup water
2 cups DOLE® Broccoli or Cauliflower
    Florets
1½ cups DOLE® Peeled Mini Carrots
1 cup DOLE® Sugar Peas or green beans
2 medium DOLE® Red, Yellow or Green
    Bell Peppers, cut into 2-inch pieces
1 package (8 ounces) mushrooms, stems
    trimmed
3 cups hot cooked brown or white rice
1 cup (4 ounces) shredded low-fat
    Cheddar cheese
⅓ cup crumbled feta cheese

• **Pour** water into large pot; bring to a boil.
Add broccoli and carrots. Reduce heat to
low; cover and cook 5 minutes. Add sugar
peas, bell peppers and mushrooms; cook
5 minutes more or until vegetables are
tender-crisp. Drain vegetables.

• **Spoon** hot rice onto large serving platter;
top with vegetables. Sprinkle with cheeses.

• **Cover** with aluminum foil; let stand
3 minutes or until cheeses melt.

Makes 4 servings

Prep Time: 15 minutes
Cook Time: 15 minutes

Vegetable & Cheese Platter

MAKE IT MEATLESS

200 EGGPLANT PASTA BAKE

4 ounces bow-tie pasta
1 pound eggplant, diced
1 clove garlic, minced
¼ cup olive oil
1½ cups shredded Monterey Jack cheese
1 cup sliced green onions
½ cup grated Parmesan cheese
1 can (14½ ounces) DEL MONTE® FRESH CUT™ Diced Tomatoes with Basil, Garlic & Oregeno

1. Preheat oven to 350°F. Cook pasta according to package directions; drain.

2. In large skillet, cook eggplant and garlic in oil over medium-high heat until tender. Toss eggplant with cooked pasta, 1 cup Monterey Jack cheese, green onions and Parmesan cheese.

3. Place in greased 9-inch square baking dish. Top with tomatoes and remaining ½ cup Monterey Jack cheese. Bake 15 minutes or until heated through.

Makes 6 servings

Prep & Cook Time: 30 minutes

Sesame Peanut Spaghetti Squash

MAKE IT MEATLESS

201 SESAME PEANUT SPAGHETTI SQUASH

Nonstick cooking spray
1 spaghetti squash (about 3 pounds)
$\frac{1}{3}$ cup sesame seeds
$\frac{1}{3}$ cup vegetable broth
2 tablespoons reduced-sodium soy sauce
1 tablespoon sugar
2 teaspoons sesame oil
1 teaspoon cornstarch
1 teaspoon crushed red pepper
1 teaspoon Worcestershire sauce
1 tablespoon vegetable oil
2 medium carrots, julienned
1 large red bell pepper, seeded and thinly sliced
$\frac{1}{4}$ pound fresh snow peas (Chinese pea pods), cut diagonally in half
$\frac{1}{2}$ cup coarsely chopped unsalted peanuts
$\frac{1}{3}$ cup minced fresh cilantro

1. Preheat oven to 350°F. Spray 13×9-inch baking dish with cooking spray. Wash squash; cut in half lengthwise. Remove and discard seeds. Place squash, cut-side down, in prepared dish. Bake 45 minutes to 1 hour or until just tender.

2. Using fork and oven mitts to protect hands, remove spaghettilike strands from hot squash; place in large bowl. Cover and keep warm.

3. Heat wok over medium-high heat until hot. Add sesame seeds; cook and stir 45 seconds or until golden brown. Remove to blender. Add broth, soy sauce, sugar, sesame oil, cornstarch, crushed red pepper and Worcestershire sauce. Process until mixture is coarsely puréed.

4. Heat wok or large skillet over medium-high heat 1 minute or until hot. Drizzle vegetable oil into wok; heat 30 seconds. Add carrots; stir-fry 1 minute. Add bell pepper; stir-fry 2 minutes or until vegetables are crisp-tender. Add snow peas; stir-fry 1 minute. Stir sesame seed mixture; add to wok. Cook and stir 1 minute or until sauce is thickened.

5. Pour vegetable mixture over spaghetti squash. Add peanuts and cilantro; toss well.

Makes 4 servings

202 PASTA WITH ROASTED VEGETABLES

1 (2-pound) butternut squash, peeled, seeded and cut into 1-inch cubes
1 (10-ounce) container fresh Brussels sprouts, each cut in half
1 small bulb fennel (about 8 ounces), trimmed, halved and thinly sliced
3 large cloves garlic, peeled and halved lengthwise
$\frac{1}{4}$ cup olive oil
$\frac{3}{4}$ teaspoon salt
$\frac{1}{2}$ teaspoon dried oregano leaves
1 (8-ounce) box penne or ziti pasta
$\frac{1}{4}$ cup pumpkin seeds
1$\frac{1}{2}$ teaspoons TABASCO® pepper sauce
$\frac{1}{2}$ cup grated Parmesan cheese

• Preheat oven to 450°F. In a roasting pan, combine squash chunks, Brussels sprouts, fennel, garlic, olive oil, salt and oregano. Bake 20 minutes, stirring occasionally.

• Meanwhile, prepare penne or ziti as package label directs. During last 2 minutes of roasting vegetables, add pumpkin seeds to the vegetables. Continue cooking until seeds are lightly toasted.

• To serve, toss cooked, drained pasta with roasted vegetables, Tabasco sauce and Parmesan cheese to mix well.

Makes 4 servings

MAKE IT MEATLESS

203 VEGETABLE LASAGNA

Tomato-Basil Sauce (recipe follows)
2 tablespoons olive oil
4 medium carrots, sliced
3 medium zucchini, sliced
6 ounces spinach leaves, stemmed and chopped
¼ teaspoon salt
¼ teaspoon ground black pepper
1 egg
3 cups ricotta cheese
½ cup plus 2 tablespoons grated Parmesan cheese, divided
12 uncooked lasagna noodles
1½ cups (6 ounces) shredded mozzarella cheese
1½ cups (6 ounces) shredded Monterey Jack cheese
½ cup water

1. Prepare Tomato-Basil Sauce.

2. Heat oil in large skillet over medium heat until hot. Add carrots; cook and stir 4 minutes. Add zucchini; cook and stir 8 minutes or until crisp-tender. Add spinach; cook and stir 1 minute or until spinach is wilted. Stir in salt and pepper.

3. Preheat oven to 350°F. Beat egg in medium bowl. Stir in ricotta cheese and ½ cup Parmesan cheese.

4. Spread 1 cup Tomato-Basil Sauce on bottom of 13×9-inch baking pan; top with 4 uncooked lasagna noodles.

5. Spoon ⅓ of ricotta cheese mixture over noodles; carefully spread with spatula.

6. Spoon ⅓ of vegetable mixture over cheese. Top with 1 cup Tomato-Basil Sauce. Sprinkle with ½ cup *each* mozzarella and Monterey Jack cheeses. Repeat layers 2 times, beginning with noodles and ending with mozzarella and Monterey Jack cheeses. Sprinkle with remaining 2 tablespoons Parmesan cheese.

7. Carefully pour water around sides of pan. Cover pan tightly with foil.

8. Bake lasagna 1 hour or until bubbly. Uncover. Let stand 10 to 15 minutes. Cut into squares. Garnish, if desired.

Makes 8 servings

TOMATO–BASIL SAUCE

2 cans (28 ounces *each*) plum tomatoes, undrained
1 teaspoon olive oil
1 medium onion, chopped
3 cloves garlic, minced
1 tablespoon sugar
1 tablespoon dried basil leaves
¼ teaspoon salt
¼ teaspoon ground black pepper

1. Drain tomatoes, reserving ½ cup juice. Seed and chop tomatoes.

2. Heat oil in large skillet over medium heat until hot. Add onion and garlic; cook and stir 5 minutes or until tender. Stir in tomatoes, reserved juice, sugar, basil, salt and pepper.

3. Bring to a boil over high heat. Reduce heat to low. Simmer, uncovered, 25 to 30 minutes or until most of juices have evaporated.

Makes 4 cups

Vegetable Lasagna

MAKE IT MEATLESS

204 VEGETABLE LASAGNA

2 cups low fat cottage cheese
(1% milkfat)
1 (10-ounce) package frozen chopped
spinach, thawed and well drained
1 cup shredded carrots
½ cup EGG BEATERS® Healthy Real Egg
Product
2 tablespoons minced onion
1 teaspoon dried Italian seasoning
2 cups no-salt-added spaghetti sauce,
divided
9 lasagna noodles, cooked in unsalted
water and drained
1 cup (4 ounces) shredded part-skim
mozzarella cheese
2 tablespoons grated Parmesan cheese

In medium bowl, combine cottage cheese,
spinach, carrots, Egg Beaters®, onion and
Italian seasoning; set aside.

Spread ½ cup spaghetti sauce on bottom of
greased 13×9×2-inch baking dish. Top with
3 noodles and ⅓ *each* spinach mixture and
remaining sauce. Repeat layers 2 more
times. Sprinkle with mozzarella and
Parmesan cheeses; cover. Bake at 375°F for
20 minutes. Uncover; bake for 25 minutes
more or until set. Let stand 10 minutes
before serving.   *Makes 8 servings*

Prep Time: 20 minutes
Cook Time: 45 minutes

205 MEXICAN CHEESE–RICE PIE

4 eggs, divided
2 cups cooked instant brown rice
1 cup (4 ounces) shredded Cheddar
cheese, divided
1 can (4 ounces) chopped green chilies,
drained
1 can (12 ounces) evaporated milk
2 tablespoons chopped green onions
½ teaspoon ground cumin
¼ teaspoon salt
1 cup shredded iceberg lettuce
¼ cup prepared chunky salsa
¼ cup sliced ripe olives

In medium bowl, beat 1 egg. Add rice; mix
well. Press rice mixture firmly onto bottom
and up side of 9-inch microwavable pie
plate. Microwave on MEDIUM (50% power)
3 to 4 minutes or until set. Sprinkle with
¾ cup Cheddar cheese and chilies; set aside.

In 1-quart glass measure or microwavable
bowl, combine remaining 3 eggs, milk,
green onions, cumin and salt. Microwave on
MEDIUM-HIGH (75% power) about
4 minutes or until hot, stirring occasionally.
Pour into prepared crust; cover loosely with
waxed paper.

Microwave on MEDIUM-HIGH 10 to
12 minutes or until center is almost set,
rotating ½ turn after 5 minutes. Uncover; let
stand 10 minutes. Remove pie from pie
plate; place on serving platter. Arrange
lettuce around edge of pie; top with salsa,
olives and remaining Cheddar cheese.
          Makes 6 servings

Favorite recipe from **National Dairy Board**

Mexican Cheese-Rice Pie

MAKE IT MEATLESS

206 PASTA ROLL–UPS

- 1 package (1.5 ounces) LAWRY'S®
  Spaghetti Sauce Seasoning Blend with
  Imported Mushrooms
- 1 can (6 ounces) tomato paste
- 2¼ cups water
- 2 tablespoons butter or vegetable oil
- 2 cups cottage cheese or ricotta cheese
- 1 cup (4 ounces) grated mozzarella cheese
- ¼ cup grated Parmesan cheese
- 2 eggs, lightly beaten
- ½ to 1 teaspoon LAWRY'S® Garlic Salt
- ½ teaspoon dried basil, crushed (optional)
- 8 ounces lasagna noodles, cooked and
  drained

In medium saucepan, prepare Spaghetti
Sauce Seasoning Blend with Imported
Mushrooms according to package directions
using tomato paste, water and butter. In
large bowl, combine remaining ingredients
except noodles; blend well. Spread ¼ cup
cheese mixture on entire length of each
lasagna noodle; roll up.

Place noodles, seam-side down, in
microwave-safe baking dish. Cover with
vented plastic wrap and microwave on HIGH
6 to 7 minutes or until cheese begins to melt.
Pour sauce over rolls and microwave on
HIGH 1 minute longer, if necessary, to heat
sauce.   *Makes 6 servings*

Pasta Roll-Up

MAKE IT MEATLESS

207 OAT BRAN 'N BROCCOLI CASSEROLE

1 package (10 ounces) frozen chopped broccoli
⅓ cup sliced green onions
¾ cup water
½ cup part-skim ricotta cheese
¼ teaspoon garlic powder
    Dash of pepper
2 cups water
½ teaspoon salt (optional)
¾ cup QUAKER® Oat Bran hot cereal, uncooked
⅔ cup QUAKER® or AUNT JEMIMA® Enriched Hominy Quick Grits*
½ cup plain low fat yogurt

To substitute QUAKER® or AUNT JEMIMA® Enriched Hominy Grits, increase water to 2½ cups and simmer time to 15 to 20 minutes. Proceed as directed.

Cook broccoli with green onions in ¾ cup water according to package directions. *Do not drain.* Stir in ricotta, garlic powder and pepper. Cook over medium heat, stirring occasionally, until heated through; set aside.

Bring 2 cups water and salt to a boil. Using a wire whisk, gradually add combined oat bran and grits, stirring constantly. Return to a boil; reduce heat. Simmer 2 to 4 minutes or until oat bran mixture is slightly thickened, stirring frequently. Add to broccoli mixture; mix well. Add yogurt; cook until heated through. Serve immediately.

Makes 6 servings

208 MAC & CHEESE WITH CRUNCHY HERB CRUST

1 pound elbow macaroni
1 cup chopped yellow onion
1 cup chopped red bell pepper
1 cup herb seasoned dry stuffing, crumbled, divided
1½ cups skim milk
12 ounces (2 cartons) ALPINE LACE® Fat Free Cream Cheese with Garlic & Herbs
1 teaspoon low sodium Worcestershire sauce
¼ teaspoon ground nutmeg
    Paprika
2 tablespoons extra virgin olive oil

• Preheat the oven to 350°F. Spray a 12-inch round or oval ovenproof baking dish with nonstick cooking spray. Cook the macaroni according to package directions until al dente. Drain well, place in the baking dish and keep warm.

• Spray a large nonstick skillet with the nonstick cooking spray and heat over medium-high heat for 1 minute. Add the onion and bell pepper and sauté for 5 minutes or until soft. Toss with the macaroni and ½ cup of the stuffing.

• In a small saucepan, bring the milk to a boil over medium heat. Add the cream cheese and stir until melted. Remove from the heat and stir in the Worcestershire and nutmeg. Pour over the macaroni mixture. *(Do not stir.)*

• Top with the remaining ½ cup of stuffing, then sprinkle with the paprika and olive oil. Cover tightly with foil and bake for 30 minutes or until bubbly and hot. Serve hot! *Makes 8 servings*

MAKE IT MEATLESS

209 STUFFED MANICOTTI

MANICOTTI
12 ounces manicotti (about 12 noodles)
2 cups (8 ounces) shredded ALPINE LACE®
    Reduced Sodium Low Moisture Part-
    Skim Mozzarella Cheese
2 cups part-skim ricotta cheese
1/3 cup slivered fresh basil leaves *or*
    2 tablespoons dried basil
1/4 cup Italian seasoned dry bread crumbs

PARMESAN SAUCE
1 1/2 cups 2% low fat milk
2 tablespoons all-purpose flour
1 teaspoon Worcestershire sauce
1/4 teaspoon crushed red pepper flakes
1 cup (4 ounces) shredded ALPINE LACE®
    Fat Free Pasteurized Process Skim
    Milk Cheese Product–For Parmesan
    Lovers, divided

1. Preheat the oven to 375°F. Spray a
13×9×2-inch baking dish with nonstick
cooking spray. Prepare the manicotti
according to package directions, transfer to
paper towels and keep warm.

2. To stuff the Manicotti: In a small bowl,
stir together the mozzarella cheese, ricotta
cheese, basil and bread crumbs. Using a
small spoon, stuff the manicotti with the
cheese mixture. Arrange in a single layer in
the baking dish.

3. To make the Parmesan Sauce: In a
medium-size saucepan, combine the milk,
flour, Worcestershire and red pepper flakes.
Bring to a boil, stirring constantly, over
medium-high heat until the sauce thickens.
Stir in 1/2 cup of the Parmesan.

4. Pour the sauce over the manicotti,
completely covering the top. Sprinkle with
the remaining 1/2 cup of the Parmesan. Cover
with foil and bake for 20 minutes or until
bubbly.

5. Uncover, turn the oven to broil and broil
4 inches from the heat for 2 minutes or until
golden brown. *Makes 6 servings*

MAKE IT MEATLESS

210 LASAGNA PRIMAVERA

- 1 (8-ounce) package lasagna noodles
- 3 carrots, cut into ¼-inch-thick slices
- 1 cup broccoli flowerets
- 1 cup zucchini, cut into ¼-inch-thick slices
- 1 crookneck squash, cut into ¼-inch-thick slices
- 2 (10-ounce) packages frozen chopped spinach, thawed
- 1 (8-ounce) package ricotta cheese
- 1 (26-ounce) jar NEWMAN'S OWN® Marinara Sauce with Mushrooms
- 3 cups (12 ounces) shredded mozzarella cheese
- ½ cup (2 ounces) grated Parmesan cheese

Bring 3 quarts water to a boil in 6-quart saucepan over high heat. Add lasagna noodles and cook 5 minutes. Add carrots; cook 2 more minutes. Add broccoli, zucchini and crookneck squash; cook for 2 minutes or until pasta is tender. Drain well.

Squeeze liquid out of spinach. Combine spinach with ricotta cheese. In a 3-quart rectangular baking pan, spread ⅓ of the Newman's Own® Marinara Sauce with Mushrooms. Line pan with lasagna noodles. Layer ½ *each* of the vegetables, spinach mixture and mozzarella cheese over the noodles; top with ½ of the remaining Newman's Own® Marinara Sauce with Mushrooms. Repeat layers. Sprinkle with Parmesan cheese.

Place baking pan on 15×10-inch baking sheet which has been lined with foil. Bake uncovered in a 400°F oven approximately 30 minutes or until hot in the center. Let stand 10 minutes before serving.

Makes 8 servings

NOTE: Casserole may be prepared up to 2 days before baking and refrigerated, covered, until 1 hour before baking. If cold, bake for 1 hour at 350°F.

211 ITALIAN EGGPLANT PARMIGIANA

- 1 large eggplant, sliced ¼ inch thick
- 2 eggs, beaten
- ½ cup dry bread crumbs
- 1 can (14½ ounces) DEL MONTE® Italian Recipe Stewed Tomatoes
- 1 can (15 ounces) DEL MONTE® Tomato Sauce
- 2 cloves garlic, minced
- ½ teaspoon dried basil
- 6 ounces mozzarella cheese, sliced

1. Dip eggplant slices into eggs, then bread crumbs; arrange in single layer on baking sheet. Broil 4 inches from heat until brown and tender, about 5 minutes per side. *Reduce oven temperature to 350°F.*

2. Place eggplant in 13×9-inch baking dish. Combine tomatoes, tomato sauce, garlic and basil; pour over eggplant and top with cheese.

3. Cover and bake at 350°F for 30 minutes or until heated through. Sprinkle with grated Parmesan cheese, if desired.

Makes 4 servings

Prep Time: 15 minutes
Cook Time: 30 minutes

MAKE IT MEATLESS

212 ITALIAN GARDEN FUSILLI

1³/₄ cups (14.5-ounce can) CONTADINA®
    Recipe Ready Diced Tomatoes,
    undrained
1 cup (4 ounces) cut fresh green beans
¹/₄ teaspoon dried rosemary leaves, crushed
¹/₂ teaspoon garlic salt
1 small zucchini, thinly sliced
    (about 1 cup)
1 small yellow squash, thinly sliced
    (about 1 cup)
1 cup (12-ounce jar) marinated artichoke
    hearts, undrained
1 cup frozen peas
¹/₂ teaspoon salt, or to taste
¹/₄ teaspoon ground black pepper, or to
    taste
8 ounces dry fusilli, cooked, drained, kept
    warm
¹/₄ cup (1 ounce) shredded Parmesan
    cheese

In large skillet, combine tomatoes and juice, green beans, rosemary and garlic salt. Bring to a boil. Reduce heat to low; cover. Simmer for 3 minutes. Add zucchini and yellow squash; cover. Simmer for 3 minutes or until vegetables are tender. Stir in artichoke hearts and juice, peas, salt and pepper; heat through. Add pasta; toss to coat well. Sprinkle with Parmesan cheese just before serving.   *Makes 6 to 8 servings*

213 OLD MEXICO BLACK BEANS & RICE

2 tablespoons vegetable oil
1 package (6.8 ounces) RICE-A-RONI®
    Spanish Rice
¹/₂ cup chopped green bell pepper
¹/₂ cup chopped onion
2 cloves garlic, minced
1 can (14¹/₂ ounces) tomatoes, undrained,
    chopped
¹/₄ to ¹/₂ teaspoon hot pepper sauce
1 can (16 ounces) black beans, rinsed and
    drained
1 can (16 ounces) pinto beans, rinsed and
    drained
¹/₂ cup (2 ounces) shredded Cheddar
    cheese or Monterey Jack cheese
2 tablespoons chopped parsley or cilantro
    (optional)

1. In large skillet, heat oil over medium heat. Add rice-vermicelli mix, green pepper, onion and garlic; sauté, stirring frequently, until vermicelli is golden brown.

2. Stir in 2 cups water, tomatoes, hot pepper sauce and contents of seasoning packet; bring to a boil over high heat.

3. Cover; reduce heat. Simmer 15 minutes.

4. Stir in black and pinto beans.

5. Cover; continue to simmer 5 minutes or until liquid is absorbed and rice is tender. Serve topped with cheese; sprinkle with parsley, if desired.   *Makes 4 servings*

Italian Garden Fusilli

Vegetable Risotto

VEGETABLE RISOTTO

2 tablespoons olive oil, divided
1 medium zucchini, cubed
1 medium yellow summer squash, cubed
1 cup shiitake mushroom slices
1 cup chopped onions
1 clove garlic, minced
6 plum tomatoes, quartered and seeded
1 teaspoon dried oregano leaves
3 cups vegetable stock
¾ cup uncooked Arborio rice
  Parmesan cheese wedge *or* ¼ cup grated
    Parmesan cheese
  Salt and pepper
½ cup frozen peas, thawed

1. Heat 1 tablespoon oil in large saucepan over medium heat until hot. Add zucchini and summer squash; cook and stir 5 minutes or until crisp-tender. Place in medium bowl; set aside.

2. Add mushrooms, onions and garlic to saucepan; cook and stir 5 minutes or until tender. Add tomatoes and oregano; cook and stir 2 to 3 minutes or until tomatoes are soft. Place in bowl with zucchini mixture. Wipe saucepan clean with paper towels.

3. Place stock in small saucepan; bring to a boil over medium heat. Reduce heat to medium-low to keep stock hot, but not boiling.

MAKE IT MEATLESS

4. Meanwhile, heat remaining 1 tablespoon oil in saucepan over medium heat until hot. Add rice; cook and stir 2 minutes.

5. Using a ladle or measuring cup, add ¾ cup stock to rice. Reduce heat to medium-low, maintaining a simmer throughout addition of stock and cooking of remaining rice. Cook and stir until rice has absorbed stock. Repeat, adding stock 3 more times, cooking and stirring until rice has absorbed stock. (Total cooking time of rice will be about 20 to 25 minutes.)

6. Grate enough cheese to measure ¼ cup. Stir cheese into rice mixture. Season to taste with salt and pepper. Stir in reserved vegetables and peas; cook until heated through. Serve immediately. Garnish, if desired. *Makes 4 to 6 servings*

215 FETTUCCINE ALFETA

```
12 ounces fettuccine
 3 tablespoons olive oil
 1 package (8 ounces) ATHENOS® Feta
     Cheese with Basil & Tomato, crumbled
 2 cups chopped tomatoes
¼ cup julienne-cut fresh basil or
     2 teaspoons dried basil leaves,
     crushed
   Fresh ground pepper
```

COOK fettuccine 8 to 10 minutes or until al dente; drain. Return to pan; toss with oil.

ADD cheese, tomatoes and basil; toss lightly. Season to taste with pepper.
Makes 6 servings

Prep Time: 10 minutes
Cook Time: 10 minutes

216 BROCCOLI AND CAULIFLOWER LINGUINE

```
 2 tablespoons olive or vegetable oil
 2 cups broccoli flowerets
 2 cups cauliflowerets
 3 cloves garlic, minced
3½ cups (28-ounce can) CONTADINA®
     Pasta Ready Chunky Tomatoes with
     Olive Oil, Garlic, Basil and Spices,
     undrained
 1 teaspoon salt
¼ teaspoon crushed red pepper flakes
½ cup dry sherry or chicken broth
 1 pound dry linguine, cooked, drained,
     kept warm
½ cup (2 ounces) grated Romano cheese
½ cup finely chopped fresh cilantro
```

In large skillet, heat oil. Add broccoli, cauliflower and garlic; sauté for 3 minutes. Add tomatoes and juice, salt and red pepper flakes. Bring to a boil. Reduce heat to low; simmer, uncovered, for 20 minutes, stirring occasionally. Add sherry; simmer for 3 minutes. In large bowl, place pasta. Add vegetable mixture, cheese and cilantro; toss to coat well. *Makes 8 servings*

MAKE IT MEATLESS

217 POLENTA WITH VEGETABLE MEDLEY

4 ounces medium Brussels sprouts (6 to 8)
1 medium fennel bulb with stalks
   Cheese Polenta (recipe follows)
1 tablespoon butter or margarine
2 teaspoons olive oil
1 cup chopped onions
2 tablespoons snipped chives
½ teaspoon sugar
2 carrots, cut into julienne strips
½ to 1 cup canned vegetable broth
   Salt
   Ground black pepper

1. To prepare Brussels sprouts, cut stems and pull off outer discolored leaves. Cut Brussels sprouts in half.

2. To prepare fennel, wash bulb. Trim stalks, reserving feathery leaves for garnish. Trim bottom of bulb leaving ⅛ inch of base. Remove any dry or discolored outer layers. Cut bulb into narrow wedges; trim core from wedges.

3. Prepare Cheese Polenta.

4. Heat butter and oil in large skillet over medium heat until butter melts. Add fennel. Cook 6 to 8 minutes or until lightly browned on both sides. Place in medium bowl.

5. Add onions, chives and sugar to skillet. Cook and stir 5 minutes or until onions are tender. Return fennel to skillet. Add carrots, Brussels sprouts and ½ cup broth. Bring to a boil over high heat. Reduce heat to low. Cover and simmer 15 to 20 minutes or until Brussels sprouts are tender, adding more broth if necessary to keep mixture moist. Season to taste with salt and pepper.

6. Spray large nonstick skillet with cooking spray. Heat over medium heat until hot. Cut Cheese Polenta into wedges. Cook 3 minutes per side or until browned. Place on serving plates; top with vegetable mixture. Garnish, if desired.   *Makes 4 to 6 servings*

CHEESE POLENTA
   1 cup cold water
   1 cup yellow cornmeal
1½ cups boiling water
   2 to 4 tablespoons crumbled Gorgonzola
   1 clove garlic, minced
   1 teaspoon salt

Stir water into cornmeal in large saucepan. Heat over medium heat until warm. Slowly stir in boiling water. Bring to a boil over medium-high heat. Reduce heat to low. Cook 15 minutes or until mixture is thick, stirring constantly. Stir in cheese, garlic and salt. Pour into greased 8-inch round pan; let stand 10 minutes or until firm.

Makes 4 to 6 servings

Polenta with Vegetable Medley

MAKE IT MEATLESS

218 EGGPLANT PARMESAN

½ cup olive or vegetable oil
1 medium eggplant (about 1½ pounds),
    peeled, sliced, divided
2 cups (15-ounce container) ricotta
    cheese, divided
1⅔ cups (15-ounce can) CONTADINA®
    Italian-Style Tomato Sauce
1 clove garlic, minced
½ teaspoon dried oregano leaves, crushed
½ cup CONTADINA® Seasoned Bread
    Crumbs
2 tablespoons grated Parmesan cheese

In large skillet, heat oil. Add eggplant; cook for 2 to 3 minutes on each side or until tender. Remove from oil with slotted spoon. Drain on paper towels. In greased 12×7½-inch baking dish, place *half* of eggplant slices. Spoon *half* of ricotta cheese over eggplant. In small bowl, combine tomato sauce, garlic and oregano. Pour *half* of tomato sauce mixture over ricotta cheese. In separate small bowl, combine bread crumbs and Parmesan cheese; sprinkle *half* over top of sauce mixture. Repeat layers. Bake in preheated 350°F oven for 30 minutes or until sauce is bubbly.   *Makes 6 servings*

219 MUSHROOM FRITTATA

1 teaspoon butter or margarine
1 medium zucchini, shredded
1 medium tomato, chopped
1 can (4 ounces) sliced mushrooms,
    drained
6 eggs, beaten
¼ cup milk
2 teaspoons Dijon mustard
½ teaspoon LAWRY'S® Seasoned Salt
½ teaspoon LAWRY'S® Seasoned Pepper
2 cups (8 ounces) grated Swiss cheese

In large, ovenproof skillet, melt butter and sauté zucchini, tomato and mushrooms 1 minute. In large bowl, combine remaining ingredients; blend well. Pour egg mixture into skillet; cook 10 minutes over low heat. To brown top, place skillet under broiler 2 to 3 minutes.   *Makes 4 servings*

PRESENTATION: Serve directly from skillet or remove frittata to serving dish. Serve with additional Swiss cheese and fresh fruit.

HINT: Try serving frittata with prepared LAWRY'S® Spaghetti Sauce Seasoning Blend with Imported Mushrooms.

Eggplant Parmesan

220 PASTA PRIMAVERA

2 tablespoons vegetable oil
½ cup sliced mushrooms
¼ cup sliced green onions
1 clove garlic, minced
1 cup cherry tomato halves
2 tablespoons chopped fresh basil leaves
½ cup half-and-half
½ cup grated Parmesan cheese
1 can (15 ounces) VEG–ALL® Mixed
    Vegetables, drained
  Salt and pepper to taste
4 ounces uncooked spaghetti, cooked,
    drained

1. Heat oil in large skillet. Add mushrooms, green onions and garlic; cook and stir 2 to 3 minutes.

2. Add tomato halves; cook 1 minute, stirring gently. Set aside.

3. Combine basil, half-and-half, cheese and VEG–ALL® in medium saucepan; cook over medium heat until just heated through. Season with salt and pepper. Stir in hot pasta and tomato mixture; serve immediately.   *Makes 4 servings*

221 CAVATELLI AND BROCCOLI

4 cloves garlic, minced
3 tablespoons olive oil
2 (13¾-fluid ounce) cans COLLEGE INN®
    Chicken Broth
1 pound frozen cavatelli pasta
4 cups chopped broccoli
1 tablespoon chopped fresh basil leaves *or*
    1 teaspoon dried basil leaves
½ cup chopped roasted red pepper
  Salt and pepper, to taste
  Grated Parmesan cheese

In 4-quart saucepan, sauté garlic in oil until tender. Stir in chicken broth; heat to a boil. Add pasta; heat to a boil. Reduce heat; cover and simmer for 5 minutes. Add broccoli; cook 10 minutes more or until pasta and broccoli are tender. Remove from heat; stir in basil and peppers. Season with salt and pepper. Serve with Parmesan cheese.
Makes 4 servings

222 SOUTHWESTERN PASTA SAUCE

¼ cup olive oil
2 medium onions, sliced
1 clove garlic, minced
3½ cups canned tomatoes, crushed or
    coarsely chopped
¾ teaspoon TABASCO® pepper sauce
¼ teaspoon salt
2 tablespoons fresh cilantro, minced
¼ teaspoon granulated sugar
12 ounces angel hair pasta, freshly cooked
  Grated Parmesan cheese

• Heat oil over medium heat in large, heavy non-aluminum saucepan. Stir in onions and garlic; sauté 10 to 12 minutes or until tender, stirring occasionally. Add tomatoes, Tabasco sauce, salt, cilantro and sugar; bring to a boil. Reduce heat to low; simmer, uncovered, 30 minutes or until slightly thickened.

• Place hot cooked pasta on heated serving platter; top with sauce. Sprinkle with Parmesan cheese.   *Makes 4 servings*

Pasta Primavera

MAKE IT MEATLESS

223 INDIAN VEGETABLE CURRY

2 to 3 teaspoons curry powder
1 can (16 ounces) sliced potatoes, drained
1 bag (16 ounces) BIRDS EYE® frozen Farm Fresh Mixtures Broccoli, Cauliflower and Carrots
1 can (15 ounces) chickpeas, drained
1 can (14½ ounces) stewed tomatoes
1 can (13¾ ounces) vegetable or chicken broth
2 tablespoons cornstarch

• Stir curry powder in large skillet over high heat until fragrant, about 30 seconds.

• Stir in potatoes, vegetables, chickpeas and tomatoes; bring to boil. Reduce heat to medium-high; cover and cook 8 minutes.

• Blend broth with cornstarch; stir into vegetables. Cook until thickened.

Makes about 6 servings

Prep Time: 5 minutes
Cook Time: 15 minutes

SERVING SUGGESTION: Serve with white or brown rice.

224 TORTELLINI WITH CREAMY PESTO

2 cups loosely packed fresh basil leaves
1 cup loosely packed parsley
⅓ cup WISH-BONE® Italian Dressing
½ cup whipping or heavy cream
¼ cup grated Parmesan cheese
⅛ teaspoon pepper
2 packages (15 ounces *each*) frozen tortellini, cooked and drained*

*Substitution: Use 1 package (16 ounces) fettuccine noodles, cooked and drained and increase grated Parmesan cheese to ½ cup.

In food processor or blender, process basil with parsley until blended. While processing, through feed cap, gradually add Italian dressing, cream, cheese and pepper until blended. Toss basil mixture with hot tortellini. Serve, if desired, with additional cheese, salt and pepper to taste. Top, if desired, with toasted pine nuts.

Makes about 6 servings

NOTE: Also terrific with WISH-BONE® Robusto Italian, Blended Italian or Lite Italian Dressing.

Indian Vegetable Curry

MAKE IT MEATLESS

225 MOSTACCIOLI WITH SPINACH AND FETA

8 ounces mostaccioli or penne
2 tablespoons olive oil
3 cups choped tomatoes
1 package (10 ounces) frozen chopped spinach, thawed, well drained
½ cup chopped green onions
1 package (8 ounces) ATHENOS® Feta Cheese with Basil & Tomato, crumbled

COOK pasta as directed on package; drain. Return to pan; toss with oil.

ADD tomatoes, spinach and onions; toss lightly. Cook and stir 2 minutes or until thoroughly heated.

ADD cheese and cook 1 minute.

Makes 8 servings

Prep Time: 10 minutes
Cook Time: 15 minutes

Louisiana Red Beans & Rice

MAKE IT MEATLESS

226 LOUISIANA RED BEANS & RICE

- 1 package (7.2 ounces) RICE-A-RONI® Herb & Butter
- 1 cup chopped green or yellow bell pepper
- ¾ cup chopped onion
- 2 cloves garlic, minced
- 2 tablespoons vegetable oil or olive oil
- 1 can (15 or 16 ounces) red beans or kidney beans, rinsed and drained
- 1 can (14½ or 16 ounces) tomatoes or stewed tomatoes, undrained
- 1 teaspoon dried thyme leaves *or* dried oregano leaves
- ⅛ teaspoon hot pepper sauce or black pepper
- 2 tablespoons chopped parsley (optional)

1. Prepare Rice-A-Roni® mix as package directs.

2. While Rice-A-Roni® is simmering, in second large skillet, sauté bell pepper, onion and garlic in oil 5 minutes.

3. Stir in beans, tomatoes, thyme and hot pepper sauce. Simmer, uncovered, 10 minutes, stirring occasionally. Stir in parsley. Serve over rice.

Makes 5 servings

227 TOMATO–ZUCCHINI PESTO

- 6 ounces pasta
- 1 cup fresh basil, chopped
- 1 teaspoon vegetable oil
- 2 cloves garlic, minced
- 1 teaspoon sugar
- ¼ cup part-skim ricotta cheese
- 1 tablespoon grated Parmesan cheese
- 1 medium zucchini, cut into ¼-inch-thick slices
- 2 teaspoons water
- 1 cup cherry tomatoes, quartered
- ½ teaspoon salt (optional)

Prepare pasta as directed on package; rinse and drain. Cover and set aside. In food processor or a blender, process basil, oil, garlic and sugar. Blend in cheeses; set aside. Place zucchini in large casserole dish. Add water; cover. Microwave on HIGH 4 minutes; drain. Stir in pasta and Parmesan cheese mixture. Garnish with tomatoes. Season with salt, if deisired.   *Makes 4 servings*

*Favorite recipe from **The Sugar Association, Inc.***

MAKE IT MEATLESS

228 ALPINE FETTUCCINE

½ pound white fettuccine, preferably fresh
½ pound green fettuccine, preferably fresh
1½ teaspoons extra virgin olive oil
1 cup sliced fresh mushrooms
1 cup chopped red bell pepper
½ cup skim milk
6 ounces (1 carton) ALPINE LACE® Fat
Free Cream Cheese with Garlic &
Herbs

• Cook the fettuccine according to package directions until al dente. Drain well and place in a large shallow pasta bowl. Toss with the oil and keep warm.

• Meanwhile, spray a medium-size nonstick skillet with nonstick cooking spray. Add the mushrooms and bell pepper and sauté until soft. Toss with the fettuccine.

• In a small saucepan, bring the milk to a boil over medium heat. Add the cream cheese; stir until melted. Toss with pasta and serve immediately.   *Makes 6 servings*

229 VEGETABLE & ORZO PASTA SAUTÉ

2 tablespoons margarine or butter
1½ pounds assorted fresh vegetables*
¾ cup orzo pasta
3 cups water
¼ cup LIPTON® Recipe Secrets® for
Seasoned Roasted Potatoes–Classic
Garlic Herb
½ teaspoon salt

Use any combination of the following, sliced: onion, zucchini, yellow squash, red, green or yellow bell peppers and carrots.

In 12-inch skillet, melt margarine over medium-high heat and cook vegetables, stirring occasionally, 5 minutes. Stir in orzo and cook, stirring occasionally, 3 minutes. Stir in remaining ingredients. Bring to a boil over high heat. Reduce heat to low and simmer uncovered, stirring occasionally, 20 minutes or until vegetables are tender.
Makes about 6 servings

NOTE: Also terrific with LIPTON® Recipe Secrets® for Seasoned Roasted Potatoes–California Onion.

Alpine Fettuccine

MAKE IT MEATLESS

230 PASTA PRIMAVERA WITH ROASTED GARLIC SAUCE

3 large heads garlic
2 tablespoons FLEISCHMANN'S®
   Margarine, melted
3 tablespoons GREY POUPON®
   COUNTRY DIJON® Mustard
3 tablespoons lemon juice
1/4 teaspoon coarsely ground black pepper
1 cup sliced fresh mushrooms
1/2 cup julienned zucchini
1/2 cup julienned carrot
1/2 cup COLLEGE INN® Lower Sodium
   Chicken Broth or water
1 cup chopped tomato
1 tablespoon chopped fresh basil leaves *or*
   1 teaspoon dried basil leaves
8 ounces angel hair pasta, cooked and
   drained

Brush each head of garlic lightly with
1 teaspoon melted margarine; wrap each
head separately in foil. Place in small baking
pan; bake at 400°F for 45 minutes or until
tender. Cool 10 minutes. Separate cloves;
squeeze cloves to extract pulp (discard
skins).

In electric blender or food processor, purée
garlic pulp, mustard, lemon juice and
pepper; set aside.

In skillet, over medium-high heat, sauté
mushrooms, zucchini and carrot in
remaining spread until tender-crisp, about
3 minutes; add garlic mixture, broth or
water, tomato and basil. Reduce heat to low;
cook and stir until sauce is heated through.
Toss with hot cooked pasta. Serve
immediately.   *Makes 4 servings*

231 PENNE WITH CREAMY TOMATO SAUCE

1 tablespoon olive or vegetable oil
1/2 cup diced onion
2 tablespoons dry vermouth, white wine
   or chicken broth
1 3/4 cups (14.5-ounce can) CONTADINA®
   Pasta Ready Chunky Tomatoes
   Primavera, undrained
1/2 cup heavy whipping cream
8 ounces dry penne or rigatoni, cooked,
   drained, kept warm
1 cup pitted ripe olives, drained, sliced
1/2 cup (2 ounces) grated Parmesan cheese
1/4 cup sliced green onions

In large skillet, heat oil. Add diced onion;
sauté for 2 to 3 minutes or until onion is
tender. Add vermouth; cook for 1 minute.
Stir in tomatoes and juice, cream, pasta,
olives and Parmesan cheese; heat
thoroughly, stirring occasionally. Sprinkle
with green onions.   *Makes 4 servings*

Penne with Creamy Tomato Sauce

232 SALSA RICE AND BLACK BEANS

1¼ cups water
1½ cups MINUTE® Brown Rice, uncooked
1 can (16 ounces) black beans, rinsed, drained
1 large tomato, chopped
1 can (4 ounces) chopped green chilies, undrained
1 tablespoon chopped cilantro or fresh parsley
1 tablespoon lime juice
⅛ teaspoon hot pepper sauce
   Suggested garnishes: light sour cream, lime slices, cilantro or fresh parsley

BRING water to boil in large saucepan on medium-high heat.

STIR in rice, beans, tomato and chilies. Return to boil. Reduce heat to low; cover and simmer 5 minutes. Remove from heat.

STIR in cilantro, lime juice and pepper sauce; cover. Let stand 5 minutes. Stir. Garnish as desired.   *Makes 4 servings*

Prep Time: 10 minutes
Cook Time: 20 minutes

233 PASTA FAGIOLE

1 cup chopped onions
2 teaspoons minced garlic
1 tablespoon vegetable oil
2 (13¾-fluid ounce) cans COLLEGE INN® Chicken Broth
1 (16-ounce) can stewed tomatoes
½ teaspoon dried basil leaves
¼ teaspoon red pepper flakes
1 (10-ounce) package frozen chopped spinach, thawed and drained
1 cup chick peas, drained
1 cup cooked ditalini pasta
   Grated Parmesan cheese

In 4-quart pot, over medium-high heat, sauté onion and garlic in oil for 2 to 3 minutes or until tender. Stir in broth, tomatoes, basil and red pepper flakes. Heat to a boil; reduce heat. Simmer for 5 minutes. Add spinach, chick peas and pasta; simmer for 6 to 8 minutes or until heated through. Serve hot with Parmesan cheese.

Makes 8 servings

Salsa Rice and Black Beans

234 WISCONSIN CHEESY PASTA PRIMAVERA

1 cup diagonally cut carrot slices
6 tablespoons butter, divided
1 cup yellow summer squash slices
2 cups mushroom quarters
1 cup Chinese pea pod halves
¼ cup green onion slices
1 tablespoon chopped fresh basil leaves *or*
    1 teaspoon dried basil leaves
8 ounces fettucini, freshly cooked
1 cup lowfat or cream-style cottage
    cheese
½ cup grated Wisconsin Parmesan cheese
    Salt and pepper

In a large skillet, sauté carrots in
4 tablespoons butter 5 minutes. Add squash;
continue cooking 2 minutes, stirring
occasionally. Add remaining vegetables;
continue cooking until vegetables are tender,
about 5 minutes. Stir in basil. Combine hot
fettucine and 2 tablespoons butter; toss until
butter is melted. Toss in cottage cheese and
Parmesan cheese. Place fettucini mixture on
serving platter; top with vegetable mixture.
Season with salt and pepper to taste.

Makes 4 servings

Favorite recipe from **Wisconsin Milk Marketing Board**

235 SESAME NOODLES

1 pound spaghetti
1 cup chunky peanut butter
1 cup orange juice
¼ cup soy sauce
¼ cup sesame oil
¼ cup vegetable oil
2 tablespoons cider vinegar
1 tablespoon TABASCO® pepper sauce
1 teaspoon salt
2 large green onions, sliced
1 medium cucumber, sliced

• Prepare spaghetti as package directs.
Drain.

• Meanwhile, in a large bowl, whisk peanut
butter, orange juice, soy sauce, sesame oil,
vegetable oil, cider vinegar, Tabasco sauce
and salt until smooth. Add cooked spaghetti
and green onions; toss well. Serve warm or
cover and refrigerate to serve cold later. Just
before serving, toss with additional orange
juice, if necessary. Garnish with cucumber
slices.   *Makes 6 servings*

Wisconsin Cheesy Pasta Primavera

Singapore Spicy Noodles

236 SINGAPORE SPICY NOODLES

1¼ cups water
2 tablespoons ketchup
2½ teaspoons packed brown sugar
1½ teaspoons chopped cilantro
1 teaspoon cornstarch
¾ teaspoon LAWRY'S® Seasoned Salt
¾ teaspoon LAWRY'S® Garlic Powder with Parsley
¼ teaspoon crushed red pepper
2½ tablespoons chunky peanut butter
¼ cup sliced green onions
8 ounces linguine, cooked and drained
1 cup shredded red cabbage

In medium saucepan, combine water, ketchup, sugar, cilantro, cornstarch and seasonings. Bring to a boil. Reduce heat; simmer, uncovered, 5 minutes. Cool 10 minutes; blend in peanut butter and green onions. Toss sauce with hot linguine and red cabbage. *Makes 4 servings*

PRESENTATION: Garnish with green onion curls. Serve with a marinated cucumber salad.

HINT: For a heartier entrée, add cooked shredded chicken or pork.

237 ORIENTAL TOFU NOODLE SALAD WITH SPICY PEANUT SAUCE

¾ **pound extra firm tofu**
   Spicy Peanut Sauce (recipe follows)
12 **ounces vermicelli noodles**
 2 **teaspoons sesame oil**
 1 **tablespoon minced green onions (green
   parts only)**
1½ **cups shredded peeled carrots**
 2 **cups bean sprouts**
½ **green pepper, cut into thin strips**
½ **red pepper, cut into thin strips**

Wrap tofu in paper towels. Top with a heavy weight, such as a pot, to press out excess water; let stand 30 minutes. Cut tofu into 1-inch cubes.

Prepare Spicy Peanut Sauce. Add to tofu; toss lightly to coat. Cover with plastic wrap; let stand at room temperature about 30 minutes.

Cook vermicelli noodles according to package directions; rinse and drain.

Heat wok or large skillet. Add sesame oil; heat until very hot. Add green onions; stir-fry 30 seconds. Add carrots, bean sprouts and peppers; stir-fry 1 minute.

Add cooked vermicelli noodles and tofu mixture; cook until heated through, stirring occasionally.   *Makes 6 servings*

SPICY PEANUT SAUCE
 1 **tablespoon minced garlic**
 1 **tablespoon minced fresh ginger**
¼ **cup smooth or crunchy reduced-fat
   peanut butter**
2½ **tablespoons low-sodium soy sauce**
 1 **tablespoon plus 1½ teaspoons rice wine
   or sake**
 2 **tablespoons Worcestershire sauce**
 1 **tablespoon plus 1½ teaspoons sugar**
 1 **teaspoon hot chili paste or crushed
   dried red chili pepper**
 3 **tablespoons chicken broth or water**

Place garlic and ginger in food processor or blender; process until finely chopped. Add all remaining ingredients; process until well blended. (If sauce seems to thick, add about 1 tablespoon additional broth or water. If sauce seems thin, add additional peanut butter.)   *Makes about ½ cup*

NOTE: Prepared peanut sauce can be stored up to 1 month in the refrigerator.

Favorite recipe from **The Sugar Association, Inc.**

MAKE IT MEATLESS

238 ZESTY MIXED VEGETABLES

8 ounces green beans
½ small head cauliflower
2 green onions with tops
2 cloves garlic
1 or 2 jalapeño or Thai chili peppers*
2 tablespoons vegetable oil
8 ounces peeled fresh baby carrots
1 cup ⅓-less-salt chicken broth, divided
1 tablespoon cornstarch
1 teaspoon sugar
¼ teaspoon salt
2 tablespoons oyster sauce

*Jalapeños can sting and irritate the skin; wear rubber globes when handling jalapeños and do not touch eyes. Wash hands after handling jalapeños.

• Trim ends from beans; discard. Cut beans diagonally into thirds or quarters. Cut cauliflower into flowerets. Cut onions into ½-inch pieces; keep white part and green tops of onions in separate piles. Chop garlic. Cut jalapeño lengthwise in half. Remove stem and seeds. Cut jalapeño crosswise into thin slices.

• Heat wok over high heat about 1 minute or until hot. Drizzle oil into wok and heat 30 seconds. Add white part of onions, beans, cauliflowerets, garlic and jalapeño; stir-fry until tender. Add carrots and ¾ cup broth. Cover; bring to a boil. Reduce heat to low; cook until carrots and beans are crisp-tender.

• Combine cornstarch, sugar and salt in cup; stir in remaining ¼ cup broth and oyster sauce until smooth. Stir into wok. Cook until sauce boils and thickens. Stir in onion tops. Transfer to serving dish. Garnish, if desired.

Makes 4 servings

239 RED AND YELLOW BELL PEPPER PASTA

3 tablespoons olive oil
2 pounds onions, thinly sliced (about 6 cups)
2 large red bell peppers, cut into thin strips
2 large yellow bell peppers, cut into thin strips
3 tablespoons sugar
¼ cup cornstarch
¼ cup water
2 cups chicken broth
1 tablespoon grated lemon rind
2 tablespoons lemon juice
1 teaspoon dried basil leaves
1 teaspoon dried mint leaves
½ teaspoon salt
12 ounces tomato and spinach twist pasta
2 tablespoons grated Parmesan cheese (optional)

Heat olive oil in large saucepan. Add onions, peppers and sugar; stir-fry 2 to 3 minutes or until softened. Remove from pan; set aside. In same saucepan, dissolve cornstarch in water. Stir in chicken broth, lemon rind, lemon juice, basil, mint and salt. Cook, stirring constantly, over medium heat until thickened. Stir chicken broth-seasoning mixture into onion-pepper mixture and heat briefly.

Meanwhile, prepare pasta according to package directions. Serve pepper sauce over hot pasta; sprinkle with Parmesan cheese.

Makes 6 servings

*Favorite recipe from **The Sugar Association, Inc.***

Zesty Mixed Vegetables

240 SZECHUAN VEGETABLE STIR–FRY

8 ounces firm tofu, drained and cut into cubes
1 cup canned vegetable broth, divided
½ cup orange juice
⅓ cup soy sauce
1 to 2 teaspoons hot chili oil
½ teaspoon fennel seeds
½ teaspoon ground black pepper
2 tablespoons cornstarch
3 tablespoons vegetable oil
1 cup sliced green onions and tops
3 medium carrots, peeled and diagonally sliced
3 cloves garlic, minced
2 teaspoons minced fresh ginger
¼ pound button mushrooms, sliced
1 medium red bell pepper, seeded and cut into 1-inch squares
¼ pound fresh snow peas (Chinese pea pods), cut diagonally in half
8 ounces broccoli flowerets, steamed
½ cup peanuts
4 to 6 cups hot cooked rice

1. Place tofu in 8-inch round or square glass baking dish. Combine ½ cup broth, orange juice, soy sauce, chili oil, fennel seeds and black pepper in 2-cup measure; pour over tofu. Let stand 15 to 60 minutes. Drain, reserving marinade.

2. Combine cornstarch and remaining ½ cup broth in medium bowl. Add reserved marinade; set aside.

3. Heat vegetable oil in wok or large skillet over high heat until hot. Add onions, carrots, garlic and ginger; stir-fry 3 minutes. Add tofu, mushrooms, bell pepper and snow peas; stir-fry 2 to 3 minutes or until vegetables are crisp-tender. Add broccoli; stir-fry 1 minute or until heated through.

4. Stir cornstarch mixture. Add to wok; cook 1 to 2 minutes or until bubbly. Stir in peanuts. Serve over rice.

Makes 4 to 6 servings

241 EGGPLANT ITALIANO

2 tablespoons olive oil, divided
2 medium onions, thinly sliced
2 ribs celery, cut into 1-inch pieces
1¼ pounds eggplant, cut into 1-inch cubes
1 can (16 ounces) diced tomatoes, drained
½ cup pitted ripe olives, cut in half
1 tablespoon sugar
1 tablespoon capers, drained
2 tablespoons balsamic vinegar
1 teaspoon dried oregano or basil leaves, crushed
Salt and black pepper to taste

• Heat wok over medium-high heat 1 minute or until hot. Drizzle 1 tablespoon oil into wok and heat 30 seconds. Add onions and celery; stir-fry about 2 minutes or until tender. Move onions and celery to side of wok. Reduce heat to medium.

• Add remaining 1 tablespoon oil to bottom of wok and heat 30 seconds. Add eggplant; stir-fry about 4 minutes or until tender. Add tomatoes; mix well. Cover and cook 10 minutes.

• Stir olives, sugar, capers, vinegar and oregano into eggplant mixture. Season with salt and black pepper. Transfer to serving dish. Garnish, if desired.

Makes 6 servings

Eggplant Italiano

242 SAVORY LO MEIN

2 tablespoons olive or vegetable oil
1 medium clove garlic, finely chopped
1 small head bok choy, cut into 2-inch
   pieces (about 5 cups)*
1 envelope LIPTON® Recipe Secrets®
   Onion Soup Mix
1 cup water
2 tablespoons sherry (optional)
1 teaspoon soy sauce
¼ teaspoon ground ginger (optional)
8 ounces linguine or spaghetti, cooked
   and drained

*Substitution: Use 5 cups coarsely shredded green
cabbage. Decrease 10 minute cook time to 3 minutes.

In 12-inch skillet, heat oil over medium heat
and cook garlic and bok choy, stirring
frequently, 10 minutes or until crisp-tender.
Stir in onion soup mix blended with water,
sherry, soy sauce and ginger. Bring to a boil
over high heat. Reduce heat to low and
simmer uncovered, stirring occasionally,
5 minutes. Toss with hot linguine. Sprinkle,
if desired, with toasted sesame seeds.

Makes about 4 servings

NOTE: Also terrific with LIPTON® Recipe
Secrets® Onion-Mushroom, Savory Herb
with Garlic, Golden Herb with Lemon or
Golden Onion Soup Mix. If using LIPTON®
Recipe Secrets® Savory Herb with Garlic
Soup Mix, omit garlic.

243 THAI NOODLES WITH PEANUT SAUCE

2 packages (3 ounces *each*) Oriental
   flavor instant ramen noodles
2 cups BIRDS EYE® frozen Farm Fresh
   Mixtures Broccoli, Carrots and Water
   Chestnuts
⅓ cup hot water
¼ cup creamy peanut butter
1 teaspoon sugar
⅛ to ¼ teaspoon crushed red pepper flakes

• Reserve seasoning packets from noodles.

• Bring 4 cups water to a boil in large
saucepan. Add noodles and vegetables.
Cook 3 minutes, stirring occasionally; drain.

• Meanwhile, whisk together hot water,
peanut butter, sugar, red pepper flakes and
reserved seasoning packets in large bowl
until blended.

• Add noodles and vegetables; toss to coat.
Serve warm.   *Makes about 4 servings*

Prep Time: 5 minutes
Cook Time: 10 minutes

SERVING SUGGESTION: Add shredded
carrot, thinly sliced cucumber or green
onion for additional flavor and color. For a
heartier main dish, add cooked seafood,
shredded cooked chicken or pork.

244 HEARTY MEATLESS CHILI

1 envelope LIPTON® Recipe Secrets®
    Onion or Onion-Mushroom Soup Mix
4 cups water
1 can (16 ounces) chickpeas or garbanzo
    beans, rinsed and drained
1 can (16 ounces) red kidney beans, rinsed
    and drained
1 can (14½ ounces) whole peeled
    tomatoes, undrained and chopped
1 cup lentils, rinsed and drained
1 large rib celery, coarsely chopped
1 tablespoon chili powder
2 teaspoons ground cumin (optional)
1 medium clove garlic, finely chopped

In 4-quart saucepan or stockpot, combine all ingredients. Bring to a boil over high heat. Reduce heat to low and simmer covered, stirring occasionally, 20 minutes or until lentils are almost tender. Remove cover and simmer, stirring occasionally, an additional 20 minutes or until liquid is almost absorbed and lentils are tender.

Makes about 4 (2-cup) servings

NOTE: For spicier chili, add ¼ teaspoon crushed red pepper flakes.

SERVING SUGGESTION: Serve over hot cooked brown or white rice and top with shredded Cheddar cheese.

245 MEATLESS ITALIAN MINESTRONE

1 tablespoon CRISCO® Vegetable Oil
1⅓ cups chopped celery
½ cup chopped onion
2 to 3 cloves garlic, minced
2 cans (14½ ounces *each*) tomatoes,
    undrained and chopped
4 cups chopped cabbage
1⅓ cups chopped carrots
1 can (46 ounces) tomato juice
1 can (19 ounces) white kidney beans
    (cannellini), drained
1 can (15½ ounces) red kidney beans,
    drained
1 can (15 ounces) garbanzo beans,
    drained
¼ cup chopped fresh parsley
1 tablespoon plus 1 teaspoon dried
    oregano leaves
1 tablespoon plus 1 teaspoon dried basil
    leaves
¾ cup (4 ounces) uncooked small elbow
    macaroni, cooked and well drained
¼ cup grated Parmesan cheese
    Salt and pepper (optional)

1. Heat Crisco® Oil in large saucepan on medium heat. Add celery, onion and garlic. Cook and stir until crisp-tender. Stir in tomatoes, cabbage and carrots. Reduce heat to low. Cover. Simmer until vegetables are tender.

2. Stir in tomato juice, beans, parsley, oregano and basil. Simmer until beans are heated. Stir in macaroni just before serving. Serve sprinkled with Parmesan cheese. Season with salt and pepper, if desired.

Makes 16 servings

Pasta Mania

246 CHICKEN–ASPARAGUS CASSEROLE

2 teaspoons vegetable oil
1 cup seeded and chopped green and/or red bell peppers
1 medium onion, chopped
2 cloves garlic, minced
1 can (10¾ ounces) condensed cream of asparagus soup
2 eggs
1 container (8 ounces) ricotta cheese
2 cups (8 ounces) shredded Cheddar cheese, divided
1½ cups chopped cooked chicken, cut into ½-inch pieces
1 package (10 ounces) frozen chopped asparagus,* thawed and drained
8 ounces egg noodles, cooked
Ground black pepper (optional)

*Or, substitute ½ pound fresh asparagus cut into ½-inch pieces. Bring 6 cups water to a boil over high heat in large saucepan. Add fresh asparagus. Reduce heat to medium. Cover and cook 5 to 8 minutes or until crisp-tender. Drain.

1. Preheat oven to 350°F. Grease 13×9-inch casserole; set aside.

2. Heat oil in small skillet over medium heat. Add bell peppers, onion and garlic; cook and stir until crisp-tender.

3. Mix soup, eggs, ricotta cheese and 1 cup Cheddar cheese in large bowl until well blended. Add onion mixture, chicken, asparagus and noodles; mix well. Season with pepper, if desired.

4. Spread mixture evenly in prepared casserole. Top with remaining 1 cup Cheddar cheese.

5. Bake 30 minutes or until center is set and cheese is bubbly. Let stand 5 minutes before serving. Garnish as desired.

Makes 12 servings

Chicken-Asparagus Casserole

Shrimp in Angel Hair Pasta Casserole

247 PASTA PRIMAVERA CASSEROLE

3 cups uncooked rotini pasta
1 can (2.8 ounces) FRENCH'S® French Fried Onions
½ cup zucchini, thinly sliced
1 tomato, chopped
1 cup frozen peas, thawed
1 cup (4 ounces) shredded mozzarella cheese
½ cup (2 ounces) grated Parmesan cheese
2 cups milk
2 tablespoons flour
1 tablespoon HERB-OX® Instant Chicken Flavor Bouillon

Cook pasta according to package directions; drain. Return pasta to saucepan. Toss lightly with ½ *can* French Fried Onions, vegetables, cheeses, milk, flour and bouillon; mix well. Pour into an 12×8-inch baking dish. Bake, uncovered, at 350°F for 35 minutes or until heated through, stirring halfway to blend sauce and pasta. Top with remaining onions. Bake, uncovered, 5 minutes or until onions are golden brown.

Makes 6 servings

248 SHRIMP IN ANGEL HAIR PASTA CASSEROLE

2 eggs
1 cup half-and-half
1 cup plain yogurt
½ cup (2 ounces) shredded Swiss cheese
⅓ cup crumbled feta cheese
⅓ cup chopped fresh parsley
¼ cup chopped fresh basil *or* 1 teaspoon dried basil leaves, crushed
1 teaspoon dried oregano leaves, crushed
1 package (9 ounces) fresh angel hair pasta, uncooked
1 jar (16 ounces) mild, thick and chunky salsa
1 pound medium shrimp, peeled and deveined
½ cup (2 ounces) shredded Monterey Jack cheese

Preheat oven to 350°F. Grease 12×8-inch baking dish. Combine eggs, half-and-half, yogurt, Swiss cheese, feta cheese, parsley, basil and oregano in medium bowl; mix well. Place half the pasta in bottom of prepared pan. Cover with salsa. Add half the shrimp. Cover with remaining pasta. Spread egg mixture over pasta and top with remaining shrimp. Sprinkle with Monterey Jack cheese. Bake 30 minutes or until bubbly. Let stand 10 minutes. Garnish as desired.

Makes 6 servings

*Favorite recipe from **Southeast United Dairy Industry Association, Inc.***

249 TUNA NOODLE CASSEROLE

1 tablespoon CRISCO® Vegetable Oil
1 cup sliced celery
⅓ cup chopped onion
¼ cup chopped green bell pepper
1 can (6½ ounces) chunk white tuna packed in water, drained and flaked
6 ounces egg noodles (3½ cups dry), cooked and well drained
½ cup sour cream
1 jar (2 ounces) sliced pimientos, drained
½ teaspoon salt
1 can (10¾ ounces) condensed cream of celery soup
½ cup milk
4 slices (¾ ounce *each*) process American cheese, chopped
2 tablespoons plain dry bread crumbs

1. Heat oven to 425°F. Oil 2-quart baking dish lightly.

2. Heat one tablespoon Crisco® Oil in large skillet on medium heat. Add celery, onion and green pepper. Cook and stir until tender. Add tuna, noodles, sour cream, pimientos and salt. Stir to blend. Remove from heat.

3. Combine soup and milk in small saucepan. Stir on medium heat until warmed. Add cheese. Stir until cheese melts. Stir into noodle mixture. Spoon into baking dish. Sprinkle with bread crumbs.

4. Bake at 425°F for 20 to 25 minutes or until hot and bubbly. *Makes 6 servings*

250 BROCCOLI CHICKEN PASTA CASSEROLE

2 teaspoons CRISCO® Vegetable Oil
2/3 cup chopped onion
2 large cloves garlic, minced
1 pound boneless, skinless chicken breast, cut into 1-inch pieces
2 cans (14½ ounces *each*) whole tomatoes, undrained and coarsely chopped
1 can (8 ounces) tomato sauce
¼ cup ketchup
1¼ teaspoons dried basil leaves
¾ teaspoon dried oregano leaves
¼ teaspoon salt
1 package (10 ounces) frozen cut broccoli, thawed and well drained
5 ounces uncooked small macaroni, cooked (without salt or fat) and well drained
½ cup grated Parmesan cheese, divided

1. Heat oven to 350°F.

2. Heat Crisco® Oil in large skillet on medium-high heat. Add onion and garlic. Cook and stir until tender. Add chicken. Cook and stir just until chicken is no longer pink in center. Stir in tomatoes, tomato sauce, ketchup, basil, oregano and salt. Bring to a boil. Reduce heat to low. Simmer 5 minutes, stirring occasionally.

3. Combine broccoli, macaroni, chicken mixture and ¼ cup cheese in large bowl. Stir well. Spoon into 13×9-inch baking dish. Sprinkle with remaining ¼ cup cheese.

4. Bake at 350°F for 20 minutes.

Makes 8 servings

251 POLISH REUBEN CASSEROLE

2 cans (10¾ ounces *each*) condensed cream of mushroom soup
1⅓ cups milk
½ cup chopped onion
1 tablespoon prepared mustard
2 cans (16 ounces *each*) sauerkraut, rinsed and drained
1 package (8 ounces) uncooked medium-width noodles
1½ pounds Polish sausage, cut into ½-inch pieces
2 cups (8 ounces) shredded Swiss cheese
¾ cup whole wheat bread crumbs
2 tablespoons butter, melted

Combine soup, milk, onion and mustard in medium bowl; blend well. Spread sauerkraut into greased 13×9-inch pan. Top with uncooked noodles. Spoon soup mixture evenly over noodles; cover with sausage. Top with cheese. Combine bread crumbs and butter in small bowl; sprinkle over cheese. Cover pan tightly with foil. Bake in preheated 350°F oven 1 hour or until noodles are tender. Garnish as desired.

Makes 8 to 10 servings

Polish Reuben Casserole

252 SAUSAGE & NOODLE CASSEROLE

1 pound BOB EVANS FARMS® Original Recipe Roll Sausage
1 cup chopped onion
¼ cup chopped green bell pepper
1 (10-ounce) package frozen peas
1 (10¾-ounce) can condensed cream of chicken soup
1 (8-ounce) package egg noodles, cooked according to package directions and drained
Salt and black pepper to taste
1 (2.8-ounce) can French fried onions, crushed

Preheat oven to 350°F. Crumble sausage into large skillet. Add onion and green pepper. Cook over medium heat until meat is browned and vegetables are tender, stirring occasionally. Drain off any drippings. Cook peas according to package directions. Drain, reserving liquid in 2-cup glass measuring cup; set aside. Add enough water to pea liquid to obtain 1⅓ cups liquid. Combine liquid and soup in large bowl; stir in sausage mixture, noodles, reserved peas, salt and black pepper. Mix well. Spoon mixture into greased 2½-quart baking dish. Sprinkle with onions. Bake 30 minutes or until bubbly. Serve hot. Refrigerate leftovers.

Makes 6 servings

253 CRAZY LASAGNA CASSEROLE

1½ pounds ground beef
1 teaspoon LAWRY'S® Seasoned Salt
1 package (1½ ounces) LAWRY'S® Original-Style Spaghetti Sauce Spices & Seasonings
1 can (8 ounces) tomato sauce
1 can (6 ounces) tomato paste
1½ cups water
1 package (10 ounces) medium-size shell macaroni, cooked and drained
1 carton (16 ounces) small curd cottage cheese
1½ cups (6 ounces) grated Cheddar cheese

In large skillet, brown ground beef until crumbly; drain fat. Add Seasoned Salt, Original-Style Spaghetti Sauce Spices & Seasonings, tomato sauce, tomato paste and water; blend well. Bring to a boil; reduce heat and simmer, uncovered, 10 minutes, stirring occasionally. In shallow 2-quart casserole, layer half of macaroni, cottage cheese and meat sauce. Sprinkle ½ cup Cheddar cheese over meat sauce. Repeat layers, ending with meat sauce. Top with remaining 1 cup Cheddar cheese. Bake, uncovered, in 350°F oven 30 to 40 minutes or until bubbly and cheese is melted.

Makes 8 servings

254 ITALIAN SAUSAGE LASAGNA

1½ pounds BOB EVANS FARMS® Italian Roll
    Sausage
2 tablespoons olive oil
2 green bell peppers, thinly sliced
1 large yellow onion, thinly sliced
4 cloves garlic, minced and divided
1 (28-ounce) can whole tomatoes,
    undrained
1 (8-ounce) can tomato sauce
2 teaspoons fennel seeds
    Salt and black pepper to taste
1 tablespoon butter or margarine
1 large yellow onion, chopped
2 (10-ounce) packages chopped frozen
    spinach, thawed and squeezed dry
1 cup grated Parmesan cheese, divided
3 cups (24 ounces) low fat ricotta cheese
1 pound shredded mozzarella or
    provolone cheese
9 uncooked lasagna noodles

Crumble sausage in large heavy skillet. Cook over medium heat until well browned, stirring occasionally. Remove sausage to paper towels; set aside. Drain off drippings and wipe skillet clean with paper towels. Heat oil in same skillet over medium-high heat until hot. Add green peppers, sliced onion and half the garlic. Cook, covered, over medium heat about 10 minutes or until vegetables are wilted, stirring occasionally. Stir in tomatoes with juice, tomato sauce and fennel seeds, stirring well to break up tomatoes. Bring to a boil. Reduce heat to low; simmer, uncovered, 20 to 30 minutes to blend flavors. Stir in reserved sausage.

Season sauce mixture with salt and black pepper; set aside. Melt butter in small saucepan over medium-high heat; add chopped onion and remaining garlic. Cook and stir about 10 minutes or until onion is tender. Stir in spinach and ¼ cup Parmesan; set aside. Combine ricotta, mozzarella and ½ cup Parmesan in medium bowl. Season with salt and black pepper. Cook noodles according to package directions; drain.

Preheat oven to 350°F. Pour ⅓ of reserved sauce mixture into greased 13×9-inch baking dish; spread evenly. Arrange 3 noodles over sauce mixture; spread half the spinach mixture over noodles. Spread half the cheese mixture evenly over spinach. Repeat layers once. Top with remaining 3 noodles and sauce mixture. Sprinkle with remaining ¼ cup Parmesan. Bake about 1 hour or until sauce is bubbly and cheese is browned on top. Let stand 10 to 15 minutes before slicing. Serve hot. Refrigerate leftovers. *Makes 8 servings*

PASTA MANIA

255 SPAGHETTI TWISTS WITH SPICY FRESH SALSA

½ cup WISH-BONE® Italian or Lite Italian Dressing
1 pound boneless chicken breasts, cut into thin strips
4 teaspoons finely chopped cilantro*
⅛ teaspoon plus ¼ teaspoon ground cumin
1 medium onion, chopped
8 small tomatoes, chopped**
1 can (4 ounces) chopped green chilies, undrained
½ teaspoon sugar
¼ teaspoon hot pepper sauce
12 ounces spaghetti twists or fusilli pasta, cooked and drained
1 cup finely shredded Monterey Jack or Cheddar cheese (about 3 ounces)

Substitution: Use 2 teaspoons dried cilantro (½ teaspoon with chicken and 1½ teaspoons stirred into sauce).

**Substitution: Use 1 can (28 ounces) crushed tomatoes.*

In 12-inch skillet, heat 2 tablespoons Italian dressing and cook chicken with 1 teaspoon cilantro and ⅛ teaspoon cumin until done; set aside. Heat an additional 2 tablespoons Italian dressing and cook onion 3 minutes or until almost tender. Add tomatoes, green chilies with liquid, sugar, hot pepper sauce, remaining ¼ cup Italian dressing and ¼ teaspoon cumin. Bring mixture to a boil, then simmer about 20 minutes. Stir in cooked chicken and remaining 3 teaspoons cilantro; heat through. To serve, spoon sauce over pasta and sprinkle with cheese.

Makes about 4 servings

256 MACARONI AND CHEESE DIJON

1¼ cups milk
12 ounces pasteurized process Cheddar cheese spread, cubed
½ cup GREY POUPON® Dijon Mustard
⅓ cup sliced green onions
6 slices bacon, cooked and crumbled
⅛ teaspoon ground red pepper
12 ounces tri-color rotelle or spiral-shaped pasta, cooked
1 (2.8-ounce) can French fried onion rings

In medium saucepan over low heat, heat milk, cheese and mustard until cheese melts and mixture is smooth. Stir in green onions, bacon and pepper; remove from heat.

In large bowl, combine hot pasta and cheese mixture, tossing until well coated; spoon into greased 2-quart casserole. Cover; bake at 350°F for 15 to 20 minutes. Uncover and stir; top with onion rings. Bake, uncovered, for 5 minutes more. Let stand 10 minutes before serving. Garnish as desired.

Makes 6 servings

Macaroni and Cheese Dijon

PASTA MANIA

257 CONTADINA® CLASSIC LASAGNE

1 tablespoon olive or vegetable oil
1 cup chopped onion
½ cup chopped green bell pepper
2 cloves garlic, minced
1½ pounds lean ground beef
3½ cups (two 14.5-ounce cans)
    CONTADINA® Recipe Ready Diced
    Tomatoes, undrained
1 cup (8-ounce can) CONTADINA®
    Tomato Sauce
⅔ cup (6-ounce can) CONTADINA®
    Tomato Paste
½ cup dry red wine or beef broth
1½ teaspoons salt
1 teaspoon dried oregano leaves, crushed
1 teaspoon dried basil leaves, crushed
½ teaspoon ground black pepper
1 egg
1 cup (8 ounces) ricotta cheese
2 cups (8 ounces) shredded mozzarella
    cheese, divided
1 pound dry lasagne noodles, cooked,
    drained, kept warm

In large skillet, heat oil. Add onion, bell pepper and garlic; sauté for 3 minutes or until vegetables are tender. Add ground beef; cook for 5 to 6 minutes or until evenly browned. Add tomatoes and juice, tomato sauce, tomato paste, wine, salt, oregano, basil and black pepper; bring to a boil. Reduce heat to low; simmer, uncovered, for 20 minutes, stirring occasionally. In medium bowl, beat egg slightly. Stir in ricotta cheese and *1 cup* mozzarella cheese. In ungreased 13×9-inch baking dish, layer noodles, *half* of meat sauce, noodles, all of ricotta cheese mixture, noodles and *remaining* meat sauce. Sprinkle with *remaining* mozzarella cheese. Bake in preheated 350°F. oven for 25 to 30 minutes or until heated through. Let stand for 15 minutes before cutting to serve.

Makes 10 servings

258 TURKEY LASAGNA

1 pound ITALIAN TURKEY SAUSAGE
1 jar (25.5 ounces) reduced-calorie
    vegetable spaghetti sauce
2 cups non-fat cottage cheese
1 cup shredded low-fat mozzarella cheese
¼ cup plus 2 tablespoons grated Parmesan
    cheese, divided
    Vegetable cooking spray
8 uncooked lasagna noodles

1. Crumble sausage into large non-stick skillet. Sauté over medium-high heat 9 minutes or until no longer pink. Drain. Stir in sauce.

2. In medium bowl combine cottage cheese, mozzarella cheese and ¼ cup Parmesan cheese.

3. Spray 13×9-inch baking pan with cooking spray. Spread 1 cup meat sauce onto bottom of prepared pan. Place 4 uncooked noodles over sauce, breaking to fit if necessary. Spread ½ of cheese mixture over noodles. Layer with ½ of remaining sauce, 4 noodles and remaining cheese mixture. Top with remaining sauce, covering all noodles. Sprinkle with 2 tablespoons Parmesan cheese. Cover pan tightly with aluminum foil. Bake at 350°F. 45 minutes or until noodles are tender. Let stand 10 to 15 minutes before cutting to serve.

Makes 8 servings

*Favorite recipe from **National Turkey Federation***

CONTADINA® Classic Lasagne

PASTA MANIA

259 COUNTRY-STYLE LASAGNA

9 lasagna noodles (2 inches wide)
2 cans (14½ ounces *each*) DEL MONTE® FRESH CUT™ Diced Tomatoes with Garlic & Onion
Milk
2 tablespoons butter or margarine
3 tablespoons all-purpose flour
1 teaspoon dried basil, crushed
1 cup diced cooked ham
2 cups shredded mozzarella cheese

Cook noodles according to package directions; rinse, drain and separate noodles. Drain tomatoes, reserving liquid; pour liquid into measuring cup. Add milk to measure 2 cups. In large saucepan, melt butter; stir in flour and basil. Cook over medium heat 3 minutes, stirring constantly. Stir in reserved liquid; cook until thickened, stirring constantly. Season to taste with salt and pepper, if desired. Stir in tomatoes. Spread thin layer of sauce on bottom of 11×7-inch or 2-quart baking dish. Top with 3 noodles and ⅓ *each* of sauce, ham and cheese; repeat layers twice ending with cheese. Bake, uncovered, at 375°F, 25 minutes. Garnish with Parmesan cheese or green onions, if desired.

Makes 6 servings

Prep Time: 15 minutes
Cook Time: 25 minutes

Country-Style Lasagna

260 SUMMER TURKEY LASAGNA

3 zucchini squash (8 to 9 inches long), sliced lengthwise into ¼-inch-thick strips
½ pound TURKEY HAM, cut into ½-inch cubes
1 can (8 ounces) no-salt tomato sauce
1 cup instant rice
½ medium onion, finely chopped
½ teaspoon Italian seasoning
⅛ teaspoon pepper
1 cup low-fat cottage cheese
½ cup (2 ounces) low-fat mozzarella cheese
1 teaspoon parsley flakes
2 tablespoons grated Parmesan cheese

1. In 8-inch square microwave-safe dish, layer zucchini strips; cover with wax paper. Microwave on HIGH (100%) 8 to 10 minutes or until zucchini are tender, rotating dish after 5 minutes. Remove zucchini; place on paper towels to drain. Drain liquid from dish.

2. In medium bowl, combine turkey, tomato sauce, rice, onions, Italian seasoning and pepper. Combine cottage cheese, mozzarella cheese and parsley in small bowl.

3. Arrange ½ of zucchini strips in single layer on bottom of same microwave-safe dish. Top with turkey-rice mixture, spreading to cover zucchini layer. Top with cheese mixture; spread gently to cover turkey mixture. Top with layer of remaining zucchini strips; sprinkle with Parmesan cheese.

4. Microwave at MEDIUM (50%) 20 to 25 minutes or until rice is tender.

Makes 4 servings

Favorite recipe from **National Turkey Federation**

261 EASY MICROWAVE TURKEY LASAGNA

1 pound GROUND TURKEY
1 clove garlic, chopped
1 cup chopped onion
1 can (14½ ounces) tomatoes, chopped
1 can (6 ounces) tomato paste
2½ teaspoons Italian seasoning *or* dried oregano leaves
8 uncooked lasagna noodles
1 container (12 ounces) low-fat cottage cheese
2 cups (8 ounces) shredded part-skim mozzarella cheese

1. In 2-quart microwave-safe casserole dish, combine turkey, garlic and onion; cover with plastic wrap. Microwave at HIGH 5 minutes, stirring halfway through cooking time. Add tomatoes, tomato paste and Italian seasoning. Microwave, uncovered, at HIGH 5 minutes.

2. Spoon ⅓ of the tomato sauce (about 1⅓ cups) onto bottom of oblong 2-quart baking dish. Top with 4 lasagna noodles, breaking noodles to fit. Spoon cottage cheese over noodles; sprinkle with mozzarella cheese. Cover with ½ of the remaining sauce and the remaining noodles. Top with remaining sauce; cover with vented plastic wrap.

3. Microwave at HIGH (100 % power) 5 minutes. Microwave at MEDIUM (50 % power) 20 to 25 minutes or until noodles are tender. Let stand, covered, 10 minutes. *Makes 8 servings*

NOTE: To absorb any spillovers in microwave, set lasagna dish on several layers of paper towels.

Favorite recipe from **National Turkey Federation**

262 SPINACH LASAGNA

1 pound ground beef
¼ pound fresh mushrooms, thinly sliced
1 medium onion, chopped
1 clove garlic, minced
1 can (28 ounces) Italian plum tomatoes, undrained
1¼ teaspoons salt, divided
¾ teaspoon dried oregano leaves, crushed
¾ teaspoon dried basil leaves, crushed
¼ teaspoon pepper, divided
9 uncooked lasagna noodles
¼ cup plus 1 tablespoon butter or margarine, divided
¼ cup all-purpose flour
⅛ teaspoon ground nutmeg
2 cups milk
1½ cups shredded mozzarella cheese (about 6 ounces), divided
½ cup freshly grated Parmesan cheese, divided
1 package (10 ounces) frozen chopped spinach, thawed and squeezed dry

1. For meat sauce, crumble ground beef into large skillet over medium-high heat. Brown 8 to 10 minutes, stirring to separate meat, until meat loses its pink color. Stir in mushrooms, onion and garlic; cook over medium heat 5 minutes or until onion is tender.

2. Press tomatoes and juice through sieve into meat mixture; discard seeds. Stir in ¾ teaspoon salt, oregano, basil and ⅛ teaspoon pepper. Bring to a boil over medium-high heat; reduce heat to low. Cover and simmer 40 minutes, stirring occasionally. Uncover and simmer 15 to 20 minutes more until sauce thickens. Set aside.

3. Add lasagna noodles, 1 at a time, to large pot of boiling salted water allowing noodles to soften and fit into pot. Cook 10 minutes or just until al dente. Drain noodles; rinse with cold water. Drain again; hang individually over pot rim to prevent sticking. Set aside.

4. For cheese sauce, melt ¼ cup butter in medium saucepan over medium heat. Stir in flour, remaining ½ teaspoon salt, remaining ⅛ teaspoon pepper and nutmeg; cook and stir until bubbly. Whisk in milk; cook and stir until sauce thickens and bubbles. Cook and stir 1 minute more. Remove from heat. Add 1 cup mozzarella and ¼ cup Parmesan cheeses; stir until smooth. Set aside.

5. Preheat oven to 350°F. With waxed paper, spread remaining 1 tablespoon butter onto bottom and sides of 12×8-inch baking dish. Spread noodles in single layer on clean kitchen (not paper) towel. Pat noodles dry.

6. Arrange 3 lasagna noodles in single layer, overlapping slightly, in bottom of baking dish. Top with ½ of reserved meat sauce; spread evenly. Spread ½ of reserved cheese sauce over meat sauce in even layer.

7. Repeat layers once, using 3 noodles, remaining meat sauce and remaining cheese sauce. Sprinkle spinach over cheese sauce in even layer; pat down lightly. Arrange remaining 3 lasagna noodles over spinach.

8. Mix remaining ½ cup mozzarella and ¼ cup Parmesan cheeses in small bowl. Sprinkle cheeses evenly on top of lasagna to completely cover noodles. Bake 40 minutes or until top is golden and edges are bubbly. Let stand 10 minutes before serving. Garnish as desired. *Makes 6 servings*

Spinach Lasagna

263 CHEESY CHICKEN ROLL–UPS

¼ cup butter
1 medium onion, diced
4 ounces fresh mushrooms, sliced
3 boneless skinless chicken breast halves,
    cut into bite-sized pieces
¾ cup dry white wine
½ teaspoon dried tarragon leaves, crushed
½ teaspoon salt
½ teaspoon pepper
6 lasagna noodles, cooked, drained
1 package (8 ounces) cream cheese,
    softened, cubed
½ cup heavy cream
½ cup dairy sour cream
1½ cups (6 ounces) shredded Swiss cheese,
    divided
1 cup (4 ounces) shredded Muenster
    cheese, divided
3 tablespoons sliced almonds, toasted*
Chopped parsley (optional)

To toast almonds, spread almonds in single layer on baking sheet. Bake in preheated 350°F oven 8 to 10 minutes or until golden brown, stirring frequently.

1. Preheat oven to 325°F. Grease 13×9-inch baking pan; set aside.

2. Melt butter in large skillet over medium-high heat. Add onion and mushrooms; cook and stir until tender. Add chicken, wine, tarragon, salt and pepper; bring to a boil over high heat. Reduce heat to low. Simmer 10 minutes.

3. Cut lasagna noodles in half lengthwise. Curl each half into a circle; arrange in prepared pan. With slotted spoon, fill center of lasagna rings with chicken mixture, reserving liquid in skillet.

4. To remaining liquid in skillet, add cream cheese, heavy cream, sour cream, ¾ cup Swiss cheese and ½ cup Muenster cheese. Cook and stir over medium-low heat until cheese melts. *Do not boil.* Pour over lasagna rings. Sprinkle remaining cheeses and almonds on top.

5. Bake 35 minutes or until bubbly. Sprinkle with parsley. Garnish as desired.

Makes 6 servings

264 CHEX® UNDER WRAPS

1½ pounds ground turkey or beef
2 cups CORN CHEX® brand cereal,
    crushed to 1 cup
1 can (10¾ ounces) condensed tomato
    soup
1 can (15¼ ounces) corn, drained
8 slices American cheese, cut in half
8 lasagna noodles, cooked and cut in half
    lengthwise
1 jar (30 ounces) prepared spaghetti sauce

1. Preheat oven to 350°F. Combine turkey, cereal, soup, corn and ¼ teaspoon salt, if desired; mix well. Divide evenly into 16 portions; form into loaves, each about 1½×2-inches. Place a cheese slice over each meat loaf; wrap with lasagna noodle.

2. Place seam side down in ungreased 13×9-inch baking dish. Pour spaghetti sauce evenly over top. Cover and bake 1 hour. Let stand 10 minutes before serving.

Makes 8 to 10 servings

Cheesy Chicken Roll-Ups

PASTA MANIA

265 LASAGNE ROLL–UPS

1 pound mild Italian sausage, casings removed
½ cup chopped onion
1 clove garlic, minced
1⅓ cups (12-ounce can) CONTADINA® Tomato Paste
1⅔ cups water
1 teaspoon dried oregano leaves, crushed
½ teaspoon dried basil leaves, crushed
1 egg
1 package (10 ounces) frozen chopped spinach, thawed, squeezed dry
2 cups (15-ounce container) ricotta cheese
1½ cups (6 ounces) shredded mozzarella cheese, divided
1 cup (4 ounces) grated Parmesan cheese
½ teaspoon salt
¼ teaspoon ground black pepper
8 dry lasagne noodles, cooked, drained, kept warm

In large skillet, crumble sausage. Add onion and garlic; cook until sausage is no longer pink. Drain. Stir in tomato paste, water, oregano and basil; cover. Bring to a boil. Reduce heat to low; simmer, uncovered, for 20 minutes. In medium bowl, beat egg lightly. Add spinach, ricotta cheese, 1 cup mozzarella cheese, Parmesan cheese, salt and pepper. Spread about ½ *cup* cheese mixture onto each noodle; roll up. Place, seam side down, in 12×7½-inch baking dish. Pour sauce over rolls; top with *remaining* mozzarella cheese. Bake in preheated 350°F. oven for 30 to 40 minutes or until heated through. *Makes 8 servings*

266 TURKEY TETRAZZINI

2 tablespoons cornstarch
1¼ cups skim milk
¾ cup turkey broth or chicken bouillon
½ teaspoon salt
½ teaspoon garlic powder
⅛ teaspoon pepper
¼ cup grated parmesan cheese
2 tablespoons dry white wine
1 can (4 ounces) mushrooms, drained
1 jar (2 ounces) chopped pimiento, drained
4 ounces spaghetti, cooked according to package instructions and drained
2 cups (½-inch) cubed COOKED TURKEY
2 tablespoons sliced almonds

1. Preheat oven to 375°F.

2. In 3-quart saucepan, combine cornstarch, milk, broth, salt, garlic powder and pepper. Bring mixture to a boil over medium heat, stirring constantly. Remove from heat; stir in cheese, wine, mushrooms, pimiento, spaghetti and turkey.

3. Spoon turkey mixture into lightly greased 9-inch square baking dish; sprinkle with almonds. Bake 25 minutes or until mixture is bubbly and top is browned.

Makes 4 servings

Favorite recipe from **National Turkey Federation**

Lasagne Roll-Up

PASTA MANIA

267 CHICKEN TETRAZZINI

8 ounces uncooked spaghetti, broken in half
3 tablespoons butter, divided
¼ cup all-purpose flour
1 teaspoon salt
½ teaspoon paprika
½ teaspoon celery salt
⅛ teaspoon pepper
2 cups milk
1 cup chicken broth
3 cups chopped cooked chicken
1 can (4 ounces) mushrooms, drained
¼ cup pimiento strips
¾ cup (3 ounces) grated Wisconsin Parmesan cheese, divided

In large saucepan, cook spaghetti according to package directions; drain. Return to same saucepan; add 1 tablespoon butter. Stir until melted. Set aside. In 3-quart saucepan, melt remaining 2 tablespoons butter over medium heat; stir in flour, salt, paprika, celery salt and pepper. Remove from heat; gradually stir in milk and chicken broth. Cook over medium heat, stirring constantly, until thickened. Add chicken, mushrooms, pimiento, spaghetti and ¼ cup cheese; heat thoroughly. Place chicken mixture on ovenproof platter or in shallow casserole; sprinkle remaining ½ cup cheese over top. Broil about 3 inches from heat until lightly browned. *Makes 6 to 8 servings*

Favorite recipe from **Wisconsin Milk Marketing Board**

268 SAUSAGE TETRAZZINI

1 pound BOB EVANS FARMS® Italian Roll Sausage
1 medium onion, chopped
1 red or green bell pepper, chopped
½ pound spaghetti, cooked according to package directions and drained
1 (10½-ounce) can condensed cream of mushroom soup
1 (10-ounce) can condensed tomato soup
1 (16-ounce) can stewed tomatoes, undrained
½ pound fresh mushrooms, chopped
1 teaspoon minced garlic
½ teaspoon black pepper
Salt to taste
1½ cups (6 ounces) shredded Cheddar cheese

Preheat oven to 350°F. Crumble sausage into large skillet. Cook over medium heat until lightly browned, stirring occasionally. Remove sausage; set aside. Add onion and red pepper to drippings in skillet; cook and stir until tender. Place in large bowl. Stir in spaghetti, soups, tomatoes with juice, mushrooms, garlic, black pepper, salt and reserved sausage; place in 3-quart casserole dish. Sprinkle with cheese; bake, uncovered, 30 to 35 minutes or until heated through. Serve hot. Refrigerate leftovers.

Makes 6 to 8 servings

Sunday Super Stuffed Shells

269 SUNDAY SUPER STUFFED SHELLS

1 package (10 ounces) frozen chopped
    spinach
2 tablespoons olive oil
3 cloves fresh garlic, peeled
¾ pound ground veal
¾ pound ground pork
1 cup parsley, finely chopped
1 cup fresh bread crumbs
2 eggs, beaten
3 cloves fresh garlic, minced
3 tablespoons grated Parmesan cheese
    Salt to taste
1 package (12 ounces) jumbo pasta shells,
    cooked, drained
3 cups spaghetti sauce

1. Cook spinach according to package directions. Place in colander to drain. Let stand until cool enough to handle. Squeeze spinach between hands to remove excess moisture. Set aside.

2. Heat oil in large skillet over medium heat. Cook and stir whole garlic cloves in hot oil until garlic is lightly browned. Discard garlic. Add veal and pork. Cook until lightly browned, stirring to separate meat; drain drippings. Cool slightly.

3. Preheat oven to 375°F. Grease 12×8-inch baking pan.

4. Combine spinach, parsley, bread crumbs, eggs, minced garlic and cheese in large bowl; blend well. Season to taste with salt. Add cooled meat mixture; blend well. Fill shells with meat mixture using spoon.

5. Spread about 1 cup spaghetti sauce onto bottom of prepared pan. Arrange shells in pan. Pour remaining sauce over shells. Cover with foil.

6. Bake 35 to 45 minutes or until bubbly. Garnish as desired.

Makes 8 to 9 servings

270 TACOS IN PASTA SHELLS

1¼ pounds ground beef
1 package (3 ounces) cream cheese with chives, cubed, softened
1 teaspoon salt
1 teaspoon chili powder
18 jumbo pasta shells, cooked, drained
2 tablespoons butter, melted
1 cup prepared taco sauce
1 cup (4 ounces) shredded Cheddar cheese
1 cup (4 ounces) shredded Monterey Jack cheese
1½ cups crushed tortilla chips
1 cup dairy sour cream
3 green onions, chopped

1. Preheat oven to 350°F. Butter 13×9-inch baking pan.

2. Cook beef in large skillet over medium-high heat until brown, stirring to separate meat; drain drippings.

3. Reduce heat to medium-low. Add cream cheese, salt and chili powder; simmer 5 minutes.

4. Toss shells with butter. Fill shells with beef mixture using spoon. Arrange shells in prepared pan. Pour taco sauce evenly over each shell. Cover with foil.

5. Bake 15 minutes. Uncover; top with Cheddar cheese, Monterey Jack cheese and chips. Bake 15 minutes more or until bubbly. Top with sour cream and onions. Garnish, if desired. *Makes 4 to 6 servings*

271 MEXICAN TURKEY STUFFED SHELLS

1 pound GROUND TURKEY
½ cup chopped onions
¼ cup chopped fresh cilantro
1 teaspoon minced garlic
1 teaspoon dried oregano leaves
½ teaspoon cumin
½ teaspoon salt
1 cup non-fat ricotta cheese
18 large pasta shells, uncooked
2 cans (10 ounces *each*) mild enchilada sauce
¼ cup (1 ounce) shredded reduced-fat Monterey Jack cheese

1. In large bowl, combine turkey, onions, cilantro, garlic, oregano, cumin and salt. Blend in ricotta cheese. Stuff each shell with 1 heaping tablespoonful turkey mixture.

2. In 2-quart oblong glass baking dish, pour 1 can enchilada sauce. Arrange shells in baking dish; dot any remaining turkey mixture over shells. Pour remaining can of sauce over shells; cover tightly with foil. Bake at 375°F 1 to 1¼ hours or until shells are tender. Sprinkle cheese over top. Re-cover and let stand 10 minutes.

Makes 6 servings

Favorite recipe from **National Turkey Federation**

Tacos in Pasta Shells

Turkey-Spinach Manicotti

272 TURKEY–SPINACH MANICOTTI

1 package (1.5 ounces) LAWRY'S®
Spaghetti Sauce Seasoning Blend with
Imported Mushrooms
1 can (28 ounces) whole tomatoes, cut up
1 can (8 ounces) tomato sauce
¼ cup chopped green onions
1 cup ricotta cheese
2 cups chopped fresh spinach*
2 cups cooked, minced turkey or chicken
2 tablespoons milk
1 teaspoon LAWRY'S® Seasoned Pepper
½ teaspoon LAWRY'S® Garlic Powder with
Parsley
8 manicotti shells, cooked and drained
⅓ cup grated Parmesan cheese

*1 package (10 ounces) frozen chopped spinach,
thawed and drained, can be substituted for fresh
spinach.

In medium saucepan, combine Spaghetti Sauce Seasoning Blend with Imported Mushrooms, tomatoes, tomato sauce and onions. Bring to a boil. Reduce heat; cover and simmer 20 minutes, stirring occasionally. In medium bowl, combine ricotta cheese, spinach, turkey, milk, Seasoned Pepper and Garlic Powder with Parsley; blend well. Carefully spoon mixture into manicotti shells. Pour ½ of sauce onto bottom of 12×8-inch baking dish. Place stuffed shells on top of sauce; pour remaining sauce over shells. Cover and bake in 375°F oven 30 minutes or until heated through. Sprinkle with Parmesan cheese.

Makes 4 to 8 servings

PRESENTATION: Sprinkle with chopped parsley. Garnish with fresh basil leaves.

PASTA MANIA

273 TURKEY MANICOTTI

1 pound ITALIAN TURKEY SAUSAGE
¼ pound fresh mushrooms, chopped
½ cup chopped onion
1 clove garlic, minced
1 cup (4 ounces) shredded part-skim
    mozzarella cheese
1½ cups low-fat ricotta cheese
1 egg, beaten
1 package (10 ounces) frozen chopped
    spinach, thawed and well drained
1 package (8 ounces) manicotti shells,
    cooked according to package
    directions and drained
    Vegetable cooking spray
¼ cup flour
⅛ teaspoon pepper
1 can (15 ounces) evaporated skim milk
½ cup low-sodium chicken broth
½ cup plus 2 tablespoons grated Parmesan
    cheese

1. In large non-stick skillet over medium heat, cook and stir turkey sausage, mushrooms, onions and garlic 5 to 6 minutes or until sausage is no longer pink. Remove skillet from heat and drain.

2. In large bowl, combine mozzarella cheese, ricotta cheese and egg. Add turkey sausage mixture and spinach; mix well.

3. Cut each manicotti shell open down long side. (This will make stuffing shells easier.) Carefully spoon about ⅓ cup turkey sausage filling down center of each shell; roll up shell to enclose filling. Arrange stuffed shells, seam side down, in 14×11-inch baking dish lightly coated with vegetable spray.

4. In medium saucepan, combine flour and pepper. Gradually add evaporated milk and chicken broth, stirring with wire whisk until well blended. Cook over medium heat, stirring constantly, until sauce comes to a boil and thickens. Remove pan from heat; whisk in ½ cup Parmesan cheese. Pour sauce over stuffed shells; sprinkle with remaining Parmesan cheese.

5. Cover baking pan with foil. Bake in 350°F oven 20 to 25 minutes or until mixture is heated through. *Makes 8 servings*

*Favorite recipe from **National Turkey Federation***

PASTA MANIA

274 SPAGHETTI ROLLS

2 pounds ground beef
1 tablespoon onion powder
1 teaspoon salt
½ teaspoon pepper
2 cups spaghetti sauce, divided
1 cup (4 ounces) shredded pizza-flavored cheese blend or mozzarella cheese
1 package (8 ounces) manicotti shells, cooked, drained

1. Preheat oven to 350°F. Grease 13×9-inch baking pan.

2. Cook beef in large skillet over medium-high heat until brown, stirring to separate meat; drain drippings. Stir in onion powder, salt and pepper. Stir in 1 cup spaghetti sauce; cool and set aside.

3. Reserve ½ cup ground beef mixture. Combine remaining beef mixture with cheese in large bowl. Fill shells with remaining beef mixture using spoon.

4. Arrange shells in prepared pan. Combine remaining spaghetti sauce with reserved beef mixture in small bowl; blend well. Pour over shells. Cover with foil.

5. Bake 20 to 30 minutes or until hot. Garnish as desired.   *Makes 4 servings*

275 EGGPLANT & FETA ZITI

1 pound ground beef
1 medium eggplant, peeled, cut into ½-inch cubes (about 6 cups)
½ cup chopped onion
1 clove garlic, minced
1 jar (32 ounces) spaghetti sauce
¼ teaspoon ground cinnamon
1 package (8 ounces) ATHENOS® Feta Cheese with Garlic & Herb, crumbled
2 cups (8 ounces) shredded low-moisture part-skim mozzarella cheese
2 cups ziti, cooked, drained

BROWN meat in large skillet; drain. Remove and set aside. Cook eggplant, onion and garlic on medium heat 10 minutes or until vegetables are tender, stirring occasionally. Stir in spaghetti sauce, cinnamon and reserved meat. Reduce heat to low; simmer 5 minutes. Mix feta and mozzarella cheese.

LAYER ziti, meat sauce and cheese mixture in greased 13×9-inch baking dish.

BAKE at 375°F for 25 to 30 minutes or until thoroughly heated and lightly browned. Let stand 10 minutes before serving.
    Makes 8 to 10 servings

Prep Time: 35 minutes
Bake Time: 30 minutes plus standing

Spaghetti Rolls

PASTA MANIA

276 CHICKEN PARMESAN NOODLE BAKE

1 package (12 ounces) extra wide noodles
4 half boneless chicken breasts, skinned
½ teaspoon rosemary, crushed
2 cans (14½ ounces *each*) DEL MONTE® Italian Recipe Stewed Tomatoes
½ cup (2 ounces) shredded mozzarella cheese
¼ cup (1 ounce) grated Parmesan cheese

1. Preheat oven to 450°F.

2. Cook noodles according to package directions; drain. Keep warm.

3. Meanwhile, sprinkle chicken with rosemary; season with salt and pepper, if desired. Arrange chicken in shallow baking dish. Bake, uncovered, 20 minutes or until chicken is no longer pink in center. Drain; remove chicken from dish.

4. Drain tomatoes, reserving liquid. In large bowl, toss reserved liquid with noodles; place in baking dish. Top with chicken and tomatoes. Sprinkle with cheeses.

5. Bake 10 minutes or until heated through. Sprinkle with additional Parmesan cheese and garnish, if desired.

Makes 4 servings

Prep & Bake Time: 35 minutes

277 COLORFUL TURKEY PASTA BAKE

2 cups (about 8 ounces) uncooked mixed vegetable rotini pasta*
1 tablespoon margarine
1 tablespoon all-purpose flour
¼ teaspoon salt
⅛ teaspoon pepper
1⅓ cups skim milk
1 cup (4 ounces) shredded natural Swiss cheese, divided
2 cups cubed COOKED TURKEY

*If desired, substitute elbow macaroni, rotelle, small shells or ziti for rotini.

1. Cook pasta according to package directions; drain. In 2-quart saucepan, melt margarine over medium heat. Stir in flour, salt and pepper. Blend in milk; cook, stirring constantly, until thickened and bubbly. Add ¾ cup cheese; stir until melted. Stir in turkey.

2. Spray 8-inch square baking dish with nonstick vegetable spray. Add pasta mixture; sprinkle with remaining ¼ cup cheese. Bake at 350°F until heated through, about 30 minutes. Cut into squares to serve.

Makes 4 servings

*Favorite recipe from **National Turkey Federation***

Chicken Parmesan Noodle Bake

278 JOHNNIE MARZETTI

1 tablespoon CRISCO® Vegetable Oil
1 cup chopped celery
1 cup chopped onion
1 medium green bell pepper, chopped
1 pound ground beef round
1 can (14½ ounces) Italian style stewed
    tomatoes
1 can (8 ounces) tomato sauce
1 can (6 ounces) tomato paste
1 cup water
1 bay leaf
1½ teaspoons dried basil leaves
1¼ teaspoons salt
¼ teaspoon black pepper
1 package (12 ounces) egg noodles,
    cooked and well drained
½ cup plain dry bread crumbs
1 cup (4 ounces) shredded sharp Cheddar
    cheese

1. Heat oven to 375°F. Oil 12½×8½×2-inch baking dish lightly.

2. Heat one tablespoon Crisco® Oil in large skillet on medium heat. Add celery, onion and green pepper. Cook and stir until tender. Remove vegetables from skillet. Set aside. Add meat to skillet. Cook until browned, stirring occasionally. Return vegetables to skillet. Add tomatoes, tomato sauce, tomato paste, water, bay leaf, basil, salt and black pepper. Reduce heat to low. Simmer 5 minutes, stirring occasionally. Remove bay leaf.

3. Place noodles in baking dish. Spoon meat mixture over noodles. Sprinkle with bread crumbs and cheese.

4. Bake at 375°F for 15 to 20 minutes or until cheese melts. Garnish, if desired.

Makes 8 servings

279 CREAMY CREOLE TURKEY BAKE

⅔ cup chopped onion
⅔ cup chopped celery
⅓ cup chopped green pepper
1 garlic clove, minced
1 tablespoon margarine
¼ pound mushrooms, sliced
4 ounces light cream cheese, softened
1 can (8 ounces) low-sodium stewed
    tomatoes, drained
1½ teaspoons creole seasoning
4 ounces fettucini, cooked according to
    package directions and drained
2 cups (½-inch) cubed COOKED TURKEY
    Vegetable cooking spray
¼ cup grated Parmesan cheese

1. In medium non-stick skillet, over medium-high heat, sauté onion, celery, green pepper and garlic in margarine 4 to 5 minutes or until vegetables are crisp-tender. Add mushrooms; sauté 2 minutes. Remove from heat.

2. In medium bowl, blend cream cheese, tomatoes and creole seasoning. Stir in vegetable mixture, fettucini and turkey.

3. Pour mixture into 9-inch square dish sprayed with cooking spray; sprinkle with cheese. Bake at 325°F 30 minutes or until bubbly.
Makes 4 servings

*Favorite recipe from **National Turkey Federation***

Johnnie Marzetti

PASTA MANIA

280 HAM & MACARONI TWISTS

2 cups rotini or elbow macaroni, cooked in unsalted water and drained
1½ cups (8 ounces) cubed cooked ham
1 can (2.8 ounces) FRENCH'S® French Fried Onions
1 package (10 ounces) frozen broccoli spears,* thawed and drained
1 cup milk
1 can (10¾ ounces) condensed cream of celery soup
1 cup (4 ounces) shredded Cheddar cheese
¼ teaspoon garlic powder
¼ teaspoon pepper

*1 small head fresh broccoli (about ½ pound) may be substituted for frozen spears. Divide into spears and cook 3 to 4 minutes before using.

Preheat oven to 350°F. In 12×8-inch baking dish, combine hot macaroni, ham and *½ can* French Fried Onions. Divide broccoli spears into 6 small bunches. Arrange bunches of spears down center of dish, alternating direction of flowerets. In small bowl, combine milk, soup, *½ cup* cheese and the seasonings; pour over casserole. Bake, covered, at 350°F for 30 minutes or until heated through. Top with remaining cheese and sprinkle onions down center; bake, uncovered, 5 minutes or until onions are golden brown.   *Makes 4 to 6 servings*

Ham & Macaroni Twists

281 TURKEY–SPAGHETTI PIE

**6 ounces spaghetti, cooked according to package directions and drained
1 egg white, lightly beaten
1/3 cup grated Parmesan cheese
2 1/2 tablespoons margarine, melted
1 cup onion, chopped
1 clove garlic, minced
1 package (10 ounces) frozen mixed vegetables, thawed and drained
2 tablespoons flour
1 teaspoon poultry seasoning
1/8 teaspoon pepper
1 1/2 cups skim milk
2 cups cubed COOKED TURKEY**

1. Preheat oven to 350° F.

2. In medium-size bowl, combine spaghetti, egg white, cheese and 1 tablespoon margarine. Press pasta mixture onto bottom and up side of well-greased 9-inch pie plate. Grease 12×10-inch piece of aluminum foil. Press foil, greased side down, on top of pasta shell. Bake 25 to 30 minutes or until pie shell is set and slightly browned around edge.

3. In medium-size saucepan, sauté onion and garlic in remaining margarine over medium-high heat 2 to 3 minutes or until onion is translucent. Stir in vegetables; cook 1 minute. Stir in flour, poultry seasoning and pepper. Remove pan from heat.

4. Gradually add milk to vegetable mixture, stirring constantly. Return saucepan to medium heat; cook and stir until mixture is thickened.

5. Add turkey. Reduce heat to medium-low; simmer 5 minutes or until heated through. Remove foil from pasta shells; fill with vegetable mixture. To serve, cut spaghetti pie into six wedges.   *Makes 6 servings*

*Favorite recipe from **National Turkey Federation***

282 TUNA MAC AND CHEESE

**1 package (7 1/4 ounces) macaroni and cheese dinner
1 can (12 ounces) STARKIST® Solid White or Chunk Light Tuna, drained and chunked
1 cup frozen peas
1/2 cup shredded Cheddar cheese
1/2 cup milk
1 teaspoon Italian herb seasoning
1/4 teaspoon garlic powder (optional)
1 tablespoon grated Parmesan cheese**

Prepare macaroni and cheese dinner according to package directions. Add remaining ingredients except Parmesan cheese. Pour into 1 1/2-quart microwavable serving dish. Cover with vented plastic wrap; microwave on HIGH 2 minutes. Stir; continue heating on HIGH 2 1/2 to 3 1/2 more minutes or until cheese is melted and mixture is heated through. Sprinkle with Parmesan cheese.

Makes 5 to 6 servings

Prep Time: 20 minutes

283 ANGEL HAIR CARBONARA

⅔ cup milk
2 tablespoons margarine or butter
1 package (4.8 ounces) PASTA RONI®
    Herb Sauce with Angel Hair Pasta
2 cups chopped cooked pork or ham
1 package (10 ounces) frozen peas
¼ cup sliced green onions

1. In round 3-quart microwaveable glass casserole, combine 1½ cups water, milk and margarine. Microwave, uncovered, on HIGH 4 to 5 minutes or until boiling.

2. Gradually add pasta while stirring. Separate pasta with a fork, if needed.

3. Stir in contents of seasoning packet.

4. Microwave, uncovered, on HIGH 4 minutes, stirring gently after 2 minutes. Separate pasta with a fork if needed. Stir in pork, frozen peas and onions. Continue to microwave 2 to 3 minutes. Sauce will be very thin, but will thicken upon standing.

5. Let stand 3 minutes or until desired consistency. Stir before serving.

Makes 4 servings

284 BAKED RIGATONI

4 ounces mild Italian sausage, casings
    removed, sliced
1 cup chopped onion
2 cloves garlic, minced
1¾ cups (14.5-ounce can) CONTADINA®
    Recipe Ready Diced Tomatoes,
    undrained
⅔ cup (6-ounce can) CONTADINA®
    Tomato Paste
1 cup chicken broth
1 teaspoon salt
1 pound dry rigatoni, cooked, drained,
    kept warm
1 cup (4 ounces) shredded mozzarella
    cheese, divided
½ cup (2 ounces) shredded Parmesan
    cheese (optional)
2 tablespoons chopped fresh basil *or*
    2 teaspoons dried basil leaves,
    crushed

In large skillet, cook sausage for 4 to 6 minutes or until no longer pink. Remove sausage from skillet, reserving any drippings in skillet. Add onion and garlic to skillet; sauté for 2 minutes. Stir in tomatoes and juice, tomato paste, broth and salt. Bring to a boil. Reduce heat to low; simmer, uncovered, for 10 minutes, stirring occasionally. In large bowl, combine pasta, tomato mixture, sausage, *½ cup* mozzarella cheese, Parmesan cheese and basil; spoon into ungreased 13×9-inch baking dish. Sprinkle with *remaining* mozzarella cheese. Bake in preheated 375°F. oven for 10 to 15 minutes or until cheese is melted.

Makes 8 servings

Angel Hair Carbonara

PASTA MANIA

285 ITALIAN ROTINI BAKE

1 tablespoon olive or vegetable oil
1½ cups chopped onion
2 small zucchini, quartered, sliced (about 1½ cups)
3 cloves garlic, minced
1 pound ground turkey
3½ cups (two 14.5-ounce cans) CONTADINA® Recipe Ready Diced Tomatoes, undrained
⅔ cup (6-ounce can) CONTADINA® Tomato Paste
1 cup water
1 tablespoon Italian herb seasoning
1 teaspoon salt
1 egg
2 cups (15-ounce container) ricotta cheese
3 cups (12 ounces) shredded mozzarella cheese, divided
8 ounces dry rotini pasta, cooked, drained, kept warm, divided

In large skillet, heat oil over medium-high heat. Add onion, zucchini and garlic; sauté for 2 to 3 minutes or until vegetables are tender. Add turkey; cook for 4 to 5 minutes or until turkey is no longer pink. Drain. Add tomatoes and juice, tomato paste, water, Italian seasoning and salt. Bring to a boil. Reduce heat to low; simmer, uncovered, for 5 minutes. In small bowl, beat egg lightly. Add ricotta cheese and *1 cup* mozzarella cheese. In ungreased 13×9-inch baking dish, layer *half* of pasta and *half* of tomato mixture. Cover with ricotta cheese mixture and *1 cup* mozzarella cheese. Top with *remaining* pasta, tomato mixture and mozzarella cheese. Bake in preheated 350°F oven for 15 to 20 minutes or until heated through. *Makes 8 to 10 servings*

286 TUNA VEGETABLE MEDLEY

8 ounces cooked egg noodles
1 package (10 ounces) frozen chopped broccoli, thawed and well drained
1 package (10 ounces) frozen carrots, thawed and well drained
1 cup corn
1 can (10¾ ounces) cream of mushroom soup
1 can (12 ounces) STARKIST® Solid White or Chunk Light Tuna, drained and chunked
⅔ cup milk
1 cup shredded Swiss, Cheddar or Monterey Jack Cheese
Salt and pepper to taste
¼ cup grated Parmesan cheese

In large bowl, combine all ingredients except Parmesan cheese; mix well. Pour mixture into 2-quart baking dish; top with Parmesan cheese. Bake in 400°F oven 20 to 30 minutes or until thoroughly heated and golden on top. *Makes 6 servings*

Prep Time: 40 minutes

287 BAKED RIGATONI WITH SAUSAGE

½ pound Italian sausage*
2 cups low fat milk
2 tablespoons all-purpose flour
½ pound rigatoni pasta, cooked and
    drained
2½ cups (10 ounces) grated mozzarella
    cheese
¼ cup grated Parmesan cheese
1 teaspoon LAWRY'S® Garlic Salt
¾ teaspoon LAWRY'S® Seasoned Pepper
2 to 3 tablespoons dry bread crumbs *or*
    ¾ cup croutons

¼ pound cooked, diced ham can replace sausage.

In large skillet, crumble Italian sausage.
Brown 5 minutes; drain fat. Stir in mixture of
milk and flour; bring to a boil, stirring
constantly. Stir in pasta, cheeses, Garlic Salt
and Seasoned Pepper. Place in 1½-quart
baking dish. Bake in 350°F oven 25 minutes.
Sprinkle with bread crumbs; place under
broiler to brown.   *Makes 6 servings*

288 MINESTRONE SOUP

2 (13¾-fluid-ounce) cans COLLEGE INN®
    Beef or Chicken Broth
¼ cup uncooked shell macaroni
1 (16-ounce) can mixed vegetables,
    undrained
1 (16-ounce) can stewed tomatoes,
    undrained and coarsely
    chopped
1 (10½-ounce) can red kidney beans,
    drained
1 teaspoon garlic powder
1 teaspoon dried basil leaves

In large saucepan, over medium-high heat,
heat broth, macaroni, mixed vegetables,
stewed tomatoes, red kidney beans, garlic
powder and basil leaves to a boil. Reduce
heat; simmer 20 minutes or until macaroni is
cooked.   *Makes 6 servings*

PASTA MANIA

289 SHRIMP NOODLE SUPREME

1 package (8 ounces) spinach noodles cooked and drained
1 package (3 ounces) cream cheese, cubed and softened
1½ pounds medium shrimp, peeled and deveined
½ cup butter, softened
Salt and pepper to taste
1 can (10¾ ounces) condensed cream of mushroom soup
1 cup dairy sour cream
½ cup half-and-half
½ cup mayonnaise
1 tablespoon chopped chives
1 tablespoon chopped parsley
½ teaspoon Dijon mustard
¾ cup (6 ounces) shredded sharp Cheddar cheese

Preheat oven to 325°F. Combine noodles and cream cheese in medium bowl. Spread noodle mixture into bottom of greased 13×9-inch glass casserole. Cook shrimp in butter in large skillet over medium-high heat until pink and tender, about 5 minutes. Season with salt and pepper. Spread shrimp over noodles.

Combine soup, sour cream, half-and-half, mayonnaise, chives, parsley and mustard in another medium bowl. Spread over shrimp. Sprinkle Cheddar cheese over top. Bake 25 minutes or until hot and cheese is melted. Garnish, if desired.   *Makes 6 servings*

290 SPAGHETTI BAKE

1 pound BOB EVANS FARMS® Dinner Link Sausage (regular or Italian)
1 (8-ounce) can tomato sauce
1 (6-ounce) can tomato paste
1 (4-ounce) can sliced mushrooms, drained
½ teaspoon salt
½ teaspoon dried basil leaves
½ teaspoon dried oregano leaves
6 ounces spaghetti, cooked according to package directions and drained
⅓ cup shredded mozzarella cheese
2 tablespoons grated Parmesan cheese
Fresh basil leaves and tomato slices (optional)

Preheat oven to 375°F. Cut sausage links into bite-size pieces. Cook in medium skillet over medium heat until browned, stirring occasionally. Drain off any drippings; set aside. Combine tomato sauce, tomato paste, mushrooms, salt, dried basil and oregano in large bowl. Add spaghetti and reserved sausage; mix well. Spoon into lightly greased 1½-quart casserole dish; sprinkle with cheeses. Bake 20 to 30 minutes or until heated through. Garnish with fresh basil and tomato slices, if desired. Serve hot. Refrigerate leftovers.   *Makes 4 servings*

Shrimp Noodle Supreme

291 SALMON LINGUINI SUPPER

8 ounces linguini, cooked in unsalted
    water and drained
1 package (10 ounces) frozen peas
1 cup milk
1 can (10¾ ounces) condensed cream of
    celery soup
¼ cup (1 ounce) grated Parmesan cheese
⅛ teaspoon dried tarragon, crumbled
    (optional)
1 can (15½ ounces) salmon, drained and
    flaked
1 egg, slightly beaten
¼ teaspoon salt
¼ teaspoon pepper
1 can (2.8 ounces) FRENCH'S® French
    Fried Onions

Preheat oven to 375°F. Return hot pasta to
saucepan; stir in peas, milk, soup, cheese
and tarragon; spoon into 12×8-inch baking
dish. In medium bowl, using fork, combine
salmon, egg, salt, pepper and ½ *can* French
Fried Onions. Shape salmon mixture into
4 oval patties. Place patties on pasta
mixture. Bake, covered, at 375°F for
40 minutes or until patties are done. Top
patties with remaining onions; bake,
uncovered, 3 minutes or until onions are
golden brown. *Makes 4 servings*

MICROWAVE DIRECTIONS: Prepare pasta
mixture as above, except increase milk to
1¼ cups; spoon into 12×8-inch microwave-
safe dish. Cook, covered, on HIGH
3 minutes; stir. Prepare salmon patties as
above using 2 eggs. Place patties on pasta
mixture. Cook, covered, 10 to 12 minutes or
until patties are done, rotating dish halfway
through cooking time. Top patties with
remaining onions; cook, uncovered,
1 minute. Let stand 5 minutes.

292 PAPRIKA PORK WITH SPINACH

1 pound boneless pork loin or leg
3 tablespoons all-purpose flour
3 tablespoons vegetable oil
1 cup frozen pearl onions, thawed
1 tablespoon paprika
1 can (14½ ounces) vegetable or chicken
    broth
8 ounces medium curly egg noodles,
    uncooked
1 package (10 ounces) frozen leaf spinach,
    thawed and well drained
½ cup sour cream

• Trim fat from pork; discard. Cut pork into
1-inch cubes. Place flour and pork in
resealable plastic food storage bag; shake
until well coated.

• Heat wok over high heat about 1 minute or
until hot. Drizzle oil into wok; heat
30 seconds. Add pork; stir-fry about
5 minutes or until well browned on all sides.
Remove pork to large bowl.

• Add onions and paprika to wok; stir-fry
1 minute. Stir in broth, noodles and pork.
Cover and bring to a boil. Reduce heat to
low; cook about 8 minutes or until noodles
and pork are tender, stirring occasionally.

• Stir spinach into pork and noodles. Cover
and cook until heated through. Add
additional water if needed. Add sour cream;
mix well. Transfer to serving dish. Garnish, if
desired. *Makes 4 servings*

Salmon Linguini Supper

293 STRING PIE

1 pound ground beef
½ cup chopped onion
¼ cup chopped green pepper
1 jar (15½ ounces) spaghetti sauce
8 ounces spaghetti, cooked and drained
⅓ cup grated Parmesan cheese
2 eggs, beaten
2 teaspoons butter
1 cup cottage cheese
½ cup (2 ounces) shredded mozzarella cheese

Preheat oven to 350°F. Cook beef, onion and green pepper in large skillet over medium-high heat until meat is browned. Drain fat. Stir in spaghetti sauce. Combine spaghetti, Parmesan cheese, eggs and butter in large bowl; mix well. Place on bottom of 13×9-inch baking pan. Spread cottage cheese over top; cover with sauce mixture. Sprinkle with mozzarella cheese. Bake until mixture is thoroughly heated and cheese is melted, about 20 minutes.   *Makes 6 to 8 servings*

Favorite recipe from **North Dakota Beef Commission**

String Pie

PASTA MANIA

294 DILLED TURKEY NOODLE BAKE

1 cup chopped celery
½ cup chopped onion
⅓ cup chopped green pepper
1 tablespoon margarine
2 tablespoons all-purpose flour
1¾ cups skim milk
2 teaspoons dried parsley flakes
1 teaspoon dried dill weed
¾ teaspoon salt
½ teaspoon pepper
4 cups uncooked egg noodles, cooked and drained
2 cups (½-inch) cubed COOKED TURKEY
1 cup non-fat sour cream
¼ cup seasoned dry bread crumbs

1. In large nonstick skillet over medium heat, sauté celery, onion and green pepper in margarine 5 minutes or until vegetables are tender. Reduce heat to low; stir in flour. Cook 1 minute, stirring constantly. Gradually add milk, stirring constantly. Stir in parsley, dill, salt and pepper; cook 1 to 2 minutes or until sauce is thickened. Remove from heat.

2. Add noodles, turkey and sour cream to ingredients in skillet; mix well. Spray 11×7-inch baking dish with vegetable cooking spray. Add noodle mixture; sprinkle with bread crumbs. Bake at 350°F 30 minutes or until hot and bubbly.

Makes 4 servings

Favorite recipe from **National Turkey Federation**

295 PIZZA PASTA

1 medium green bell pepper, chopped
1 medium onion, chopped
1 cup sliced mushrooms
½ teaspoon LAWRY'S® Garlic Powder with Parsley or Garlic Salt
1 tablespoon vegetable oil
¼ cup sliced ripe olives
1 package (1.5 ounces) LAWRY'S® Original-Style Spaghetti Sauce Spices & Seasonings
1¾ cups water
1 can (6 ounces) tomato paste
10 ounces mostaccioli, cooked and drained
3 ounces thinly sliced pepperoni
¾ cup shredded mozzarella cheese

In large skillet, sauté bell pepper, onion, mushrooms and Garlic Powder with Parsley in vegetable oil until vegetables are tender. Stir in olives, Spaghetti Sauce Spices & Seasonings, water and tomato paste; blend well. Bring sauce to a boil; reduce heat. Simmer, uncovered, 10 minutes. Add mostaccioli and pepperoni; blend well. Pour into 12×8-inch casserole; top with cheese. Bake at 350°F 15 minutes or until cheese is melted. *Makes 6 servings*

PASTA MANIA

296 FOOLPROOF CLAM FETTUCINE

1 package (6 ounces) fettucine-style noodles with creamy cheese sauce mix
¾ cup milk
1 can (6½ ounces) chopped clams, undrained
¼ cup (1 ounce) grated Parmesan cheese
1 teaspoon parsley flakes
1 can (4 ounces) mushroom stems and pieces, drained
2 tablespoons diced pimiento
1 can (2.8 ounces) FRENCH'S® French Fried Onions

Preheat oven to 375°F. In large saucepan, cook noodles according to package directions; drain. Return hot noodles to saucepan; stir in sauce mix, milk, undrained clams, Parmesan cheese, parsley flakes, mushrooms, pimiento and ½ can French Fried Onions. Heat and stir 3 minutes or until bubbly. Pour into 10×6-inch baking dish. Bake, covered, at 375°F for 30 minutes or until thickened. Place remaining onions around edges of casserole; bake, uncovered, 3 minutes or until onions are golden brown.

Makes 4 servings

MICROWAVE DIRECTIONS: Prepare noodle mixture as above; pour into 10×6-inch microwave-safe dish. Cook, covered, on HIGH 4 to 6 minutes or until heated through, stirring noodle mixture halfway through cooking time. Top with remaining onions as above; cook, uncovered, 1 minute. Let stand 5 minutes.

297 COUNTRY CHICKEN DINNER

¼ cup milk
2 tablespoons margarine or butter
1 package (4.7 ounces) PASTA RONI® Chicken & Broccoli Sauce with Linguine Pasta
2 cups frozen mixed broccoli, cauliflower and carrots vegetable medley
2 cups chopped cooked chicken or turkey
1 teaspoon dried basil

1. In round 3-quart microwaveable glass casserole, combine 1¾ cups water, milk and margarine. Microwave, uncovered, on HIGH 4 to 5 minutes or until boiling.

2. Gradually add pasta while stirring.

3. Stir in contents of seasoning packet, frozen vegetables, chicken and basil.

4. Microwave, uncovered, on HIGH 14 to 15 minutes, stirring gently after 7 minutes. Sauce will be thin, but will thicken upon standing.

5. Let stand 4 to 5 minutes or until desired consistency. Stir before serving.

Makes 4 servings

Country Chicken Dinner

Mustard Chicken & Vegetables

298 BACON–TUNA PARMESANO

½ cup milk
2 tablespoons margarine or butter
1 package (4.8 ounces) PASTA RONI®
  Parmesano with Tenderthin Pasta
1 package (10 ounces) frozen peas
1 can (6⅛ ounces) white tuna in water,
  drained, flaked
4 slices crisply cooked bacon, crumbled
½ cup sliced green onions

1. In round 3-quart microwaveable glass casserole, combine 1⅔ cups water, milk and margarine. Microwave, uncovered, on HIGH 4 to 5 minutes or until boiling.

2. Stir in pasta, contents of seasoning packet, frozen peas, tuna, bacon and onions.

3. Microwave, uncovered, on HIGH 9 to 10 minutes or until peas are tender, stirring after 3 minutes.

4. Cover; let stand 3 to 4 minutes. Sauce will thicken upon standing. Stir before serving.
Makes 4 servings

299 MUSTARD CHICKEN & VEGETABLES

2 cups (8 ounces) fusilli or rotini, cooked
   in unsalted water and drained
¼ cup FRENCH'S® Dijon or CLASSIC
   YELLOW® Mustard
¼ cup vegetable oil
1 tablespoon red wine vinegar
½ teaspoon dried oregano, crumbled
¼ teaspoon pepper
¼ teaspoon salt
2 pounds chicken pieces, fat trimmed
1 can (10¾ ounces) condensed cream of
   chicken soup
½ cup milk
1 cup *each* (1-inch) zucchini and yellow
   squash chunks
1 can (2.8 ounces) FRENCH'S® French
   Fried Onions
1 medium tomato, cut into wedges

Preheat oven to 375°F. In large bowl,
combine mustard, oil, vinegar and
seasonings; mix well. Toss chicken in
mustard sauce until coated. Reserve
remaining mustard sauce. Arrange chicken
in 13×9-inch baking dish. Bake, uncovered,
at 375°F for 30 minutes. Stir soup, milk, hot
pasta, squash and ½ *can* French Fried
Onions into remaining mustard sauce. Spoon
pasta mixture into baking dish, placing it
under and around chicken. Bake, uncovered,
15 to 20 minutes or until chicken is done.
Top pasta mixture with tomato wedges and
top chicken with remaining onions. Bake,
uncovered, 3 minutes or until onions are
golden brown. *Makes 4 to 6 servings*

MICROWAVE DIRECTIONS: Prepare
mustard sauce as directed; add chicken and
toss until coated. Reserve remaining
mustard sauce. In 12×8-inch microwave-
safe dish, arrange chicken with meatiest
parts toward edges of dish. Cook,
uncovered, on HIGH 10 minutes. Rearrange
chicken. Prepare pasta mixture and add to
chicken as above. Cook, uncovered, 15 to
17 minutes or until chicken and vegetables
are done, stirring vegetables and pasta and
rotating dish halfway through cooking time.
Top with tomato wedges and remaining
onions as directed; cook, uncovered,
1 minute. Let stand 5 minutes.

300 ITALIAN PASTA BAKE

1 lb. ground beef
5 cups cooked pasta
1 jar (30 oz.) spaghetti sauce
½ cup KRAFT® 100% Grated Parmesan
   Cheese
2 cups (8 oz.) KRAFT® Natural Shredded
   Low Moisture Part Skim Mozzarella
   Cheese

COOK ground beef in large skillet and
drain.

STIR in pasta, spaghetti sauce and
Parmesan cheese. Spoon into 13×9-inch
baking dish.

TOP with mozzarella cheese. Bake at 375°F
for 20 minutes. *Makes 4 servings*

301 TUNA PESTO & PASTA

1 box (10 ounces) BIRDS EYE® frozen Peas
   and Onions
3 cups cooked rotini or other shaped
   pasta
1 can (6⅛ ounces) tuna packed in water,
   drained
¼ cup mayonnaise
2 to 4 tablespoons prepared pesto
   Grated Parmesan cheese

• Prepare vegetables in medium saucepan
according to package directions.

• Stir in pasta, tuna, mayonnaise and pesto;
heat through.

• Serve with cheese.

Makes about 2 servings

Prep Time: 5 minutes
Cook Time: 12 minutes

SERVING SUGGESTION: Chill Tuna Pesto &
Pasta and serve as a cold pasta salad.

302 ITALIAN BEEF AND PASTA

1¼ pounds boneless beef round steak
      (full cut) or boneless beef chuck steak,
      cut ½ inch thick
1 tablespoon vegetable oil
1 medium onion, chopped
1 large clove garlic, minced
1 teaspoon Italian seasoning
1 can (14½ ounces) Italian-style stewed
   tomatoes, undrained, chopped
1 can (13¾ ounces) beef broth
¼ cup red wine
½ pound mushrooms, halved
1½ cups (4 ounces) uncooked mostaccioli
2 tablespoons grated Parmesan cheese
1 tablespoon chopped parsley (optional)

Cut steak into 1-inch pieces. Heat oil in large
skillet or Dutch oven over medium heat until
hot. Add half of steak; cook and stir until
browned. Pour off any drippings; discard.
Set cooked steak aside. Repeat with
remaining steak. Return all steak to pan. Stir
in onion, garlic and Italian seasoning; cook
2 minutes. Add tomatoes, broth and wine.
Bring to a boil. Reduce heat to low; cover
tightly and cook on top of range or in 300°F
oven 1½ hours, or until meat is tender. Add
mushrooms and mostaccioli, stirring to
separate pasta. Cook, covered, 20 minutes.
Remove cover; continue cooking 10 minutes
or until mostaccioli is tender. Transfer to
deep serving dish; stir in Parmesan cheese.
Sprinkle with parsley, if desired.

Makes 4 servings

*Favorite recipe from **National Cattlemen's Beef
Association***

Tuna Pesto & Pasta

303 MANHATTAN TURKEY À LA KING

8 ounces wide egg noodles
1 pound boneless turkey or chicken, cut into strips
1 tablespoon vegetable oil
1 can (14½ ounces) DEL MONTE® FRESH CUT™ Diced Tomatoes with Garlic & Onion, undrained
1 can (10¾ ounces) condensed cream of celery soup
1 medium onion, chopped
2 stalks celery, sliced
1 cup sliced mushrooms

1. Cook noodles according to package directions; drain.

2. Meanwhile, in large skillet, brown turkey in oil over medium-high heat. Season with salt and pepper, if desired.

3. Add remaining ingredients except noodles; cover. Cook 5 minutes. Remove cover; cook 5 minutes or until thickened, stirring occasionally.

4. Serve over hot noodles. Sprinkle with chopped parsley, if desired.

Makes 6 servings

Prep Time: 7 minutes
Cook Time: 20 minutes

HELPFUL HINT: Cook pasta ahead; rinse and drain. Cover and refrigerate. Just before serving, heat in microwave or dip in boiling water.

304 CHICKEN PAPRIKASH

2 tablespoons margarine or butter
1 pound skinless, boneless chicken breasts or thighs, cut into 1-inch pieces
½ cup chopped onion
1 clove garlic, minced
1 tablespoon paprika
½ cup milk
1 package (4.7 ounces) PASTA RONI® Alfredo with Fettuccine Pasta
1 medium green bell pepper, cut into strips
½ cup sour half-and-half or sour cream

1. In large skillet, melt margarine over medium heat. Add chicken, onion and garlic; cook 1 minute, stirring occasionally. Add paprika; continue cooking 2 minutes.

2. Add 1½ cups water, milk, pasta, contents of seasoning packet and green pepper. Bring just to a boil. Reduce heat to medium-low.

3. Boil, uncovered, stirring frequently, 9 to 11 minutes or until pasta is desired tenderness and chicken is no longer pink inside. (Sauce will thicken upon standing.) Stir in sour half-and-half before serving.

Makes 4 servings

Manhattan Turkey à la King

305 ANGEL HAIR AL FRESCO

¾ cup skim milk
1 tablespoon margarine or butter
1 package (4.8 ounces) PASTA RONI®
    Herb Sauce with Angel Hair Pasta
1 can (6⅛ ounces) white tuna in water,
    drained, flaked, *or* 1½ cups chopped
    cooked chicken
2 medium tomatoes, chopped
⅓ cup sliced green onions
¼ cup dry white wine or water
¼ cup slivered almonds, toasted (optional)
1 tablespoon chopped fresh basil *or*
    1 teaspoon dried basil

1. In 3-quart saucepan, combine 1⅓ cups water, skim milk and margarine. Bring just to a boil.

2. Stir in pasta, contents of seasoning packet, tuna, tomatoes, onions, wine, almonds and basil. Return to a boil; reduce heat to medium.

3. Boil, uncovered, stirring frequently, 6 to 8 minutes. Sauce will be thin, but will thicken upon standing.

4. Let stand 3 minutes or until desired consistency. Stir before serving.

Makes 4 servings

306 MAC & STUFF

1 package (7¼ ounces) KRAFT® Macaroni
    and Cheese Dinner
1¼ cups water
1 cup frozen green peas, thawed
4 OSCAR MAYER® Wieners, sliced
2 tablespoons margarine or butter
2 cups STOVE TOP® Chicken Flavor
    Stuffing Mix in the Canister

PREPARE Dinner as directed on package.

MEANWHILE, bring water, peas, wieners and margarine to boil in large saucepan. Stir in stuffing mix just to moisten; cover. Remove from heat. Let stand 5 minutes.

STIR stuffing mixture lightly into prepared Dinner. Serve immediately.

Makes 4 to 6 servings

Prep Time: 10 minutes
Cook Time: 15 minutes

Angel Hair al Fresco

307 CHEESEBURGER MACARONI

- 2 cups mostaccioli or elbow macaroni
- 1 pound ground beef
- 1 medium onion, chopped
- 1 can (14½ ounces) DEL MONTE® Original or Italian Recipe Stewed Tomatoes
- ¼ cup DEL MONTE® Tomato Ketchup
- 1 cup (4 ounces) shredded Cheddar cheese

1. Cook pasta according to package directions; drain.

2. In large skillet, brown meat with onion; drain. Season with salt and pepper, if desired. Stir in tomatoes, ketchup and pasta; heat through.

3. Top with cheese. Garnish, if desired.

Makes 4 servings

Prep Time: 8 minutes
Cook Time: 15 minutes

308 SKILLET SPAGHETTI AND SAUSAGE

- ¼ pound mild or hot Italian sausage links, sliced
- ½ pound ground beef
- ¼ teaspoon dried oregano, crushed
- 4 ounces spaghetti, broken in half
- 1 can (26 ounces) DEL MONTE® Chunky Spaghetti Sauce with Garlic & Herb
- 1½ cups sliced fresh mushrooms
- 2 stalks celery, sliced

In large skillet, brown sausage over medium-high heat. Add beef and oregano; season to taste with salt and pepper, if desired. Cook, stirring occasionally, until beef is browned; drain. Add pasta, 1 cup water, spaghetti sauce, mushrooms and celery. Bring to boil, stirring occasionally. Reduce heat; cover and simmer 12 to 14 minutes or until spaghetti is tender. Garnish with grated Parmesan cheese and chopped parsley, if desired. Serve immediately.

Makes 4 to 6 servings

Prep Time: 5 minutes
Cook Time: 30 minutes

PASTA MANIA

309 PASTA, BEEF & ZUCCHINI DINNER

1 pound extra lean ground beef
1 medium onion, chopped
1 clove garlic, crushed
½ teaspoon salt
2 (14-ounce) cans ready-to-serve beef broth
1 teaspoon Italian seasoning
¼ teaspoon crushed red pepper
2 cups uncooked mini lasagna or rotini pasta
2 cups sliced zucchini (cut ⅜ inch thick)
1 tablespoon cornstarch
¼ cup water
3 plum tomatoes, each cut into 4 wedges
2 tablespoons grated Parmesan cheese

In large nonstick skillet, cook ground beef with onion, garlic and salt over medium heat 8 to 10 minutes or until beef is browned, stirring occasionally to break up beef into 1-inch crumbles. Remove beef mixture with slotted spoon; pour off drippings. Set aside.

Add broth, Italian seasoning and red pepper to same skillet. Bring to a boil; add pasta. Reduce heat to medium; simmer, uncovered, for 6 minutes, stirring occasionally. Add zucchini; continue cooking for an additional 6 to 8 minutes or until pasta is tender, yet firm. Push pasta and zucchini to side of skillet. Mix cornstarch with water and add to broth in skillet; bring to a boil. Return beef mixture to skillet. Add tomatoes; heat through, stirring occasionally. Spoon into serving dish; sprinkle with Parmesan cheese.

Makes 5 servings

Favorite recipe from **North Dakota Wheat Commission**

310 SKILLET PASTA ROMA

½ pound Italian sausage, sliced or crumbled
1 large onion, coarsely chopped
1 large clove garlic, minced
1 can (26 ounces) DEL MONTE® Chunky Spaghetti Sauce with Garlic & Herb
1 cup water
8 ounces uncooked rotini or other spiral pasta
8 sliced mushrooms, optional
Grated Parmesan cheese and fresh parsley sprigs, optional

In large skillet, brown sausage. Add onion and garlic. Cook until onion is soft; drain. Stir in spaghetti sauce, water and pasta. Cover and bring to a boil; reduce heat. Simmer, covered, 25 to 30 minutes or until pasta is tender, stirring occasionally. Stir in mushrooms; simmer 5 minutes. Serve in skillet garnished with cheese and parsley, if desired.

Makes 4 servings

311 RIGATONI WITH MEAT SAUCE

10 ounces dry rigatoni, cooked, drained and kept warm
2 tablespoons extra-virgin olive oil
½ cup finely chopped onion
¼ cup chopped celery
¼ cup chopped, peeled carrot
3 cloves garlic, finely chopped
8 ounces lean ground beef
3½ cups (28-ounce can) CONTADINA® Crushed Tomatoes
½ cup beef broth
⅓ cup dry red wine
¼ cup chopped fresh Italian parsley

HEAT oil in large skillet over medium-high heat. Add onion, celery, carrot and garlic; cook over medium-high heat for 3 to 5 minutes or until tender. Add meat, stirring to break up. Cook, stirring occasionally, for 5 to 7 minutes or until meat is just browned. Stir in crushed tomatoes, broth, wine and parsley. Bring to a boil. Reduce heat to low; cover. Cook, stirring occasionally, for 20 to 25 minutes or until sauce begins to thicken.

ADD pasta to skillet; toss gently. Cover; let stand over low heat for 1 to 2 minutes or until pasta absorbs some of sauce.

Makes 6 to 8 servings

312 SPICY BEEF STIR–FRY

1 boneless beef sirloin, top loin or tenderloin steak, cut 1 inch thick (about 1 pound)
5 tablespoons low sodium teriyaki sauce, divided
1 teaspoon hot chili oil *or* ½ teaspoon crushed Szechuan peppercorns
1 tablespoon cornstarch
1 tablespoon dry sherry
2 tablespoons peanut oil or vegetable oil, divided
2 cups sliced fresh mushrooms
1 small onion, cut into 1-inch pieces
Hot cooked angel hair pasta

• Trim fat from beef; discard. Cut beef across grain into ⅛-inch-thick slices; cut each slice into 1½-inch pieces. Combine 1 tablespoon teriyaki and chili oil in medium bowl. Add beef and toss to coat; set aside.

• Combine cornstarch, remaining 4 tablespoons teriyaki and sherry in small bowl; stir until smooth. Set aside.

• Heat wok over high heat about 1 minute or until hot. Drizzle 1 tablespoon peanut oil into wok and heat 30 seconds. Add half the beef mixture; stir-fry 2 minutes or until beef is barely pink in center. Remove beef to large bowl. Repeat with remaining beef mixture. Reduce heat to medium-high.

• Add remaining 1 tablespoon peanut oil to wok and heat 30 seconds. Add mushrooms and onion; stir-fry 5 minutes or until vegetables are tender.

• Stir cornstarch mixture until smooth and add to wok. Stir-fry 30 seconds or until sauce boils and thickens.

• Return beef and any accumulated juices to wok; cook until heated through. Serve over pasta. Garnish, if desired.

Makes 4 servings

Spicy Beef Stir-Fry

313 PAD THAI (THAI FRIED NOODLES)

7¼ cups water, divided
12 ounces dried thin rice stick noodles*
4 tablespoons vegetable oil, divided
3 tablespoons brown sugar
¼ cup soy sauce
2 tablespoons lime juice
1 tablespoon anchovy paste
2 eggs, lightly beaten
12 ounces medium shrimp, peeled and deveined
2 cloves garlic, minced
1 tablespoon paprika
¼ to ½ teaspoon crushed red pepper
1 cup canned bean sprouts, rinsed and drained, divided
½ cup coarsely chopped unsalted dry roasted peanuts
4 green onions with tops, cut into 1-inch pieces

*If rice stick noodles are unavailable, use fine egg noodles, thin spaghetti, vermicelli or angel hair pasta.

• Place 6 cups water in wok; bring to a boil over high heat. Add noodles; cook 2 minutes or until tender but still firm, stirring frequently. Drain; rinse under cold running water to stop cooking. Drain again and place noodles in large bowl. Add 1 tablespoon oil and toss lightly to coat; set aside.

• Combine remaining 1¼ cups water, brown sugar, soy sauce, juice and anchovy paste in small bowl; set aside.

• Heat wok over medium heat 2 minutes or until hot. Drizzle 1 tablespoon oil into wok and heat 30 seconds. Add eggs; stir-fry 1 minute or just until set on bottom. Turn eggs over; stir to scramble. Remove to medium bowl. Increase heat to high.

• Drizzle 1 tablespoon oil into wok and heat 30 seconds. Add shrimp and garlic; stir-fry 2 minutes or until shrimp begin to turn pink and opaque. Remove shrimp to bowl with eggs. Reduce heat to medium.

• Drizzle remaining 1 tablespoon oil into wok and heat 15 seconds. Stir in paprika and red pepper to taste. Add noodles and anchovy mixture; cook and stir about 5 minutes or until noodles are softened. Stir in ¾ cup bean sprouts. Add peanuts and onions; toss and cook about 1 minute or until onions are tender. Add eggs and shrimp; stir-fry until heated through. Transfer to serving plate; top with remaining bean sprouts. Garnish, if desired.

Makes 4 servings

Pad Thai

PASTA MANIA

314 BEEF ORIENTAL

3 cups corkscrew pasta
1 pound ground beef
7 green onions, cut diagonally into 3-inch
    pieces
3 tablespoons soy sauce
¼ teaspoon ground ginger
2 to 3 ribs celery, cut diagonally into
    1-inch pieces
8 mushrooms, sliced (optional)
1 package (20 ounces) frozen pea pods,
    thawed and drained
1 can (8 ounces) tomato sauce
3 fresh tomatoes, cut into wedges
1 cup (4 ounces) shredded Cheddar
    cheese, divided
1 green pepper, cut into thin slices

1. Cook pasta according to package
directions. Drain in colander. Set aside.

2. Cook beef, onions, soy sauce and ginger
in wok over medium-high heat until meat is
browned, stirring to separate meat. Push
mixture up the side of wok. Add celery and
mushrooms; stir-fry 2 minutes. Push mixture
up the side. Add pea pods and tomato sauce;
cook 4 to 5 minutes, stirring every minute.

3. Add pasta, tomatoes and ¾ cup cheese.
Stir gently to combine all ingredients. Cook
1 minute. Add green pepper; sprinkle
remaining ¼ cup cheese over top. Reduce
heat to low; cook until heated through.

Makes 4 servings

315 BEEF À LA STROGANOFF

1¼ pounds boneless beef sirloin
1 large onion
1 tablespoon butter
2 tablespoons water
½ pound sliced mushrooms
2 tablespoons all-purpose flour
1 cup beef broth
¼ cup dry red wine
¼ teaspoon salt
1 cup low fat sour cream
¼ teaspoon dried dill weed
    Hot cooked noodles

• Trim fat from beef; discard. Slice beef
across grain into thin slices. Cut onion
lengthwise in half and slice across into
¼-inch slices.

• Heat wok over medium-high heat 1 minute
or until hot. Add butter and swirl to coat
bottom. Add beef; stir-fry about 2 minutes or
until well browned. Remove beef to large
bowl. Reduce heat to medium.

• Add water, mushrooms and onion to wok;
stir-fry about 2 minutes or until onion is
tender. Add flour; mix well. Gradually stir in
broth, wine and salt. Bring to a boil. Simmer
5 minutes. Stir in sour cream and dill weed.
Return beef and any accumulated juices to
wok; cook until heated through. Serve over
noodles. *Makes 4 servings*

Beef Oriental

PASTA MANIA

316 CANTONESE TOMATO BEEF

1 pound fresh Chinese-style thin wheat
  noodles *or* 12 ounces dry spaghetti
2 pounds ripe tomatoes, cored
3 small onions
1 small beef flank steak or filet mignon tail
  (about 1 pound)
2 tablespoons sesame oil, divided
2 tablespoons soy sauce
1 tablespoon plus 1 teaspoon cornstarch,
  divided
1 cup beef broth
2 tablespoons brown sugar
1 tablespoon cider vinegar
2 tablespoons vegetable oil, divided
1 tablespoon minced fresh ginger
1 green onion with tops, diagonally cut
  into thin slices

• Cook noodles in stockpot according to
package directions just until tender.
Meanwhile, cut each tomato into 8 wedges.
Cut each onion into 8 wedges. Cut beef
lengthwise in half. Cut across grain into
$2 \times \frac{1}{4}$-inch slices. Set aside.

• Drain noodles in colander and return to
stockpot. Add 1 tablespoon sesame oil; toss
until well coated. Cover; keep warm.

• Combine soy sauce, remaining
1 tablespoon sesame oil and 1 teaspoon
cornstarch in medium bowl; stir until
smooth. Add beef and toss to coat; set aside.

• Stir broth, brown sugar and vinegar into
remaining 1 tablespoon cornstarch in small
bowl; stir until smooth. Set aside.

• Heat wok over high heat about 1 minute or
until hot. Drizzle 1 tablespoon vegetable oil
into wok and heat 30 seconds. Add ginger;
stir-fry about 30 seconds or until fragrant.
Add beef mixture; stir-fry 5 minutes or until
lightly browned. Remove beef mixture to
large bowl. Reduce heat to medium.

• Add remaining 1 tablespoon vegetable oil
to wok and heat 30 seconds. Add onion
wedges; cook and stir about 2 minutes or
until tender. Stir in half the tomatoes. Stir
broth mixture until smooth and add to wok.
Cook and stir until liquid boils and thickens.

• Return beef and any accumulated juices to
wok. Add remaining tomatoes; cook and stir
until heated through. Transfer noodles to
shallow serving bowl. Spoon beef mixture
over noodles. Sprinkle with green onion.

Makes 4 servings

Cantonese Tomato Beef

317 FIVE–SPICE BEEF AND BOK CHOY

1 boneless beef sirloin steak (about 1 pound)
¼ cup soy sauce
2 tablespoons dry sherry
2 teaspoons minced fresh ginger
2 cloves garlic, minced
1 teaspoon sugar
½ teaspoon Chinese five-spice powder
¼ teaspoon crushed red pepper (optional)
1 large head bok choy
2 teaspoons cornstarch
2 tablespoons peanut oil or vegetable oil, divided
Hot cooked Chinese egg noodles

• Trim fat from beef; discard. Cut beef across grain into ⅛-inch-thick slices; cut each slice into 2-inch pieces. Combine soy sauce, sherry, ginger, garlic, sugar, five-spice powder and red pepper, if desired, in medium bowl. Add beef and toss to coat; set aside.

• Separate bok choy leaves from stems; rinse and pat dry. Stack leaves and cut crosswise into 1-inch slices. Cut stems diagonally into ½-inch slices. Keep leaves and stems separate.

• Drain beef, reserving marinade. Stir reserved marinade into cornstarch in small bowl; stir until smooth. Set aside.

• Heat wok over medium-high heat 1 minute or until hot. Drizzle 1 tablespoon oil into wok and heat 30 seconds. Add beef; stir-fry 2 minutes or until beef is barely pink in center. Remove beef to large bowl.

• Add remaining 1 tablespoon oil and heat 30 seconds. Add bok choy stems; stir-fry 3 minutes. Add bok choy leaves; stir-fry 2 minutes.

• Stir marinade mixture until smooth; add to wok. Stir-fry 1 minute or until sauce boils and thickens.

• Return beef and any accumulated juices to wok; cook until heated through. Serve over noodles. Garnish, if desired.

Makes 4 servings

318 ORIENTAL BEEF & NOODLE TOSS

1 pound lean ground beef
2 packages (3 ounces *each*) Oriental flavor instant ramen noodles, divided
2 cups water
2 cups thawed frozen Oriental vegetable mixture
⅛ teaspoon ground ginger
2 tablespoons thinly sliced green onions

1. In large nonstick skillet, brown ground beef over medium heat 8 to 10 minutes or until beef is no longer pink. Remove with slotted spoon; pour off drippings. Season beef with one seasoning packet from noodles; set aside.

2. In same skillet, combine water, vegetables, noodles, ginger and remaining seasoning packet. Bring to a boil; reduce heat. Cover; simmer 3 minutes or until noodles are tender, stirring occasionally.

3. Return beef to skillet; heat through. Stir in green onions before serving.

Makes 4 servings

*Favorite recipe from **National Cattlemen's Beef Association***

Five-Spice Beef and Bok Choy

319 PASTA FAGIOLI (BEAN) SOUP

2 medium onions, chopped
2 medium carrots, sliced
½ medium red bell pepper, cut into thin strips
4 garlic cloves, finely chopped
2 tablespoons olive oil
8 ounces smoked ham, diced
½ teaspoon dried basil leaves
1 (16-ounce) can FRANK'S or SNOWFLOSS Italian Style Diced Tomatoes, drained
6 cups chicken broth
2 (15½-ounce) cans dark red kidney beans, drained
2½ cups rotini pasta, uncooked
Salt and pepper
¾ cup fresh mushrooms, sliced
⅓ cup sliced green onions
Grated Parmesan cheese

1. In a stock pot, sauté onions, carrots, bell pepper and garlic in olive oil until tender. Add ham and basil; cook and stir 2 minutes.

2. Add diced tomatoes, crushing them with back of spoon until liquid has a thick consistency.

3. Add chicken broth and kidney beans; bring to a boil. Reduce heat to low; simmer 20 minutes.

4. Before serving, return soup to a boil. Add rotini; cook until pasta is tender. Spoon off any excess grease just before serving.

5. Remove from heat. Season wth salt and pepper to taste. Add mushrooms; cover. Let stand 5 minutes. Top with green onion just before serving. Serve with Parmesan cheese.

Makes 8 servings

Prep Time: 15 minutes
Cook Time: 50 minutes

320 KOREAN BEEF

1 pound beef flank steak
¼ cup low-sodium soy sauce
2 tablespoons sugar
1 tablespoon sesame oil
1 teaspoon ground ginger
¼ teaspoon crushed red pepper
¼ small head napa cabbage
3 tablespoons vegetable oil
1 can (14½ ounces) beef broth
1 cup peeled baby carrots
2 cups frozen cauliflowerets, thawed
1 cup frozen green bean cuts, thawed
Hot cooked rice noodles

• Slice beef across grain into ¼-inch-thick slices. Combine soy sauce, sugar, sesame oil, ginger and red pepper in medium bowl. Add beef and toss to coat. Cut cabbage crosswise into 1-inch slices. Set aside.

• Heat wok over high heat about 1 minute or until hot. Drizzle half the vegetable oil into wok and heat 30 seconds. Drain beef, reserving marinade. Add half the beef to wok; stir-fry until browned. Remove to large bowl. Repeat with remaining vegetable oil and beef.

• Add reserved marinade and broth to wok. Cover; bring to a boil. Add carrots; cook, uncovered, 5 minutes or until crisp-tender. Stir in cabbage, cauliflowerets and beans; cook until tender. Return beef to wok; heat through. Serve over noodles in bowls.

Makes 4 servings

Korean Beef

PASTA MANIA

321 CREAMY SALMON WITH GREEN BEANS

1 large red salmon steak (about ¾ pound)
2 tablespoons butter or margarine
1 large ripe tomato, cut into ½-inch pieces
1 small onion, coarsely chopped
2 tablespoons all-purpose flour
1 cup vegetable or chicken broth
1 package (9 ounces) frozen cut green beans, partially thawed
1 cup half-and-half
¼ teaspoon salt
¼ teaspoon ground white pepper
5 tablespoons grated Parmesan cheese, divided
Hot cooked angel hair pasta

• Rinse salmon and pat dry with paper towels. Remove skin and bones; discard. Cut salmon into ¾-inch pieces. Set aside.

• Heat wok over medium-high heat 1 minute or until hot. Add butter; swirl to coat bottom and heat 30 seconds. Add salmon; stir-fry gently 3 to 4 minutes or until fish flakes easily when tested with fork. Remove to large bowl; cover and keep warm.

• Add tomato and onion to wok; stir-fry about 5 minutes or until onion is tender. Stir in flour until well mixed. Increase heat to high. Stir in broth and beans; stir-fry until sauce boils and thickens. Add salmon, half-and-half, salt and pepper; stir-fry until heated through. Add half of cheese; toss until well mixed. Spoon salmon mixture over angel hair pasta. Sprinkle with remaining cheese. Garnish, if desired.

Makes 4 servings

322 ALPHABET TURKEY SOUP

4 cups turkey broth or reduced-sodium chicken bouillon
1 can (16 ounces) tomatoes, undrained
1 cup chopped onion
1 cup thinly sliced carrots
2 teaspoons dried Italian seasoning
½ teaspoon salt
¼ teaspoon pepper
4 cups thinly sliced cabbage
2 cups (½-inch) cubed COOKED TURKEY
½ cup alphabet pasta

1. In 5-quart saucepan over medium-high heat, combine broth, tomatoes, onion, carrots, Italian seasoning, salt and pepper; bring to a boil. Reduce to low; simmer 10 to 15 minutes or until carrots are tender.

2. Add cabbage, turkey and pasta; return to a boil. Cook 5 to 10 minutes or until cabbage and pasta are tender. *Makes 8 servings*

Favorite recipe from **National Turkey Federation**

Creamy Salmon with Green Beans

323 PASTA AND VEGETABLE CHOWDER

2½ cups rainbow-colored rotini
6 slices bacon, cut into 1-inch pieces
1 cup chopped onions
½ cup (1-inch) celery pieces
3 tablespoons all-purpose flour
6 cups chicken broth, divided
3 cups zucchini (2 cups shredded, 1 cup diced)
¾ cup sliced carrots
1 cup skim milk
¼ cup celery leaves, chopped
½ teaspoon pepper

Cook pasta according to package directions; drain.

Cook bacon in large saucepan until crisp. Remove bacon from saucepan; drain all but 1 tablespoon bacon drippings from saucepan. Add onions and celery to saucepan; cook and stir until crisp-tender.

Add flour to 1 cup chicken broth in small bowl; mix until smooth. Add to ingredients in saucepan. Gradually stir in remaining broth; bring to a boil. Add shredded zucchini and carrots; return to a boil. Reduce heat to low; simmer 10 minutes. Add diced zucchini; simmer until vegetables are tender, about 12 minutes. Add cooked pasta, milk, celery leaves and pepper; bring to a boil and serve.

Makes 6 servings

Favorite recipe from **North Dakota Wheat Commission**

324 ZESTY NOODLE SOUP

1 pound BOB EVANS FARMS® Zesty Hot Roll Sausage
1 (16-ounce) can whole tomatoes, undrained
½ pound fresh mushrooms, sliced
1 large onion, chopped
1 small green bell pepper, chopped
2½ cups tomato juice
2½ cups water
¼ cup chopped fresh parsley
1 teaspoon lemon juice
1 teaspoon Worcestershire sauce
1 teaspoon celery seeds
½ teaspoon salt
½ teaspoon dried thyme leaves
1 cup uncooked egg noodles

Crumble sausage into 3-quart saucepan. Cook over medium-high heat until browned, stirring occasionally. Drain off any drippings. Add tomatoes with juice, mushrooms, onion and pepper; cook until vegetables are tender, stirring well to break up tomatoes. Stir in all remaining ingredients except noodles. Bring to a boil over high heat. Reduce heat to low; simmer, covered, 30 minutes. Add noodles; simmer just until noodles are tender, yet firm. Serve hot. Refrigerate leftovers. *Makes 6 servings*

SERVING SUGGESTION: Serve with crusty French bread.

Zesty Noodle Soup

325 HERB-OX® TORTELLINI VEGETABLE SOUP

1 package (14 ounces) turkey or pork
    breakfast sausage, crumbled
2 quarts water
6 HERB-OX® Beef Bouillon cubes
½ teaspoon garlic powder
1 package (9 ounces) fresh tortellini
    cheese pasta
1 package (16 ounces) frozen vegetable
    combination (broccoli, cauliflower,
    red pepper), thawed

In Dutch oven over medium-high heat, cook sausage until browned; drain. Add water, bouillon and garlic powder; bring to a boil. Add pasta; boil 5 minutes. Stir in vegetables. Simmer, uncovered, 10 minutes until vegetables and pasta are tender.

Makes 8 servings

326 CREAMY SHELL SOUP

4 cups water
3 or 4 chicken pieces
1 cup chopped onion
¼ cup chopped celery
¼ cup minced fresh parsley *or*
  1 tablespoon dried parsley flakes
1 bay leaf
1 teaspoon salt
¼ teaspoon white pepper
2 medium potatoes, diced
4 or 5 green onions, sliced
3 chicken bouillon cubes
½ teaspoon seasoned salt
½ teaspoon poultry seasoning
4 cups milk
2 cups medium shell macaroni, cooked
  and drained
¼ cup butter or margarine
¼ cup all-purpose flour

Combine water, chicken, chopped onion, celery, minced parsley, bay leaf, salt and pepper in Dutch oven. Bring to a boil. Reduce heat to low; simmer until chicken is tender. Remove bay leaf; discard. Remove chicken; cool. Skin, debone and cut meat into small cubes; set aside.

Add potatoes, green onions, bouillon cubes, seasoned salt and poultry seasoning to broth. Simmer 15 minutes. Add milk, macaroni and chicken; return to simmer.

Melt butter in skillet over medium heat. Add flour, stirring constantly, until mixture begins to brown. Add to soup; blend well. Let soup simmer on very low heat 20 minutes to blend flavors. Season with additional salt and pepper to taste, if desired. Sprinkle with ground nutmeg and additional chopped parsley, if desired.

Makes 8 servings

Favorite recipe from **North Dakota Wheat Commission**

327 WHITE CHEDDAR SEAFOOD CHOWDER

2 tablespoons margarine or butter
½ cup chopped onion
2¼ cups water
1 package (6.2 ounces) PASTA RONI®
  White Cheddar Sauce with Shells
1 cup sliced carrots
½ teaspoon salt (optional)
¾ pound fresh or thawed frozen firm white
  fish, cut into ½-inch pieces
1¼ cups milk
2 tablespoons chopped parsley (optional)

1. In 3-quart saucepan, melt margarine over medium heat. Add onion; sauté 1 minute.

2. Add water; bring to a boil over high heat.

3. Stir in pasta, carrots and salt.

4. Bring just to a boil. Reduce heat to medium. Boil, uncovered, stirring frequently, 12 minutes.

5. Add fish, milk, parsley and contents of seasoning packet. Continue cooking 3 to 4 minutes, stirring occasionally, or until pasta is desired tenderness and fish is opaque. *Makes 4 servings*

Creamy Shell Soup

328 RAVIOLI SOUP

8 ounces sweet Italian sausage, casing removed
1 clove garlic, crushed
2 (13¾-fluid ounce) cans lower sodium chicken broth
2 cups water
1 (9-ounce) package frozen miniature cheese-filled ravioli
1 (15-ounce) can garbanzo beans, drained
1 (14½-ounce) can stewed tomatoes
⅓ cup GREY POUPON® Dijon Mustard
½ teaspoon dried oregano leaves
¼ teaspoon coarsely ground black pepper
1 cup torn fresh spinach leaves
  Grated Parmesan cheese

In 4-quart heavy pot, over medium heat, brown sausage and cook garlic until tender, stirring to break up sausage, about 5 minutes. Pour off excess fat; remove sausage mixture from pot and set aside.

In same pot, over medium-high heat, heat chicken broth and water to a boil. Add ravioli; cook for 4 to 5 minutes or until tender. Stir in beans, stewed tomatoes, sausage mixture, mustard, oregano and pepper; heat through. Stir in spinach and cook until wilted, about 1 minute. Serve topped with Parmesan cheese.

Makes 8 servings

329 RAVIOLI STEW

2 tablespoons olive or vegetable oil
1 medium onion, chopped
2 medium carrots, diced
2 ribs celery, diced
1 medium green bell pepper, chopped
1 clove garlic, finely chopped
1 can (15 to 19 ounces) red kidney beans, rinsed and drained
4 plum tomatoes, chopped
1 envelope LIPTON® Recipe Secrets® Golden Herb with Lemon Soup Mix
2½ cups water
1 package (8 or 10 ounces) refrigerated cheese ravioli

In Dutch oven or 6-quart saucepot, heat oil over medium heat and cook onion, carrots, celery, green pepper and garlic, stirring occasionally, 5 minutes or until tender. Stir in beans, tomatoes and golden herb with lemon soup mix blended with water. Bring to a boil over high heat. Stir in ravioli. Reduce heat to medium and cook, stirring gently, 5 minutes or until ravioli are tender. Serve, if desired, with grated Parmesan cheese.

Makes about 4 (2-cup) servings

Ravioli Soup

Breakfast & Brunch Buffet

330 MAKE-AHEAD BREAKFAST CASSEROLE

2½ cups seasoned croutons
1 pound BOB EVANS FARMS® Original Recipe Roll Sausage
4 eggs
2¼ cups milk
1 (10½-ounce) can condensed cream of mushroom soup
1 (10-ounce) package frozen chopped spinach, thawed and squeezed dry
1 (4-ounce) can mushrooms, drained and chopped
1 cup (4 ounces) shredded sharp Cheddar cheese
1 cup (4 ounces) shredded Monterey Jack cheese
¼ teaspoon dry mustard
Fresh herb sprigs and carrot strips (optional)
Picante sauce or salsa (optional)

Spread croutons on bottom of greased 13×9-inch baking dish. Crumble sausage into medium skillet. Cook over medium heat until browned, stirring occasionally. Drain off any drippings. Spread over croutons. Whisk eggs and milk in large bowl until blended. Stir in soup, spinach, mushrooms, cheeses and mustard. Pour egg mixture over sausage and croutons. Refrigerate overnight. Preheat oven to 325°F. Bake egg mixture 50 to 55 minutes or until set and lightly browned on top. Garnish with herb sprigs and carrot strips, if desired. Serve hot with picante sauce, if desired. Refrigerate leftovers.   *Makes 10 to 12 servings*

Make-Ahead Breakfast Casserole

331 MUSHROOM & ONION EGG BAKE

1 tablespoon vegetable oil
4 green onions, chopped
4 ounces mushrooms, sliced
1 cup low-fat cottage cheese
1 cup sour cream
6 eggs
2 tablespoons all-purpose flour
1/4 teaspoon salt
1/8 teaspoon freshly ground pepper
   Dash hot pepper sauce

1. Preheat oven to 350°F. Grease shallow 1-quart baking dish.

2. Heat oil in medium skillet over medium heat. Add onions and mushrooms; cook until tender. Set aside.

3. In blender or food processor, process cottage cheese until almost smooth. Add sour cream, eggs, flour, salt, pepper and hot pepper sauce; process until combined. Stir in onions and mushrooms. Pour into prepared baking dish. Bake about 40 minutes or until knife inserted near center comes out clean.

Makes about 6 servings

332 SUNRISE SQUARES

1 pound BOB EVANS FARMS® Original
   Recipe Roll Sausage
2 slices bread, cut into 1/2-inch cubes
   (about 2 cups)
1 cup (4 ounces) shredded sharp Cheddar
   cheese
6 eggs
2 cups milk
1/2 teaspoon salt
1/2 teaspoon dry mustard

Preheat oven to 350°F. Crumble sausage into medium skillet. Cook over medium heat until browned, stirring occasionally. Drain off any drippings. Spread bread cubes in greased 11×7-inch baking dish; top with sausage and cheese. Whisk eggs, milk, salt and mustard until well blended; pour over cheese. Bake 30 to 40 minutes or until set. Let stand 5 minutes before cutting into squares; serve hot. Refrigerate leftovers.

Makes 6 servings

TIP: You can make this tasty meal ahead and refrigerate overnight before baking.

SERVING SUGGESTION: Serve squares between toasted English muffins.

Mushroom & Onion Egg Bake

333 SPINACH-CHEDDAR SQUARES

1½ cups EGG BEATERS® Healthy Real Egg
     Product
¾ cup skim milk
1 tablespoon dried onion flakes
1 tablespoon grated Parmesan cheese
¼ teaspoon garlic powder
⅛ teaspoon ground black pepper
¼ cup plain dry bread crumbs
¾ cup shredded fat-free Cheddar cheese,
     divided
1 (10-ounce) package frozen chopped
     spinach, thawed and well drained
¼ cup diced pimentos

In medium bowl, combine Egg Beaters®,
milk, onion flakes, Parmesan cheese, garlic
powder and pepper; set aside.

Sprinkle bread crumbs evenly onto bottom
of lightly greased 8×8×2-inch baking dish.
Top with ½ cup Cheddar cheese and
spinach. Pour egg mixture evenly over
spinach; top with remaining Cheddar cheese
and pimentos.

Bake at 350°F for 35 to 40 minutes or until
knife inserted in center comes out clean. Let
stand 10 minutes before serving.
Makes 16 appetizer servings

Prep Time: 15 minutes
Cook Time: 40 minutes

334 CHILIES RELLENOS CASSEROLE

3 eggs, separated
¾ cup milk
¾ cup all-purpose flour
½ teaspoon salt
1 tablespoon butter or margarine
½ cup chopped onion
2 cans (7 ounces *each*) whole green
     chilies, drained
8 slices (1 ounce *each*) Monterey Jack
     cheese, cut into halves
Garnishes: sour cream, sliced green
     onions, pitted ripe olive slices,
     guacamole and salsa

1. Preheat oven to 350°F.

2. Combine egg yolks, milk, flour and salt in
blender or food processor container. Cover;
process until smooth. Pour into bowl; let
stand until ready to use.

3. Melt butter in small skillet over medium
heat. Add onion; cook and stir until tender.

4. Pat chilies dry with paper towels. Slit
each chili lengthwise and carefully remove
seeds. Place 2 cheese halves and
1 tablespoon onion in each chili; reshape
chilies to cover cheese. Place in single layer
in greased 13×9-inch baking dish.

5. In small clean bowl, beat egg whites until
soft peaks form; fold into yolk mixture. Pour
over chilies.

6. Bake 20 to 25 minutes or until topping is
puffed and knife inserted in center comes
out clean. Broil 4 inches below heat
30 seconds or until topping is golden brown.
Serve with desired garnishes.
Makes 4 servings

335 WEEKEND BRUNCH CASSEROLE

1 pound BOB EVANS FARMS® Original
   Recipe Roll Sausage
1 (8-ounce) can refrigerated crescent
   dinner rolls
2 cups (8 ounces) shredded mozzarella
   cheese
4 eggs, beaten
¾ cup milk
¼ teaspoon salt
⅛ teaspoon black pepper

Preheat oven to 425°F. Crumble sausage into
medium skillet. Cook over medium heat
until browned, stirring occasionally. Drain
off any drippings. Line bottom of greased
13×9-inch baking dish with crescent roll
dough, firmly pressing perforations to seal.
Sprinkle with sausage and cheese. Combine
remaining ingredients in medium bowl until
blended; pour over sausage. Bake
15 minutes or until set. Let stand 5 minutes
before cutting into squares; serve hot.
Refrigerate leftovers.

Makes 6 to 8 servings

SERVING SUGGESTION: Serve with fresh
fruit or sliced tomatoes.

336 BAKED HAM & CHEESE MONTE CRISTO

6 slices bread
2 cups (8 ounces) shredded Cheddar
   cheese
1 can (2.8 ounces) FRENCH'S® French
   Fried Onions
1 package (10 ounces) frozen broccoli
   spears, thawed, drained and cut into
   1-inch pieces
2 cups (10 ounces) cubed cooked ham
5 eggs
2 cups milk
½ teaspoon ground mustard
½ teaspoon seasoned salt
¼ teaspoon coarsely ground black pepper

Preheat oven to 325°F. Cut 3 bread slices
into cubes; place in greased 12×8-inch
baking dish. Top bread with *1 cup* cheese,
½ can French Fried Onions, broccoli and
ham. Cut remaining bread slices diagonally
into halves. Arrange bread halves down
center of casserole, overlapping slightly,
crusted points all in same direction. In
medium bowl, beat eggs, milk and
seasonings; pour evenly over casserole.
Bake, uncovered, at 325°F for 1 hour or until
center is set. Top with remaining cheese and
onions; bake, uncovered, 5 minutes or until
onions are golden brown. Let stand
10 minutes before serving.

Makes 6 to 8 servings

BREAKFAST & BRUNCH BUFFET

337 CHEDDAR AND LEEK STRATA

2 small leeks
8 eggs, lightly beaten
2 cups milk
½ cup ale or beer
2 cloves garlic, minced
¼ teaspoon salt
¼ teaspoon black pepper
1 loaf (16 ounces) sourdough bread, cut into ½-inch cubes
1 red bell pepper, chopped
1½ cups (6 ounces) shredded Swiss cheese
1½ cups (6 ounces) shredded sharp Cheddar cheese

1. To prepare leeks, remove any withered outer leaves. Use chef's knife to cut off leaf tops down to where the dark green begins to pale; discard. Cut off roots; make 1 or 2 deep cuts into leeks to within 1 inch of root end. Hold leeks under cold running water; separate layers slightly and wash thoroughly to remove all embedded soil. Coarsely chop with chef's knife; set aside.

2. Combine eggs, milk, ale, garlic, salt and black pepper in large bowl. Beat with wire whisk until well blended.

3. Place ½ of bread cubes on bottom of greased 13×9-inch baking dish. Sprinkle ½ of leeks and ½ of bell pepper over bread cubes. Top with ¾ cup Swiss cheese and ¾ cup Cheddar cheese. Repeat layers with remaining ingredients, ending with Cheddar cheese.

4. Pour egg mixture evenly over top. Cover tightly with plastic wrap or foil. Weigh down top of strata with slightly smaller baking dish. Refrigerate strata at least 2 hours or overnight.

5. Preheat oven to 350°F. Bake strata uncovered 40 to 45 minutes or until center is set. Garnish, if desired. Serve immediately.

Makes 12 servings

338 MEXICAN STRATA OLÉ

4 (6-inch) corn tortillas, halved, divided
1 cup chopped onion
½ cup chopped green bell pepper
1 clove garlic, crushed
1 teaspoon dried oregano leaves
½ teaspoon ground cumin
1 teaspoon FLEISCHMANN'S® Margarine
1 cup dried kidney beans, cooked in unsalted water according to package directions
½ cup (2 ounces) shredded reduced-fat Cheddar cheese
1½ cups skim milk
1 cup EGG BEATERS® Healthy Real Egg Product
1 cup thick and chunky salsa

Arrange half of tortilla pieces on bottom of greased 12×8-inch baking dish; set aside.

In large nonstick skillet, over medium-high heat, sauté onion, bell pepper, garlic, oregano and cumin in margarine until tender; stir in beans. Spoon half of mixture over tortillas; repeat layers once. Sprinkle with cheese.

In medium bowl, combine milk and Egg Beaters®; pour evenly over cheese. Bake at 350°F for 40 minutes or until puffed and golden brown. Let stand 10 minutes before serving. Serve topped with salsa.

Makes 8 servings

Prep Time: 25 minutes
Cook Time: 50 minutes

Cheddar and Leek Strata

BREAKFAST & BRUNCH BUFFET

339 CHEESE STRATA

BASIC STRATA
3 tablespoons butter or margarine
6 slices bread, crusts removed
3 cups (12 ounces) shredded Cheddar
    cheese
6 eggs
2 cups milk
1 tablespoon LAWRY'S® Minced Onion
    with Green Onion Flakes
1 teaspoon LAWRY'S® Seasoned Salt
¼ teaspoon LAWRY'S® Garlic Powder with
    Parsley

Lightly grease 13×9×2-inch baking dish
with butter; arrange bread slices in bottom
of dish. Sprinkle with half of Cheddar
cheese. In medium bowl, beat together eggs,
milk, Minced Onion with Green Onion
Flakes, Seasoned Salt and Garlic Powder
with Parsley. Pour mixture over bread and
cheese. Sprinkle with remaining Cheddar
cheese. Bake, uncovered, in 350°F oven
35 minutes or until light golden brown. Let
stand 5 minutes before serving.

Makes 6 servings

MEXICAN STRATA: Pour 1 bottle
(8½ ounces) LAWRY'S® Chunky Taco Sauce
over strata 5 minutes before baking time is
completed. Continue to bake as directed.

HERB STRATA: Add 2 tablespoons LAWRY'S®
Pinch of Herbs to BASIC STRATA egg-and-
milk mixture.

ITALIAN-HERB STRATA: To HERB variation,
add ¼ cup sliced black olives to each cheese
layer and top with diced tomatoes. Serve
with LAWRY'S® Original-Style Spaghetti
Sauce Spices & Seasonings prepared as
directed on package.

340 VEGETABLE STRATA

2 slices white bread, cubed
¼ cup shredded reduced-fat Swiss cheese
½ cup sliced carrots
½ cup sliced mushrooms
¼ cup chopped onion
1 clove garlic, crushed
1 teaspoon FLEISCHMANN'S® Margarine
½ cup chopped tomato
½ cup snow peas
1 cup EGG BEATERS® Healthy Real Egg
    Product
¾ cup skim milk

Place bread cubes evenly on bottom of
greased 1½-quart casserole dish. Sprinkle
with cheese; set aside.

In medium nonstick skillet, over medium
heat, sauté carrots, mushrooms, onion and
garlic in margarine until tender. Stir in
tomato and snow peas; cook 1 to 2 minutes
more. Spoon over cheese. In small bowl,
combine Egg Beaters® and milk; pour over
vegetable mixture. Bake at 375°F for 45 to
50 minutes or until knife inserted in center
comes out clean. Let stand 10 minutes
before serving. *Makes 6 servings*

Prep Time: 15 minutes
Cook Time: 55 minutes

Vegetable Strata

BREAKFAST & BRUNCH BUFFET

341 EASY MORNING STRATA

1 pound BOB EVANS FARMS® Original Recipe Roll Sausage
8 eggs
10 slices bread, cut into cubes (about 10 cups)
3 cups milk
2 cups (8 ounces) shredded Cheddar cheese
2 cups (8 ounces) sliced fresh mushrooms
1 (10-ounce) package frozen cut asparagus, thawed and drained
2 tablespoons butter or margarine, melted
2 tablespoons all-purpose flour
1 tablespoon dry mustard
2 teaspoons dried basil leaves
1 teaspoon salt

Crumble sausage into large skillet. Cook over medium heat until browned, stirring occasionally. Drain off any drippings. Whisk eggs in large bowl. Add sausage and remaining ingredients; mix well. Spoon into greased 13×9-inch baking dish. Cover; refrigerate 8 hours or overnight. Preheat oven to 350°F. Bake 60 to 70 minutes or until knife inserted near center comes out clean. Let stand 5 minutes before cutting into squares; serve hot. Refrigerate leftovers.

Makes 10 to 12 servings

342 SPINACH-CHEESE STRATA

6 slices whole wheat bread
2 tablespoons butter or margarine, softened
1 cup (4 ounces) shredded Cheddar cheese
½ cup (2 ounces) shredded Monterey Jack cheese
1¼ cups milk
6 eggs, lightly beaten
1 package (10 ounces) frozen spinach, thawed and well drained
¼ teaspoon salt
⅛ teaspoon pepper

1. Spread bread with butter; arrange in single layer in greased 13×9-inch baking dish. Sprinkle with cheeses.

2. Combine milk, eggs, spinach, salt and pepper in large bowl; stir well. Pour over bread and cheese. Cover; refrigerate at least 6 hours or overnight.

3. Bake, uncovered, at 350°F about 1 hour or until puffy and lightly golden.

Makes 4 to 6 servings

Easy Morning Strata

BREAKFAST & BRUNCH BUFFET

343 ELEGANT CRABMEAT FRITTATA

3 tablespoons butter or margarine, divided
¼ pound fresh mushrooms, sliced
2 green onions, cut into thin slices
½ pound lump crabmeat or imitation crabmeat, diced
8 eggs, separated
¼ cup milk
¼ teaspoon salt
½ teaspoon hot pepper sauce
½ cup (2 ounces) shredded Swiss cheese

1. Melt 2 tablespoons butter in large ovenproof skillet over medium-high heat. Add mushrooms and onions; cook and stir 3 to 5 minutes or until vegetables are tender. Remove from skillet; set aside.

2. To remove cartilage and shell from crabmeat, gently squeeze 1 teaspoonful at a time between fingers. Feel carefully for small bits. The shell may be white or orange, and cartilage is milky white and thin. Flake crabmeat with fork.

3. Beat egg yolks with electric mixer at high speed until slightly thickened and lemon colored. Stir in milk, salt and hot pepper sauce.

4. Beat egg whites in clean large bowl with electric mixer at high speed until foamy. Gradually add to egg yolk mixture, whisking just until blended.

5. Melt remaining 1 tablespoon butter in skillet. Pour egg mixture into skillet; cook until almost set. Remove from heat.

6. Preheat broiler. Broil frittata 4 to 6 inches from heat until top is set.

7. Top with crabmeat and cheese. Return frittata to broiler; broil until cheese is melted. Garnish, if desired. Serve immediately. *Makes 4 servings*

344 VEGETABLE-CHEESE FRITTATA

½ cup fresh green beans, cut into 1-inch pieces
1 small onion, chopped
3 tablespoons butter or margarine
¼ red bell pepper, chopped
¼ cup sliced fresh mushrooms
¼ cup dry bread crumbs
½ cup prepared HIDDEN VALLEY RANCH® Original Ranch® salad dressing mix
6 eggs, beaten
⅓ cup shredded Cheddar cheese
¼ cup grated Parmesan cheese

Preheat oven to 350°F. In medium saucepan, steam green beans over boiling water until crisp-tender, about 4 minutes. In medium skillet, sauté onion in butter until onion is softened; stir in beans, bell pepper and mushrooms. Fold vegetables, bread crumbs and salad dressing into eggs. Pour into buttered quiche dish. Sprinkle with cheeses. Bake until set, about 25 minutes.

Makes 6 servings

NOTE: Substitute chopped tomatoes, diced green chili peppers, sliced black olives, chopped zucchini or any vegetable combination for green beans, onion and mushrooms.

BREAKFAST & BRUNCH BUFFET

345 GARDEN FRITTATA

1 tablespoon extra-virgin olive oil
1 cup sliced, unpeeled, small red-skinned
   potatoes (about 4 ounces)
½ cup chopped red onion
½ cup chopped red bell pepper
1 teaspoon minced garlic
1 cup chopped fresh asparagus
½ cup fresh corn kernels or frozen corn,
   thawed and drained
1 cup diced ALPINE LACE® Boneless
   Cooked Ham (4 ounces)
¾ cup egg substitute *or* 3 large eggs
3 large egg whites
1 cup (4 ounces) shredded ALPINE LACE®
   Reduced Fat Lightly Smoked
   Provolone Cheese
¼ cup slivered fresh basil leaves *or*
   1 tablespoon dried basil
½ teaspoon salt
¼ teaspoon freshly ground black pepper

1. Preheat the broiler. In a large broilerproof nonstick skillet, heat the oil over medium-high heat. Add the potatoes, onion, bell pepper and garlic. Cook, stirring occasionally, for 7 minutes or until the potatoes are almost tender. Stir in the asparagus, corn and ham and cook 3 minutes more or until the vegetables are crisp-tender.

2. In a medium-size bowl, whisk the egg substitute (or the whole eggs), the egg whites, cheese, basil, salt and black pepper together until blended. Pour over the vegetables. Reduce the heat and cook, uncovered, for 8 minutes or just until the egg mixture is set around the edges.

3. Slide the skillet under the broiler for 1 minute or until the eggs are set in the center. Serve immediately.

Makes 4 servings

346 HASH BROWN FRITTATA

1 (10-ounce) package BOB EVANS
   FARMS® Skinless Link Sausage
6 eggs
1 (12-ounce) package frozen hash brown
   potatoes, thawed
1 cup (4 ounces) shredded Cheddar
   cheese
⅓ cup whipping cream
¼ cup chopped green and/or red bell
   peppers
¼ teaspoon salt
   Dash black pepper

Preheat oven to 350°F. Cut sausage into bite-size pieces. Cook in small skillet over medium heat until lightly browned, stirring occasionally. Drain off any drippings. Whisk eggs in medium bowl; stir in sausage and remaining ingredients. Pour into greased 2-quart casserole dish. Bake, uncovered, 30 minutes or until eggs are almost set. Let stand 5 minutes before cutting into squares; serve hot. Refrigerate leftovers.

Makes 6 servings

347 ASPARAGUS-SWISS SOUFFLÉ

¼ cup unsalted butter substitute
½ cup chopped yellow onion
¼ cup all-purpose flour
½ teaspoon salt
¼ teaspoon cayenne pepper
1 cup 2% low fat milk
1 cup (4 ounces) shredded ALPINE LACE®
   Reduced Fat Swiss Cheese
1 cup egg substitute *or* 4 large eggs
1 cup coarsely chopped fresh asparagus
   pieces, cooked, or frozen asparagus
   pieces, thawed and drained
3 large egg whites

1. Preheat the oven to 325°F. Spray a 1½-quart soufflé dish with nonstick cooking spray.

2. In a large saucepan, melt the butter over medium heat, add the onion and sauté for 5 minutes or until soft. Stir in the flour, salt and pepper and cook for 2 minutes or until bubbly. Add the milk and cook, stirring constantly, for 5 minutes or until the sauce thickens. Add the cheese and stir until melted.

3. In a small bowl, whisk the egg substitute (or the whole eggs). Whisk in a little of the hot cheese sauce, then return this egg mixture to the saucepan and whisk until well blended. Remove from the heat and fold in the drained asparagus.

4. In a medium-size bowl, using an electric mixer set on high, beat the egg whites until stiff peaks form. Fold the hot cheese sauce into the whites, then spoon into the soufflé dish.

5. Place the soufflé on a baking sheet and bake for 50 minutes or until golden brown and puffy.   *Makes 8 servings*

348 HAM & CHEESE GRITS SOUFFLÉ

3 cups water
¾ cup quick-cooking grits
½ teaspoon salt
½ cup (2 ounces) shredded mozzarella
   cheese
2 ounces ham, finely chopped
2 tablespoons minced chives
2 eggs, separated
   Dash hot pepper sauce

1. Preheat oven to 375°F. Grease 1½-quart soufflé dish or deep casserole.

2. Bring water to a boil in medium saucepan. Stir in grits and salt. Cook, stirring frequently, about 5 minutes or until thickened. Stir in cheese, ham, chives, egg yolks and hot pepper sauce.

3. In small clean bowl, beat egg whites until stiff but not dry; fold into grits mixture. Pour into prepared dish. Bake about 30 minutes or until puffed and golden. Serve immediately.   *Makes 4 to 6 servings*

Asparagus-Swiss Soufflé

Broccoli & Cheese Quiche

349 DOUBLE ONION QUICHE

3 cups thinly sliced yellow onions
3 tablespoons butter or margarine
1 cup thinly sliced green onions
3 eggs
1 cup heavy cream
½ cup grated Parmesan cheese
¼ teaspoon hot pepper sauce
1 package (1 ounce) HIDDEN VALLEY®
   Milk Recipe Original Ranch® salad
   dressing mix
1 (9-inch) deep-dish pastry shell, baked
   and cooled

Preheat oven to 350°F. In medium skillet, sauté yellow onions in butter, stirring occasionally, about 10 minutes. Add green onions and cook 5 minutes longer. Remove from heat and let cool.

In large bowl, whisk eggs until frothy. Whisk in cream, cheese, pepper sauce and salad dressing mix. Stir in onion mixture. Pour egg-onion mixture into pastry shell. Bake until top is browned and knife inserted in center comes out clean, 35 to 40 minutes. Cool on wire rack 10 minutes before slicing. Garnish if desired. *Makes 8 servings*

350 BROCCOLI & CHEESE QUICHE

2 cups zwieback crumbs
$\frac{1}{2}$ teaspoon ground nutmeg
$\frac{1}{3}$ cup honey
2 cups fresh broccoli florets or frozen broccoli florets, thawed and drained
$\frac{1}{2}$ tablespoon unsalted butter substitute
1 cup chopped yellow onion
1 cup (4 ounces) shredded ALPINE LACE® Reduced Fat Swiss Cheese
1 cup (4 ounces) shredded ALPINE LACE® Reduced Fat Colby Cheese
1 cup chopped red bell pepper
$\frac{3}{4}$ cup egg substitute *or* 3 large eggs
2 large egg whites
$\frac{3}{4}$ cup 2% low fat milk
$\frac{1}{2}$ teaspoon dry mustard
$\frac{1}{2}$ teaspoon salt
$\frac{1}{4}$ teaspoon freshly ground white pepper

1. Preheat the oven to 400°F. Spray a 10-inch pie plate with nonstick cooking spray. To make the crumb crust: Toss the crumbs and nutmeg with the honey until the crumbs are thoroughly coated. Press onto the bottom and up the side of the pie plate.

2. To make the filling: Coarsely chop the broccoli. Half-fill a medium-size saucepan with water and bring to a boil over medium-high heat. Add the broccoli and cook, uncovered, for 5 minutes or just until crisp-tender. Drain.

3. In a small nonstick skillet, melt the butter over medium-high heat. Add the onion and sauté for 5 minutes or until soft. Layer both of the cheeses, then the onion, bell pepper and broccoli in the crust.

4. In a medium-size bowl, whisk the egg substitute (or the whole eggs), the egg whites, milk, mustard, salt and pepper together until blended. Pour evenly over the vegetables in the crust.

5. Bake for 10 minutes. Reduce the oven temperature to 350°F. Bake 20 minutes longer or until golden brown and puffy and a knife inserted in the center comes out clean.
Makes 8 servings

351 EASY CRAB ASPARAGUS PIE

4 ounces crabmeat, shredded
12 ounces fresh asparagus, cut into 1-inch pieces and cooked
$\frac{1}{2}$ cup chopped onion, cooked
1 cup (4 ounces) shredded Monterey Jack cheese
$\frac{1}{4}$ cup (1 ounce) grated Parmesan cheese
Freshly ground pepper
$\frac{3}{4}$ cup all-purpose flour
$\frac{3}{4}$ teaspoon baking powder
$\frac{1}{2}$ teaspoon salt
2 tablespoons cold butter or margarine
1$\frac{1}{2}$ cups milk
4 eggs, slightly beaten

1. Preheat oven to 350°F. Lightly grease 10-inch quiche dish or pie plate.

2. Layer crabmeat, asparagus and onion in prepared pie plate; top with cheeses. Season with pepper.

3. Combine flour, baking powder and salt in large bowl. With pastry blender or 2 knives, cut in butter until mixture forms coarse crumbs. Stir in milk and eggs; pour over cheese mixture.

4. Bake 30 minutes or until filling is puffed and knife inserted near center comes out clean. Serve hot. *Makes 6 servings*

BREAKFAST & BRUNCH BUFFET

352 TURKEY AND RICE QUICHE

3 cups cooked rice, cooled to room
    temperature
1½ cups chopped cooked turkey
1 medium tomato, seeded and finely diced
¼ cup sliced green onions
¼ cup finely diced green pepper
1 tablespoon chopped fresh basil *or*
    1 teaspoon dried basil
½ teaspoon seasoned salt
⅛ to ¼ teaspoon ground red pepper
½ cup skim milk
3 eggs, beaten
    Vegetable cooking spray
½ cup (2 ounces) shredded Cheddar
    cheese
½ cup (2 ounces) shredded mozzarella
    cheese

Combine rice, turkey, tomato, onions, green
pepper, basil, salt, red pepper, milk and eggs
in 13×9-inch pan coated with cooking spray.
Top with cheeses. Bake at 375°F for
20 minutes or until knife inserted near
center comes out clean. To serve, cut quiche
into 8 squares; cut each square diagonally
into 2 triangles.   *Makes 8 servings*
                          (2 triangles each)

Favorite recipe from **USA Rice Council**

353 BROWN RICE-SPINACH QUICHE

1 bag SUCCESS® Brown Rice
6 egg whites, divided
¼ cup (1 ounce) grated Parmesan cheese,
    divided
    Vegetable cooking spray
1 tablespoon reduced-calorie margarine
½ cup chopped onion
1 package (10 ounces) frozen chopped
    spinach, thawed and drained
1 teaspoon black pepper
½ teaspoon salt
½ teaspoon ground nutmeg
½ cup fat-free sour cream
2 tablespoons flour
1 cup skim milk

Prepare rice according to package
directions. Cool.

Preheat oven to 425°F.

Combine rice, 3 egg whites and
2 tablespoons cheese; mix well. Spray 9-inch
pie plate with cooking spray. With back of
spoon, firmly press rice mixture onto bottom
and up side of prepared pie plate to form
shell. Bake 5 minutes. Remove from oven.
Melt margarine in small skillet. Add onion;
cook and stir until tender. Combine onion,
spinach, pepper, salt and nutmeg in medium
bowl; mix well. Spoon spinach mixture into
rice shell; sprinkle with remaining
2 tablespoons cheese. Slightly beat
remaining 3 egg whites in medium bowl. Stir
in sour cream, flour and milk. Pour over
spinach mixture. Bake 10 minutes. Reduce
oven temperature to 350°F. Continue baking
until quiche is firm, about 30 minutes.
                          Makes 6 servings

Turkey and Rice Quiche

354 RANCH QUICHE LORRAINE

2 cups crushed butter-flavored crackers
6 tablespoons butter or margarine, melted
2 cups shredded Swiss cheese
4 eggs
2 cups heavy cream
1 package (1.2 ounces) HIDDEN VALLEY RANCH® Original Ranch® with Bacon salad dressing mix
1 tablespoon dehydrated minced onion

Preheat oven to 375°F. In medium bowl, combine crackers and butter. Press crumb mixture evenly into 10-inch pie pan or quiche dish. Bake until golden, about 7 minutes. Remove and cool pan on wire rack.

Increase oven temperature to 425°F. Sprinkle cheese over cooled pie crust. In medium bowl, whisk eggs until frothy. Add cream, salad dressing mix and onion. Pour egg mixture over cheese. Bake 15 minutes; reduce temperature to 350°F and continue baking until knife inserted in center comes out clean, about 20 minutes longer. Cool on wire rack 10 minutes before slicing.

Makes 8 servings

355 SAUSAGE & APPLE QUICHE

1 unbaked (9-inch) pastry shell
½ pound bulk spicy pork sausage
½ cup chopped onion
¾ cup shredded, peeled tart apple
1 tablespoon lemon juice
1 tablespoon sugar
⅛ teaspoon crushed red pepper
1 cup (4 ounces) shredded Cheddar cheese
3 eggs
1½ cups half-and-half
¼ teaspoon salt
   Ground black pepper

1. Preheat oven to 425°F.

2. Place piece of foil inside pastry shell; partially fill with uncooked beans or rice. Bake 10 minutes. Remove foil and beans; continue baking pastry 5 minutes or until lightly browned. Let cool.

3. Reduce oven temperature to 375°F.

4. Crumble sausage into large skillet; add onion. Cook over medium heat until meat is browned and onion is tender. Spoon off and discard pan drippings.

5. Add apple, lemon juice, sugar and red pepper to skillet. Cook on medium-high, stirring constantly, 4 minutes or until apple is just tender and all liquid is evaporated. Let cool.

6. Spoon sausage mixture into pastry shell; top with cheese. Whisk eggs, half-and-half, salt and dash of black pepper in medium bowl. Pour over sausage mixture.

7. Bake 35 to 45 minutes or until filling is puffed and knife inserted in center comes out clean. Let stand 10 minutes before cutting to serve. *Makes 6 servings*

356 ACAPULCO EGGS

3 corn tortillas, cut into 2-inch strips
3 tablespoons butter or margarine
½ cup chopped onion
1½ cups DEL MONTE® Thick & Chunky Salsa, Mild
1 cup cooked ham, cut into thin strips, or shredded cooked turkey
½ cup green pepper strips
6 eggs, beaten
¾ cup shredded Monterey Jack cheese

In large skillet, cook tortilla strips in butter until golden. Remove and set aside. Cook onion in same skillet until tender. Stir in salsa, meat and green pepper; heat through. Reduce heat to low; add tortillas and eggs. Cover and cook 4 to 6 minutes or until eggs are set. Sprinkle with cheese; cover and cook 1 minute or until cheese is melted. Garnish with chopped cilantro or parsley, if desired.   *Makes 4 to 6 servings*

Prep Time: 10 minutes
Cook Time: 15 minutes

357 HUEVOS CON ARROZ

1 package (6.8 ounces) RICE-A-RONI® Spanish Rice
2 cups chopped tomatoes
4 eggs
½ cup (2 ounces) shredded Cheddar cheese or Monterey Jack cheese
2 tablespoons chopped cilantro or parsley
¼ cup salsa or picante sauce (optional)

1. Prepare Rice-A-Roni® mix as package directs, substituting fresh tomatoes for 1 can (14½ ounces) tomatoes. Bring to a boil over high heat. Cover; reduce heat. Simmer 20 minutes.

2. Make 4 round indentations in rice with back of large spoon. Break 1 egg into each indentation. Cover; cook over low heat 5 to 7 minutes or until eggs are cooked to desired doneness.

3. Sprinkle with cheese and cilantro. Serve topped with salsa, if desired.
       Makes 4 servings

358 BRUNCH EGGS OLÉ

8 eggs
½ cup all-purpose flour
1 teaspoon baking powder
¾ teaspoon salt
2 cups (8 ounces) shredded Monterey Jack
   cheese with jalapeño peppers
1½ cups (12 ounces) small curd cottage
   cheese
1 cup (4 ounces) shredded sharp Cheddar
   cheese
1 jalapeño pepper, seeded, chopped*
½ teaspoon hot pepper sauce
   Fresh Salsa (recipe follows)

Jalapeño peppers can sting and irritate the skin; wear rubber gloves when handling peppers and do not touch eyes. Wash hands after handling.

1. Preheat oven to 350°F. Grease 9-inch square baking pan.

2. Beat eggs in large bowl at high speed with electric mixer 4 to 5 minutes or until slightly thickened and lemon colored.

3. Combine flour, baking powder and salt in small bowl. Stir flour mixture into eggs until blended.

4. Combine Monterey Jack cheese, cottage cheese, Cheddar cheese, jalapeño and hot pepper sauce in medium bowl; mix well. Fold into egg mixture until well blended. Pour into prepared pan.

5. Bake 45 to 50 minutes or until golden brown and firm in center. Let stand 10 minutes before cutting into squares to serve. Serve with Fresh Salsa. Garnish as desired. *Makes 8 servings*

FRESH SALSA

3 medium plum tomatoes, seeded and
   chopped
2 tablespoons chopped onion
1 small jalapeño pepper, stemmed, seeded
   and minced
1 tablespoon chopped fresh cilantro
1 tablespoon lime juice
¼ teaspoon salt
⅛ teaspoon black pepper

Stir together tomatoes, onion, jalapeño pepper, cilantro, lime juice, salt and black pepper in small bowl. Refrigerate until ready to serve. *Makes 1 cup*

359 EGGS AND RICE DISH

1 bag SUCCESS® Rice
8 ounces egg substitute
½ cup finely chopped turkey ham
½ cup chopped green onions
¼ cup chopped pimentos (optional)
¼ teaspoon salt
⅛ teaspoon black pepper
2 tablespoons margarine
¼ cup (1 ounce) shredded low-fat Cheddar
   cheese

Prepare rice according to package directions.

Combine rice, egg substitute, turkey ham, green onions, pimentos, salt and black pepper in large bowl; mix well. Melt margarine in large skillet over medium heat. Add rice mixture. Cook, stirring occasionally, until eggs are set, about 2 minutes. (Do not overcook.) Sprinkle with cheese. Remove from heat; stir gently. Serve immediately. *Makes 4 servings*

Brunch Eggs Olé

360 HAM AND EGG ENCHILADAS

2 tablespoons butter or margarine
1 small red bell pepper, chopped
3 green onions with tops, sliced
½ cup diced ham
8 eggs
8 (7- to 8-inch) flour tortillas
2 cups (8 ounces) shredded Colby-Jack cheese or Monterey Jack cheese with jalapeño peppers, divided
1 can (10 ounces) enchilada sauce
½ cup prepared salsa
   Sliced avocado, fresh cilantro and red pepper slices for garnish

1. Preheat oven to 350°F.

2. Melt butter in large nonstick skillet over medium heat. Add bell pepper and onions; cook and stir 2 minutes. Add ham; cook and stir 1 minute.

3. Lightly beat eggs with wire whisk in medium bowl. Add eggs to skillet; cook until set, but still soft, stirring occasionally.

4. Spoon about ⅓ cup egg mixture evenly down center of each tortilla; top with 1 tablespoon cheese. Roll tortillas up and place seam side down in shallow 11×7-inch baking dish.

5. Combine enchilada sauce and salsa in small bowl; pour evenly over enchiladas.

6. Cover enchiladas with foil; bake 20 minutes. Uncover; sprinkle with remaining cheese. Continue baking 10 minutes or until enchiladas are hot and cheese is melted. Garnish, if desired. Serve immediately. *Makes 4 servings*

361 BREAKFAST HASH

1 pound BOB EVANS FARMS® Special Seasonings or Sage Roll Sausage
2 cups chopped potatoes
¼ cup chopped red and/or green bell peppers
2 tablespoons chopped onion
6 eggs
2 tablespoons milk

Crumble sausage into large skillet. Add potatoes, peppers and onion. Cook over low heat until sausage is browned and potatoes are fork-tender, stirring occasionally. Drain off any drippings. Whisk eggs and milk in small bowl until blended. Add to sausage mixture; scramble until eggs are set but not dry. Serve hot. Refrigerate leftovers.
Makes 6 to 8 servings

Breakfast Hash

BREAKFAST & BRUNCH BUFFET

362 CREAMY CHICKEN & VEGETABLES WITH PUFF PASTRY

2 whole chicken breasts, split (about 2 pounds)
1 medium onion, sliced
4 carrots, coarsely chopped, divided
4 ribs celery with leaves, cut into 1-inch pieces, divided
1 frozen puff pastry sheet, thawed
2 tablespoons butter or margarine
1 medium onion, chopped
½ pound fresh mushrooms, sliced
½ cup all-purpose flour
1 teaspoon dried basil leaves
1 teaspoon salt
¼ to ½ teaspoon white pepper
1 cup milk
1 cup frozen peas, thawed

1. To make chicken stock, place chicken, sliced onion, ⅓ *each* of carrots and celery in Dutch oven. Add enough cold water to cover. Cover and bring to a boil over medium heat. Reduce heat to low. Simmer 5 to 7 minutes or until chicken is no longer pink in center.

2. Remove chicken; cool. Strain stock through large sieve lined with several layers of dampened cheesecloth; discard vegetables. Refrigerate stock; skim off any fat that forms on top. Measure 2 cups stock.

3. When chicken is cool enough to handle, remove skin and bones; discard. Cut chicken into bite-sized pieces.

4. Place remaining carrots, celery and enough water to cover in medium saucepan. Cover; bring to a boil. Reduce heat to medium-low; simmer 8 minutes or until vegetables are crisp-tender. Set aside.

5. Preheat oven to 400°F. Roll puff pastry out on lightly floured surface to 12×8-inch rectangle. Place on ungreased baking sheet; bake 15 minutes. Set aside.

6. Melt butter in large saucepan over medium-high heat. Add chopped onion and mushrooms; cook and stir 5 minutes or until tender. Stir flour, basil, salt and pepper. Slowly pour in reserved chicken stock and milk. Cook until mixture begins to boil. Cook 1 minute longer, stirring constantly.

7. Stir in reserved chicken, peas, carrots and celery. Cook until heated through. Pour mixture into 12×8-inch baking dish; top with hot puff pastry. Bake 5 minutes until puff pastry is brown. Garnish as desired.

Makes 6 servings

Creamy Chicken & Vegetables with Puff Pastry

BREAKFAST & BRUNCH BUFFET

363 CHICKEN WITH MUSHROOM SAUCE

MUSHROOM SAUCE
   3 tablespoons butter or margarine
   8 ounces fresh mushrooms, sliced
   3 tablespoons all-purpose flour
1½ cups chicken broth
   1 tablespoon minced chives
   1 tablespoon minced fresh parsley
   1 teaspoon Dijon mustard
¼ teaspoon salt
⅛ teaspoon freshly ground pepper
½ cup sour cream

CHICKEN
   1 tablespoon vegetable oil
   4 boneless skinless chicken breast halves
   4 ham slices
   4 slices Monterey Jack cheese
   2 English muffins, split and toasted
½ red bell pepper, cut into thin strips

1. For Mushroom Sauce, melt butter in medium saucepan over medium heat. Add mushrooms; cook and stir until tender. Remove mushrooms from saucepan with slotted spoon; set aside. Stir flour into pan; cook, stirring constantly, until bubbly. Slowly whisk in broth.

2. Add mushrooms, chives, parsley, mustard, salt and pepper. Cook, stirring constantly, until thickened. Stir in sour cream; heat until hot. Do not boil. Keep warm on very low heat.

3. For Chicken, heat oil in large skillet over medium heat. Add chicken; cook, turning occasionally, about 8 minutes or until chicken is browned and no longer pink in center.

4. Reduce heat to low; place ham and then cheese on chicken. Cover and cook 1 to 2 minutes or just until cheese is melted. Place chicken on English muffins. Spoon sauce over chicken and top with pepper strips. *Makes 4 servings*

364 BRUNCH RICE

   1 teaspoon margarine
¾ cup shredded carrots
¾ cup diced green pepper
¾ cup (about 3 ounces) sliced fresh mushrooms
   6 egg whites, beaten
   2 eggs, beaten
½ cup skim milk
½ teaspoon salt
¼ teaspoon ground black pepper
   3 cups cooked brown rice
½ cup (2 ounces) shredded Cheddar cheese
   6 corn tortillas, warmed (optional)

Melt margarine in large skillet over medium-high heat. Add carrots, green pepper and mushrooms; cook and stir 2 minutes. Combine egg whites, eggs, milk, salt and black pepper in small bowl. Reduce heat to medium; pour egg white mixture over vegetables in skillet. Continue cooking 2 minutes, stirring occasionally. Add rice and cheese; stir to gently separate grains. Cook 2 minutes or until rice is heated through and cheese is melted. Spoon mixture into warmed corn tortillas, if desired. Serve immediately. *Makes 6 servings*

Favorite recipe from **USA Rice Council**

Brunch Rice

365 BREAKFAST IN A LOAF

Scrambled Eggs (recipe follows)
1 round loaf bread (8- to 9-inch diameter)
4 ounces sliced ham
½ red bell pepper, thinly sliced crosswise
½ cup (2 ounces) shredded Monterey Jack cheese
½ cup (2 ounces) shredded Cheddar cheese
½ cup sliced pitted ripe olives
1 medium tomato, thinly sliced
8 ounces mushrooms, sliced, cooked

1. Prepare Scrambled Eggs. Remove from heat; cover to keep warm.

2. Preheat oven to 350°F. Cut 2-inch slice from top of loaf; set aside for lid. Remove soft interior of loaf, leaving a 1-inch-thick wall and bottom.

3. Place ham on bottom of loaf. Top with bell pepper rings; sprinkle with half of cheeses. Layer Scrambled Eggs, olives and tomato over cheeses. Top with remaining cheeses and mushrooms.

4. Place lid on loaf. Wrap in foil. Place on baking sheet. Bake about 30 minutes or until heated through. Cut into 8 wedges.

Makes 8 servings

SCRAMBLED EGGS
1 tablespoon butter or margarine
6 eggs, lightly beaten
½ teaspoon salt
¼ teaspoon ground pepper

1. Melt butter in 10-inch skillet over medium heat.

2. Season eggs with salt and pepper. Add eggs to skillet; cook, stirring gently and lifting to allow uncooked eggs to flow under cooked portion. (Do not overcook; eggs should be soft with no liquid remaining.)

Makes 4 servings

Breakfast in a Loaf

ACKNOWLEDGMENTS

The publisher would like to thank the companies and organizations listed below for the use of their recipes and photos in this publication.

Alpine Lace Brands, Inc.
American Lamb Council
Blue Diamond Growers
Bob Evans Farms®
Canned Food Information Council
Chef Paul Prudhomme's Magic Seasoning
    Blends®
Dean Foods Vegetable Company
Del Monte Corporation
Dole Food Company, Inc.
Florida Department of Agriculture and
    Consumer Services, Bureau of Seafood &
    Aquaculture
The Fremont Company, Makers of Frank's &
    SnowFloss Kraut and Tomato Products
Golden Grain/Mission Pasta
Hunt-Wesson, Inc.
The HVR Company
Kraft Foods, Inc.
Lawry's® Foods, Inc.
Thomas J. Lipton Co.
McIlhenny Company
Minnesota Cultivated Wild Rice Council
Nabisco, Inc.

National Broiler Council
National Cattlemen's Beef Association
National Dairy Board
National Turkey Federation
Nestlé Food Company
Newman's Own, Inc.
North Dakota Wheat Commission
North Dakota Beef Commission
Perdue® Farms
The Procter & Gamble Company
The Quaker Oats Company
Ralston Foods, Inc.
Reckitt & Colman Inc.
RED STAR® Yeast & Products, A Division of
    Universal Foods Corporation
Riviana Foods Inc.
Southeast United Dairy Industry Association,
    Inc.
StarKist Seafood Company
The Sugar Association, Inc.
USA Dry Pea & Lentil Council
USA Rice Council
Wisconsin Milk Marketing Board

INDEX

A

Acapulco Eggs, 315
Albacore Vegetable Pilaf, 147
Alphabet Turkey Soup, 286
Alpine Fettuccine, 203
Angel Hair al Fresco, 270
Angel Hair Carbonara, 253
Arizona Turkey Stew, 58
Arroz con Pollo, 33
Artichokes
    Company Crab, 157
    Italian Garden Fusilli, 188
    Vegetarian Paella, 172
Asparagus
    Asparagus Chicken, 36
    Asparagus-Swiss Soufflé, 308
    Chicken-Asparagus Casserole,
        218
    Easy Crab Asparagus Pie, 311
    Easy Morning Strata, 304
    Fancy Chicken Puff Pie, 9
    Garden Frittata, 307
    Superb Fillet of Sole &
        Vegetables, 142

B

Bacon-Tuna Parmesano, 264
Baked Fish with Potatoes and
    Onions, 130
Baked Ham & Cheese Monte Cristo,
    299
Baked Rigatoni, 253
Baked Rigatoni with Sausage, 255
Bean and Rice Soup, 92
Bean Sprouts
    Ground Beef Chow Mein, 80
    Pad Thai (Thai Fried Noodles),
        276
    Stir-Fried Corkscrew Shrimp with
        Vegetables, 154
    Teriyaki Chop Suey, 87
Beans, Black
    Black Bean & Pork Stew, 119
    Old Mexico Black Beans & Rice,
        188
    Salsa Rice and Black Beans, 206
Beans, Dried
    Dijon Ham and Lentil Soup, 119
    Harvest Casserole, 171
    Hearty Meatless Chili, 217
    Lamb & Pork Cassoulet, 125
    Prize Potluck Casserole, 97
Beans, Green
    Chicken Pot Pie, 15
    Chicken Skillet Supper, 30
    Chop Suey Casserole, 64
    Creamy Salmon with Green
        Beans, 286
    Family Favorite Hamburger
        Casserole, 67

Beans, Green *(continued)*
    Homespun Turkey 'n' Vegetables,
        48
    Italian Garden Fusilli, 188
    Korean Beef, 284
    Old-Fashioned Beef Stew, 88
    Sesame Steak, 79
    Southwestern Beef Stew, 90
    Vegetable-Cheese Frittata, 306
    Zesty Mixed Vegetables, 212
Beans, Kidney
    Hearty Meatless Chili, 217
    Louisiana Red Beans & Rice, 201
    Meatless Italian Minestrone, 217
    Mexican Strata Olé, 301
    Minestrone Soup, 255
    Pasta Fagioli (Bean) Soup, 284
    Ravioli Stew, 292
    Spicy Quick and Easy Chili, 92
    Spinach Ziti Casserole, 168
    Tex-Mex Chicken & Rice Chili, 40
    Texas-Style Deep-Dish Chili Pie,
        64
Beans, White
    Bean and Rice Soup, 92
    Dijon Lamb Stew, 125
    Hearty Meatless Chili, 217
    Indian Vegetable Curry, 198
    Meatless Italian Minestrone, 217
    Mexican Skillet Rice, 102
    Minestrone, 120
    Old Mexico Black Beans & Rice,
        188
    Pasta Fagiole, 206
    Quick Cassoulet, 104
    Ravioli Soup, 292
    20-Minute White Bean Chili, 57
    Vegetarian Paella, 172
Beef *(see also* **Beef, Ground;**
    Corned Beef)
    Beef à la Stroganoff, 278
    Beef and Broccoli, 87
    Beef Benihana, 84
    Beef Sausage Skillet Dinner, 100
    Bistro Burgundy Stew, 90
    Cantonese Tomato Beef, 280
    Chop Suey Casserole, 64
    Countdown Casserole, 60
    Easy Beef and Rice Stew, 88
    Five-Spice Beef and Bok Choy,
        282
    Hunan Chili Beef, 85
    Italian Beef and Pasta, 267
    Korean Beef, 284
    Mandarin Tomato Beef, 80
    Quick Skillet Supper, 79
    Ranch Stroganoff, 76
    Sesame Steak, 79
    Sherried Beef, 75
    Southwestern Beef Stew, 90

Beef *(continued)*
    Spanish Style Beef and Rice
        Casserole, 68
    Spicy Beef Stir-Fry, 275
    Teriyaki Beef, 81
    Teriyaki Chop Suey, 87
    Texas-Style Deep-Dish Chili Pie,
        64
    Three-Pepper Steak, 82
Beef Oriental, 278
Beef Sausage Skillet Dinner, 100
Beef Sonoma & Rice, 77
Beef, Ground
    Beef Oriental, 278
    Beef Sonoma & Rice, 77
    Cheeseburger Macaroni, 272
    Chunky Chili Casserole, 67
    CONTADINA® Classic Lasagne,
        228
    Crazy Lasagna Casserole, 224
    Eggplant & Feta Ziti, 245
    Family Favorite Hamburger
        Casserole, 67
    Ground Beef Chow Mein, 80
    Heartland Shepherd's Pie, 62
    Hungarian Goulash Stew, 91
    Italian Pasta Bake, 265
    Johnnie Marzetti, 248
    Meatball Stroganoff with Rice, 77
    Mexican Lasagna, 73
    Moussaka-Style Beef and
        Zucchini, 82
    Old-Fashioned Beef Pot Pie, 70
    Oriental Beef & Noodle Toss, 282
    Oven-Easy Beef & Potato Dinner,
        71
    Pasta, Beef & Zucchini Dinner,
        273
    Patchwork Casserole, 62
    Rigatoni with Meat Sauce, 275
    Skillet Spaghetti and Sausage, 272
    Spaghetti Rolls, 245
    Speedy Stuffed Peppers, 66
    Spicy Quick and Easy Chili, 92
    Spinach Lasagna, 232
    String Pie, 260
    Taco Bake, 70
    Tacos in Pasta Shells, 241
    Tex-Mex Lasagna, 68
Biscuit-Topped Tuna Bake, 135
Bistro Burgundy Stew, 90
Black Bean & Pork Stew, 119
Breakfast Hash, 318
Breakfast in a Loaf, 324
Broccoli
    Baked Ham & Cheese Monte
        Cristo, 299
    Beef and Broccoli, 87
    Broccoli and Cauliflower
        Linguine, 191

Broccoli (continued)
Broccoli & Cheddar Noodle Casserole, 165
Broccoli & Cheese Quiche, 311
Broccoli Chicken Pasta Casserole, 222
Broccoli Lasagna, 166
Broccoli Lasagna Bianca, 160
Broccoli Stuffed Shells, 172
Cavatelli and Broccoli, 196
Chicken Walnut Stir-Fry, 34
Creamy Turkey & Broccoli, 55
Fish Broccoli Casserole, 133
Ham & Macaroni Twists, 250
Ham & Potato Scallop, 102
Harvest Casserole, 171
Herb-Baked Fish & Rice, 128
HERB-OX® Tortellini Vegetable Soup, 289
Lasagna Primavera, 187
Mandarin Cashew Chicken, 38
Oat Bran 'n Broccoli Casserole, 185
Orange Ginger Chicken & Rice, 29
Rainbow Stir-Fried Fish, 148
Skillet Chicken Divan, 31
Sweet & Sour Mustard Pork, 110
Szechuan Vegetable Stir-Fry, 214
Thai Noodles with Peanut Sauce, 216
Tuna and Broccoli Bake, 140
Tuna Tortilla Roll-Ups, 132
Tuna Vegetable Medley, 254
Vegetable & Cheese Platter, 176
"Wildly" Delicious Casserole, 22
Brown Rice Chicken Bake, 10
Brown Rice-Spinach Quiche, 313
Brunch Eggs Olé, 317
Brunch Rice, 322
Brussels Sprouts
Pasta with Roasted Vegetables, 179
Polenta with Vegetable Medley, 193

C
Cabbage (see also **Sauerkraut**)
Alphabet Turkey Soup, 286
Five-Spice Beef and Bok Choy, 282
Korean Beef, 284
Meatless Italian Minestrone, 217
Pork and Cabbage Rice, 110
Savory Lo Mein, 216
Singapore Spicy Noodles, 210
Sweet & Sour Mustard Pork, 110
Cajun Chili, 41
Cantonese Tomato Beef, 280

Casseroles, Beef (see also **Casseroles, Ground Beef**)
Chop Suey Casserole, 64
Countdown Casserole, 60
French Veal Casserole, 73
Reuben Casserole, 74
Spanish Style Beef and Rice Casserole, 68
Casseroles, Chicken (see also **Casseroles, Turkey**)
Broccoli Chicken Pasta Casserole, 222
Brown Rice Chicken Bake, 10
Chicken-Asparagus Casserole, 218
Chicken Biscuit Bake, 22
Chicken Mexicana Casserole, 20
Chicken, Rice and Biscuits, 143
Dairyland Confetti Chicken, 10
Home-Style Chicken Casserole, 23
Individual Chicken Rice Casseroles, 7
Lattice-Top Chicken, 12
Savory Chicken & Biscuits, 9
Tortilla Chicken Bake, 15
"Wildly" Delicious Casserole, 22
Casseroles, Fish & Seafood (see also **Casseroles, Tuna**)
Company Crab, 157
Crab and Brown Rice Casserole, 157
Fish Broccoli Casserole, 133
Foolproof Clam Fettucine, 262
Louisiana Seafood Bake, 136
Shrimp in Angel Hair Pasta Casserole, 221
Shrimp Noodle Supreme, 256
Casseroles, Ground Beef
Crazy Lasagna Casserole, 224
Eggplant & Feta Ziti, 245
Family Favorite Hamburger Casserole, 67
Italian Pasta Bake, 265
Johnnie Marzetti, 248
Patchwork Casserole, 62
Casseroles, Ham
Baked Ham & Cheese Monte Cristo, 299
Ham & Macaroni Twists, 250
Ham Starburst Casserole, 97
Casseroles, Meatless (see also **Casseroles, Meatless Pasta**)
Brunch Eggs Olé, 317
Chilies Rellenos Casserole, 298
Harvest Casserole, 171
Mushroom & Onion Egg Bake, 296
Spinach-Cheddar Squares, 298

Casseroles, Meatless Pasta
Broccoli & Cheddar Noodle Casserole, 165
Eggplant Pasta Bake, 178
Mac & Cheese with Crunchy Herb Crust, 185
Macaroni and Cheese Dijon, 226
Pasta Primavera Casserole, 220
Rigatoni with Four Cheeses, 168
Spinach Ziti Casserole, 168
Casseroles, Sausage
Baked Rigatoni, 253
Baked Rigatoni with Sausage, 255
Italian Sausage Supper, 99
Make-Ahead Breakfast Casserole, 294
Pizza Pasta, 261
Polish Reuben Casserole, 222
Prize Potluck Casserole, 97
Rice & Sausage Casserole, 94
Sausage & Noodle Casserole, 224
Spaghetti Bake, 256
Stuffed Franks 'n Taters, 94
Weekend Brunch Casserole, 299
Casseroles, Tuna
Biscuit-Topped Tuna Bake, 135
Creamy Scalloped Potatoes and Tuna, 128
Mushroom and Tuna Bake, 144
Old-Fashioned Tuna Noodle Casserole, 135
Tag-Along Tuna Bake, 133
Tuna and Broccoli Bake, 140
Tuna Noodle Casserole, 221
Tuna, Rice and Biscuits, 143
Tuna Vegetable Medley, 254
Casseroles, Turkey (see also **Casseroles, Chicken**)
Creamy Creole Turkey Bake, 248
Dilled Turkey Noodle Bake, 261
Easy Turkey and Rice, 55
Italian Rotini Bake, 254
Mexican Rice and Turkey Bake, 50
One-Dish Meal, 54
Turkey Olé, 58
Turkey Wild Rice Supreme, 48
Cauliflower
Broccoli and Cauliflower Linguine, 191
Ham and Cauliflower Chowder, 118
HERB-OX® Tortellini Vegetable Soup, 289
Korean Beef, 284
Zesty Mixed Vegetables, 212
Cavatelli and Broccoli, 196
Cheddar and Leek Strata, 301

Cheese, Swiss
Asparagus-Swiss Soufflé, 308
Broccoli & Cheese Quiche, 311
Cheddar and Leek Strata, 301
Cheesy Chicken Roll-Ups, 234
Colorful Turkey Pasta Bake, 246
Elegant Crabmeat Frittata, 306
Lasagna Roll-Ups, 163
Mushroom Frittata, 194
Polish Reuben Casserole, 222
Ranch Quiche Lorraine, 314
Reuben Casserole, 74
Shrimp in Angel Hair Pasta
    Casserole, 221
STARKIST® Swiss Potato Pie, 140
Superb Fillet of Sole &
    Vegetables, 142
Tomato, Bacon and Cheese
    Supper, 96
Tuna-Swiss Pie, 138
Tuna Vegetable Medley, 254
Turkey Cottage Pie, 46
Vegetable Strata, 302
Vegetarian Lasagna, 163
Wisconsin Swiss Linguine Tart, 165
Cheeseburger Macaroni, 272
Cheese Polenta, 193
Cheese Strata, 302
Cheesy Chicken Roll-Ups, 234
Chesapeake Crab Strata, 156
CHEX® Under Wraps, 234
Chicken (*see also* **Chicken,
    Cooked**)
Arroz con Pollo, 33
Asparagus Chicken, 36
Cajun Chili, 41
Chicken à la Bourguignonne, 14
Chicken and Vegetables with
    Mustard Sauce, 36
Chicken and Zucchini Casserole, 19
Chicken Breasts Florentine, 19
Chicken Cacciatore, 26
Chicken Enchiladas, 4
Chicken Fiesta, 17
Chicken in French Onion Sauce, 7
Chicken Mexicana Casserole, 20
Chicken Paprikash, 268
Chicken Parmesan, 30
Chicken Parmesan Noodle Bake,
    246
Chicken Pot Pie, 15
Chicken Skillet Supper, 30
Chicken Thighs with Peas, 34
Chicken Vegetable Skillet, 27
Chicken Walnut Stir-Fry, 34
Chicken with Mushroom Sauce, 322
Country Chicken Stew, 38
Creamy Chicken & Vegetables
    with Puff Pastry, 320
Creamy Shell Soup, 290

Chicken (*continued*)
Crispy Chicken Roll-Ups, 234
Down-Home Corn and Chicken
    Casserole, 20
Festive Chicken and Stuffing, 24
Home-Style Chicken Casserole, 23
Lemon-Garlic Chicken & Rice, 33
Mandarin Cashew Chicken, 38
Microwaved Garlic and Herb
    Chicken, 13
Mustard Chicken & Vegetables, 265
Orange Ginger Chicken & Rice, 29
Oven Chicken & Rice, 12
Paella, 29
Paella à la Española, 12
Savory Chicken & Biscuits, 9
Skillet Chicken Divan, 31
Southwestern Pumpkin Stew, 46
Spaghetti Twists with Spicy Fresh
    Salsa, 226
Spanish-Style Chicken & Rice, 6
Tortilla Chicken Bake, 15
"Wildly" Delicious Casserole, 22
Chicken, Cooked
Brown Rice Chicken Bake, 10
Chicken-Asparagus Casserole, 218
Chicken Biscuit Bake, 22
Chicken, Rice and Biscuits, 143
Chicken Tetrazzini, 238
Country Chicken Dinner, 262
Curried Chicken Pot Pie, 18
Dairyland Confetti Chicken, 10
Dijon Roasted Vegetable Soup, 41
Fancy Chicken Puff Pie, 9
Hearty Chicken Bake, 17
Individual Chicken Rice
    Casseroles, 7
Lattice-Top Chicken, 12
Polynesian Chicken and Rice, 24
Tex-Mex Chicken & Rice Chili, 40
Chicken, Ground (*see* **Chicken**)
Chilaquiles, 170
Chilies Rellenos Casserole, 298
Chilis (*see also* **Soups; Stews**)
Cajun Chili, 41
Hearty Meatless Chili, 217
Spicy Quick and Easy Chili, 92
Tex-Mex Chicken & Rice Chili,
    40
20-Minute White Bean Chili, 57
Chop Suey Casserole, 64
Chunky Chili Casserole, 67
Clams
Foolproof Clam Fettucine, 262
Southern Italian Clam Chowder,
    158
Colorful Turkey Pasta Bake, 246
Company Crab, 157
Confetti Topping, 10
CONTADINA® Classic Lasagne, 228

Corn
Albacore Vegetable Pilaf, 147
CHEX® Under Wraps, 234
Chicken Fiesta, 17
Chicken Mexicana Casserole, 20
Chunky Chili Casserole, 67
Corn, Bacon & Rice Chowder, 120
Down-Home Corn and Chicken
    Casserole, 20
Garden Frittata, 307
Hunan Chili Beef, 85
Hungarian Goulash Stew, 91
Mexican Rice and Turkey Bake, 50
Navajo Lamb Stew with Cornmeal
    Dumplings, 122
Quick Skillet Supper, 79
Southwestern Beef Stew, 90
Southwest Pork and Dressing, 112
Spicy Quick and Easy Chili, 92
Tuna Vegetable Medley, 254
20-Minute White Bean Chili, 57
Corned Beef
Corned Beef, Potato and Pepper
    Hash, 74
Reuben Casserole, 74
Cornmeal Dumplings, 122
Cottage Cheese (*see also* **Ricotta
    Cheese**)
Broccoli Lasagna, 166
Brunch Eggs Olé, 317
Crazy Lasagna Casserole, 224
Easy Microwave Turkey Lasagna,
    231
Easy Spinach Pie, 97
Mushroom & Onion Egg Bake,
    296
Pasta Roll-Ups, 184
Rice Lasagna, 43
Spinach Ziti Casserole, 168
String Pie, 260
Summer Turkey Lasagna, 231
Tex-Mex Lasagna, 68
Tuna and Broccoli Bake, 140
Turkey Lasagna, 228
Vegetable Lasagna, 182
Wisconsin Cheesy Pasta
    Primavera, 208
Countdown Casserole, 60
Country Chicken Dinner, 262
Country Chicken Stew, 38
Country Skillet Hash, 104
Country-Style Lasagna, 230
Crabmeat
Chesapeake Crab Strata, 156
Company Crab, 157
Crab and Brown Rice Casserole,
    157
Easy Crab Asparagus Pie, 311
Elegant Crabmeat Frittata,
    306

Crazy Lasagna Casserole, 224
Creamy Chicken & Vegetables with
    Puff Pastry, 320
Creamy Creole Turkey Bake, 248
Creamy Salmon with Green Beans,
    286
Creamy Scalloped Potatoes and
    Tuna, 128
Creamy Shell Soup, 290
Creamy Turkey & Broccoli, 55
Crispy Chicken Roll-Ups, 234
Crunchy Tuna Squares, 143
Curried Chicken Pot Pie, 18

D
Dairyland Confetti Chicken, 10
Dijon Ham and Lentil Soup, 119
Dijon Lamb Stew, 125
Dijon Roasted Vegetable Soup, 41
Dilled Turkey Noodle Bake, 261
Double Onion Quiche, 310
Down-Home Corn and Chicken
    Casserole, 20

E
Easy Beef and Rice Stew, 88
Easy Crab Asparagus Pie, 311
Easy Microwave Turkey Lasagna,
    231
Easy Morning Strata, 304
Easy Spinach Pie, 97
Easy Three Cheese Tuna Souffle,
    126
Easy Turkey and Rice, 55
Eggplant
    Eggplant & Feta Ziti, 245
    Eggplant Italiano, 214
    Eggplant Parmesan, 194
    Eggplant Pasta Bake, 178
    Italian Eggplant Parmigiana, 187
    Valley Eggplant Parmigiano, 162
Eggs and Rice Dish, 317
Elegant Crabmeat Frittata, 306

F
Family Baked Bean Dinner, 99
Family Favorite Hamburger
    Casserole, 67
Fancy Chicken Puff Pie, 9
Festive Chicken and Stuffing, 24
Fettuccine Alfeta, 191
Fish, Fillets (*see also* **Salmon;**
    Tuna)
    Baked Fish with Potatoes and
        Onions, 130
    Fish Broccoli Casserole, 133
    Louisiana Seafood Bake, 136
    New England Fisherman's Skillet,
        147
    Rainbow Stir-Fried Fish, 148

Fish, Fillets (*continued*)
    Saucy Stir-Fried Fish, 148
    Seafood Gumbo, 153
    Sicilian Fish and Rice Bake, 138
    So-Easy Fish Divan, 130
    Sole Almondine, 144
    Superb Fillet of Sole & Vegetables,
        142
    White Cheddar Seafood Chowder,
        290
Five-Spice Beef and Bok Choy, 282
Foolproof Clam Fettucine, 262
French Veal Casserole, 73
Fresh Salsa, 317
Frittatas
    Elegant Crabmeat Frittata, 306
    Garden Frittata, 307
    Hash Brown Frittata, 307
    Mushroom Frittata, 194
    Tuna and Pasta Frittata, 145
    Vegetable-Cheese Frittata, 306

G
Garden Frittata, 307
Garlic Shrimp with Wilted Spinach,
    152
Ground Beef (*see* **Beef, Ground**)
Ground Beef Chow Mein, 80

H
Ham
    Acapulco Eggs, 315
    Baked Ham & Cheese Monte
        Cristo, 299
    Black Bean & Pork Stew, 119
    Breakfast in a Loaf, 324
    Chicken with Mushroom Sauce,
        322
    Country-Style Lasagna, 230
    Dijon Ham and Lentil Soup, 119
    Easy Spinach Pie, 97
    Fancy Chicken Puff Pie, 9
    Garden Frittata, 307
    Ham and Cauliflower Chowder,
        118
    Ham & Cheese Grits Soufflé,
        308
    Ham and Egg Enchiladas, 318
    Ham & Macaroni Twists, 250
    Ham & Potato Scallop, 102
    Ham Starburst Casserole, 97
    Pasta Fagioli (Bean) Soup, 284
    Sausage Ham Jambalaya, 103
Harvest Casserole, 171
Hash Brown Frittata, 307
Heartland Shepherd's Pie, 62
Hearty Chicken Bake, 17
Hearty Manicotti, 174
Hearty Meatless Chili, 217
Herb-Baked Fish & Rice, 128

Herbed Tomato Pork Chops and
    Stuffing, 109
HERB-OX® Tortellini Vegetable
    Soup, 289
Herb Strata, 302
Home-Style Chicken Casserole, 23
Homespun Turkey 'n' Vegetables, 48
Homestyle Tuna Pot Pie, 136
Hot 'n Spicy Pork, 116
Huevos con Arroz, 315
Hunan Chili Beef, 85
Hungarian Goulash Stew, 91

I
Indian Vegetable Curry, 198
Individual Chicken Rice
    Casseroles, 7
Italian Beef and Pasta, 267
Italian Eggplant Parmigiana, 187
Italian Garden Fusilli, 188
Italian-Herb Strata, 302
Italian Pasta Bake, 265
Italian Rotini Bake, 254
Italian Sausage Lasagna, 225
Italian Sausage Supper, 99
Ivory, Rubies and Jade, 115

J
Johnnie Marzetti, 248

K
Korean Beef, 284

L
Lamb
    Dijon Lamb Stew, 125
    Lamb & Pork Cassoulet, 125
    Navajo Lamb Stew with Cornmeal
        Dumplings, 122
    Shepherd's Pie, 124
Lasagna Primavera, 187
Lasagnas
    Broccoli Lasagna, 166
    Broccoli Lasagna Bianca, 160
    CONTADINA® Classic Lasagne,
        228
    Country-Style Lasagna, 230
    Easy Microwave Turkey Lasagna,
        231
    Italian Sausage Lasagna, 225
    Lasagna Primavera, 187
    Mexican Lasagna, 73
    Mexican Turkey Lasagna, 43
    Rice Lasagna, 43
    Spinach Lasagna, 232
    Summer Turkey Lasagna, 231
    Tex-Mex Lasagna, 68
    Turkey Lasagna, 228
    Vegetable Lasagna: 180, 182
    Vegetarian Lasagna, 163

Lattice-Top Chicken, 12
Lemon-Garlic Chicken & Rice, 33
Lemon-Garlic Shrimp, 150
Lentils (*see* **Beans, Dried**)
Louisiana Red Beans & Rice, 201
Louisiana Seafood Bake, 136

M
Mac & Cheese with Crunchy Herb
   Crust, 185
Mac & Stuff, 270
Macaroni and Cheese Dijon, 226
Make-Ahead Breakfast Casserole,
   294
Mandarin Cashew Chicken, 38
Mandarin Pork Stir-Fry, 116
Mandarin Tomato Beef, 80
Manhattan Turkey à la King, 268
Manicotti
   Hearty Manicotti, 174
   Spaghetti Rolls, 245
   Stuffed Manicotti, 186
   Turkey Manicotti, 243
   Turkey-Spinach Manicotti, 242
Meatball Stroganoff with Rice, 77
Meatless Italian Minestrone, 217
Mexican Cheese-Rice Pie, 182
Mexican Lasagna, 73
Mexican Rice and Turkey Bake, 50
Mexican Skillet Rice, 102
Mexican Strata, 302
Mexican Strata Olé, 301
Mexican Turkey Lasagna, 43
Mexican Turkey Rice, 57
Mexican Turkey Stuffed Shells, 241
Microwave, Beef
   Chunky Chili Casserole, 67
   Countdown Casserole, 60
Microwave, Chicken (*see also*
   Microwave, Turkey)
   Chicken and Zucchini Casserole, 19
   Chicken Breasts Florentine, 19
   Chicken in French Onion Sauce, 7
   Country Chicken Dinner, 262
   Lattice-Top Chicken, 12
   Microwaved Garlic and Herb
      Chicken, 13
   Mustard Chicken & Vegetables,
      265
Microwave, Fish & Seafood
   (*see also* **Microwave, Tuna**)
   Foolproof Clam Fettucine, 262
   Herb-Baked Fish & Rice, 128
   Louisiana Seafood Bake, 136
   Salmon Linguini Supper, 258
   Shrimp Classico, 154
Microwave, Meatless
   Chilaquiles, 170
   Mexican Cheese-Rice Pie, 182
   Tomato-Zucchini Pesto, 201

Microwave, Pork
   Angel Hair Carbonara, 253
   Easy Spinach Pie, 97
   Family Baked Bean Dinner, 99
   Mexican Skillet Rice, 102
   Stuffed Franks 'n Taters, 94
   Tomato, Bacon and Cheese
      Supper, 96
Microwave, Tuna
   Bacon-Tuna Parmesano, 264
   Surfin' Tuna Casserole, 139
   Tuna Mac and Cheese, 251
Microwave, Turkey
   Creamy Turkey & Broccoli, 55
   Easy Microwave Turkey Lasagna,
      231
   Mexican Rice and Turkey Bake,
      50
   One-Dish Meal, 54
   Summer Turkey Lasagna, 231
   Turkey Cottage Pie, 46
   Turkey 'n Stuffing Pie, 52
   Turkey Parmesan, 44
Microwaved Garlic and Herb
   Chicken, 13
Minestrone, 120
Minestrone Soup, 255
Mostaccioli with Spinach and Feta,
   200
Moussaka-Style Beef and Zucchini,
   82
Mushroom & Onion Egg Bake, 296
Mushroom and Tuna Bake, 144
Mushroom Frittata, 194
Mustard Chicken & Vegetables,
   265

N
Navajo Lamb Stew with Cornmeal
   Dumplings, 122
New England Fisherman's Skillet,
   147
New Orleans Rice and Sausage, 100

O
Oat Bran 'n Broccoli Casserole, 185
Old-Fashioned Beef Pot Pie, 70
Old-Fashioned Beef Stew, 88
Old-Fashioned Tuna Noodle
   Casserole, 135
Old Mexico Black Beans & Rice,
   188
One-Dish Meal, 54
Orange Ginger Chicken & Rice, 29
Oriental Beef & Noodle Toss, 282
Oriental Tofu Noodle Salad with
   Spicy Peanut Sauce, 211
Oven Chicken & Rice, 12
Oven-Easy Beef & Potato Dinner,
   71

P
Pad Thai (Thai Fried Noodles), 276
Paella, 29
Paella à la Española, 27
Paprika Pork with Spinach, 258
Pasta, Stuffed Shells
   Broccoli Stuffed Shells, 172
   Mexican Turkey Stuffed Shells,
      241
   Sunday Super Stuffed Shells, 239
   Tacos in Pasta Shells, 241
Pasta and Vegetable Chowder, 288
Pasta, Beef & Zucchini Dinner, 273
Pasta Fagiole, 206
Pasta Fagioli (Bean) Soup, 284
Pasta Primavera, 196
Pasta Primavera Casserole, 220
Pasta Primavera with Roasted
   Garlic Sauce, 204
Pasta Roll-Ups, 184
Pasta with Roasted Vegetables, 179
Patchwork Casserole, 62
Pea Pods (*see* **Snow Peas**)
Penne with Creamy Tomato Sauce,
   204
Pizza Pasta, 261
Polenta with Vegetable Medley,
   193
Polish Reuben Casserole, 222
Polynesian Chicken and Rice, 24
Pork (*see also* **Ham; Pork Chops;
   Pork, Ground**)
   Angel Hair Carbonara, 253
   Hot 'n Spicy Pork, 116
   Ivory, Rubies and Jade, 115
   Mandarin Pork Stir-Fry, 116
   Minestrone, 120
   Paprika Pork with Spinach, 258
   Pork and Cabbage Rice, 110
   Savory Pork & Apple Stir-Fry,
      113
   See the Lite Pork Fried Rice, 115
   Southwest Pork and Dressing,
      112
   Sweet & Sour Mustard Pork, 110
   Sweet & Sour Pork, 113
Pork Chops
   Country Skillet Hash, 104
   Herbed Tomato Pork Chops and
      Stuffing, 109
   Lamb & Pork Cassoulet, 125
   Pork Chops O'Brien, 106
   Pork Chops with Apples and
      Stuffing, 107
   Quick Cassoulet, 104
   Savory Pork Chop Supper, 107
Pork, Ground
   Mexican Skillet Rice, 102
   Sunday Super Stuffed Shells,
      239

Potatoes, Cooked Mashed
Heartland Shepherd's Pie, 62
Hearty Chicken Bake, 17
Turkey Cottage Pie, 46
Potatoes, Fresh
Arizona Turkey Stew, 58
Baked Fish with Potatoes and
Onions, 130
Breakfast Hash, 318
Chicken Skillet Supper, 30
Chicken Vegetable Skillet, 27
Corned Beef, Potato and Pepper
Hash, 74
Country Chicken Stew, 38
Creamy Scalloped Potatoes and
Tuna, 128
Creamy Shell Soup, 290
Garden Frittata, 307
Navajo Lamb Stew with Cornmeal
Dumplings, 122
New England Fisherman's Skillet,
147
Old-Fashioned Beef Stew, 88
Savory Pork Chop Supper, 107
Shepherd's Pie, 124
Turkey-Olive Ragoût en Croûte,
50
Potatoes, Frozen Hash Brown
Countdown Casserole, 60
Family Favorite Hamburger
Casserole, 67
Hash Brown Frittata, 307
Oven-Easy Beef & Potato Dinner,
71
Patchwork Casserole, 62
Pork Chops O'Brien, 106
STARKIST® Swiss Potato Pie, 140
Stuffed Franks 'n Taters, 94
Pot Pies
Chicken Pot Pie, 15
Curried Chicken Pot Pie, 18
Fancy Chicken Puff Pie, 9
Homestyle Tuna Pot Pie, 136
Old-Fashioned Beef Pot Pie, 70
Shepherd's Pie, 124
Tasty Turkey Pot Pie, 52
Texas-Style Deep-Dish Chili Pie, 64
Turkey-Olive Ragoût en Croûte,
50
Prize Potluck Casserole, 97

Q
Quiches
Broccoli & Cheese Quiche, 311
Brown Rice-Spinach Quiche, 313
Double Onion Quiche, 310
Easy Crab Asparagus Pie, 311
Ranch Quiche Lorraine, 314
Sausage & Apple Quiche, 314
Turkey and Rice Quiche, 313

Quick and Easy Tuna Rice with
Peas, 145
Quick Cassoulet, 104
Quick Paella, 109
Quick Skillet Supper, 79

R
Rainbow Stir-Fried Fish, 148
Ranch Quiche Lorraine, 314
Ranch Stroganoff, 76
Ravioli Soup, 292
Ravioli Stew, 292
Red and Yellow Bell Pepper Pasta,
212
Reuben Casserole, 74
Rice & Sausage Casserole, 94
Rice Lasagna, 43
Rice, Wild
Chicken à la Bourguignonne, 14
Oven Chicken & Rice, 12
Turkey Wild Rice Supreme, 48
"Wildly" Delicious Casserole, 22
Ricotta Cheese (*see also* **Cottage
Cheese**)
Broccoli Lasagna Bianca, 160
Broccoli Stuffed Shells, 172
Chicken-Asparagus Casserole,
218
CONTADINA® Classic Lasagne,
228
Eggplant Parmesan, 194
Hearty Manicotti, 174
Italian Rotini Bake, 254
Italian Sausage Lasagna, 225
Lasagna Primavera, 187
Lasagna Roll-Ups, 163
Lasagne Roll-Ups, 236
Mexican Lasagna, 73
Mexican Turkey Stuffed Shells,
241
Oat Bran 'n Broccoli Casserole,
185
Spinach-Cheese Lasagna Rolls,
170
Stuffed Manicotti, 186
Tomato, Bacon and Cheese
Supper, 96
Tomato-Zucchini Pesto, 201
Turkey Florentine Spaghetti Pie,
45
Turkey Manicotti, 243
Turkey-Spinach Manicotti, 242
Valley Eggplant Parmigiano,
162
Vegetable Lasagna: 180, 182
Vegetarian Lasagna, 163
Rigatoni with Four Cheeses, 168
Rigatoni with Meat Sauce, 275
Roasted Vegetables with Fettuccine,
176

S
Salmon
Creamy Salmon with Green
Beans, 286
Salmon Linguini Supper, 258
Salsa Rice and Black Beans, 206
Saucy Stir-Fried Fish, 148
Sauerkraut
Lasagna Roll-Ups, 163
Polish Reuben Casserole, 222
Reuben Casserole, 74
Vegetarian Lasagna, 163
Sausage (*see also* **Sausage: Bulk
Pork, Italian, Polish**)
Beef Sausage Skillet Dinner, 100
Black Bean & Pork Stew, 119
Cajun Chili, 41
Hash Brown Frittata, 307
HERB-OX® Tortellini Vegetable
Soup, 289
Lamb & Pork Cassoulet, 125
Mac & Stuff, 270
New Orleans Rice and Sausage,
100
Pizza Pasta, 261
Sausage Ham Jambalaya, 103
Spaghetti Bake, 256
Stuffed Franks 'n Taters, 94
Turkey Lasagna, 228
Turkey Manicotti, 243
Sausage, Bulk Pork
Chicken Fiesta, 17
Easy Morning Strata, 304
Italian Sausage Lasagna, 225
Make-Ahead Breakfast Casserole,
294
Rice & Sausage Casserole, 94
Sausage & Apple Quiche, 314
Sausage & Noodle Casserole, 224
Sausage Tetrazzini, 238
Sunrise Squares, 296
Weekend Brunch Casserole, 299
Zesty Noodle Soup, 288
Sausage, Italian
Baked Rigatoni, 253
Baked Rigatoni with Sausage, 255
Black Bean & Pork Stew, 119
Italian Sausage Supper, 99
Lasagne Roll-Ups, 236
Quick Paella, 109
Ravioli Soup, 292
Skillet Pasta Roma, 273
Skillet Spaghetti and Sausage, 272
Turkey Manicotti, 243
Sausage, Polish
Family Baked Bean Dinner, 99
Polish Reuben Casserole, 222
Prize Potluck Casserole, 97
Savory Chicken & Biscuits, 9
Savory Lo Mein, 216

Savory Pork & Apple Stir-Fry, 113
Savory Pork Chop Supper, 107
Savory Rice Pilaf with Tuna, 150
Scallops: Stir-Fried Scallops with
    Vegetables, 158
Scrambled Eggs, 324
Seafood Gumbo, 153
See the Lite Pork Fried Rice, 115
Sesame Noodles, 208
Sesame Peanut Spaghetti Squash,
    179
Sesame Steak, 79
Shepherd's Pie, 124
Sherried Beef, 75
Shrimp
  Garlic Shrimp with Wilted
    Spinach, 152
  Lemon-Garlic Shrimp, 150
  Louisiana Seafood Bake, 136
  Pad Thai (Thai Fried Noodles),
    276
  Paella, 29
  Paella à la Española, 27
  Quick Paella, 109
  Seafood Gumbo, 153
  Shrimp à la Louisiana, 153
  Shrimp Classico, 154
  Shrimp in Angel Hair Pasta
    Casserole, 221
  Shrimp Noodle Supreme, 256
  Stir-Fried Corkscrew Shrimp with
    Vegetables, 154
Sicilian Fish and Rice Bake, 138
Singapore Spicy Noodles, 210
Skillet Chicken Divan, 31
Skillet Meals, Beef (*see also*
    Skillet Meals, Ground Beef;
    Stir-Fries, Beef)
  Beef Sonoma & Rice, 77
  Corned Beef, Potato and Pepper
    Hash, 74
  Italian Beef and Pasta, 267
  Meatball Stroganoff with Rice, 77
  Oriental Beef & Noodle Toss, 282
  Quick Skillet Supper, 79
  Ranch Stroganoff, 76
  Sesame Steak, 79
  Sherried Beef, 75
Skillet Meals, Chicken & Turkey
    (*see also* **Stir-Fries, Chicken**)
  Arroz con Pollo, 33
  Chicken Cacciatore, 26
  Chicken Paprikash, 268
  Chicken Parmesan, 30
  Chicken Skillet Supper, 30
  Chicken Vegetable Skillet, 27
  Chicken with Mushroom Sauce,
    322
  Eggs and Rice Dish, 317
  Festive Chicken and Stuffing, 24

Skillet Meals, Chicken & Turkey
    (*continued*)
  Lemon-Garlic Chicken & Rice, 33
  Manhattan Turkey à la King, 268
  Mexican Turkey Rice, 57
  Orange Ginger Chicken & Rice, 29
  Paella, 29
  Paella à la Española, 27
  Polynesian Chicken and Rice, 24
  Skillet Chicken Divan, 31
  Spaghetti Twists with Spicy Fresh
    Salsa, 226
Skillet Meals, Fish & Seafood
    (*see also* **Frittatas; Stir-Fries,**
    Fish & Seafood)
  Garlic Shrimp with Wilted
    Spinach, 152
  New England Fisherman's Skillet,
    147
  Shrimp à la Louisiana, 153
Skillet Meals, Ground Beef
    (*see also* **Stir-Fries, Beef**)
  Cheeseburger Macaroni, 272
  Pasta, Beef & Zucchini Dinner, 273
  Rigatoni with Meat Sauce, 275
  Skillet Spaghetti and Sausage, 272
Skillet Meals, Meatless (*see also*
    Frittatas; Skillet Meals,
    Meatless Pasta; Stir-Fries,
    Meatless)
  Brunch Rice, 322
  Huevos con Arroz, 315
  Indian Vegetable Curry, 198
  Louisiana Red Beans & Rice, 201
  Oat Bran 'n Broccoli Casserole, 185
  Old Mexico Black Beans & Rice,
    188
  Polenta with Vegetable Medley,
    193
  Salsa Rice and Black Beans, 206
  Vegetable & Cheese Platter, 176
  Vegetable Risotto, 190
Skillet Meals, Meatless Pasta
    (*see also* **Stir-Fries, Meatless**)
  Alpine Fettuccine, 203
  Broccoli and Cauliflower
    Linguine, 191
  Cavatelli and Broccoli, 196
  Fettuccine Alfeta, 191
  Italian Garden Fusilli, 188
  Mostaccioli with Spinach and
    Feta, 200
  Pasta Fagiole, 206
  Pasta Primavera, 196
  Pasta Primavera with Roasted
    Garlic Sauce, 204
  Penne with Creamy Tomato
    Sauce, 204
  Red and Yellow Bell Pepper Pasta,
    212

Skillet Meals, Meatless Pasta
    (*continued*)
  Savory Lo Mein, 216
  Sesame Noodles, 208
  Singapore Spicy Noodles, 210
  Southwestern Pasta Sauce, 196
  Thai Noodles with Peanut Sauce,
    216
  Tortellini with Creamy Pesto, 198
  Vegetable & Orzo Pasta Sauté, 203
  Wisconsin Cheesy Pasta
    Primavera, 208
Skillet Meals, Pork (*see also*
    Frittatas; Skillet Meals,
    Sausage; Stir-Fries, Pork)
  Acapulco Eggs, 315
  Country Skillet Hash, 104
  Ham & Potato Scallop, 102
  Herbed Tomato Pork Chops and
    Stuffing, 109
  Mexican Skillet Rice, 102
  Pork and Cabbage Rice, 110
  Pork Chops with Apples and
    Stuffing, 107
  Quick Cassoulet, 104
  Quick Paella, 109
  Sausage Ham Jambalaya, 103
  Savory Pork Chop Supper, 107
  Southwest Pork and Dressing, 112
Skillet Meals, Sausage (*see also*
    Frittatas)
  Beef Sausage Skillet Dinner, 100
  Breakfast Hash, 318
  Mac & Stuff, 270
  New Orleans Rice and Sausage, 100
  Skillet Pasta Roma, 273
Skillet Meals, Tuna (*see also*
    Frittatas)
  Albacore Vegetable Pilaf, 147
  Angel Hair al Fresco, 270
  Quick and Easy Tuna Rice with
    Peas, 145
  Savory Rice Pilaf with Tuna, 150
  Tuna and Rice Skillet Dinner, 145
  Tuna Pesto & Pasta, 267
Skillet Pasta Roma, 273
Skillet Spaghetti and Sausage, 272
Snow Peas
  Beef Oriental, 278
  Chicken Walnut Stir-Fry, 34
  Ivory, Rubies and Jade, 115
  Mandarin Tomato Beef, 80
  Rainbow Stir-Fried Fish, 148
  See the Lite Pork Fried Rice, 115
  Sesame Peanut Spaghetti Squash,
    179
  Stir-Fried Corkscrew Shrimp with
    Vegetables, 154
  Stir-Fried Scallops with
    Vegetables, 158

INDEX

Snow Peas (continued)
Szechuan Vegetable Stir-Fry, 214
Vegetable & Cheese Platter, 176
Vegetable Strata, 302
Wisconsin Cheesy Pasta
Primavera, 208
So-Easy Fish Divan, 130
Sole Almondine, 144
Soufflés
Asparagus-Swiss Soufflé, 308
Easy Three Cheese Tuna Souffle,
126
Ham & Cheese Grits Soufflé, 308
Soups (see also **Chilis; Stews**)
Alphabet Turkey Soup, 286
Bean and Rice Soup, 92
Corn, Bacon & Rice Chowder, 120
Creamy Shell Soup, 290
Dijon Ham and Lentil Soup, 119
Dijon Roasted Vegetable Soup, 41
Ham and Cauliflower Chowder, 118
HERB-OX® Tortellini Vegetable
Soup, 289
Meatless Italian Minestrone, 217
Minestrone, 120
Minestrone Soup, 255
Pasta and Vegetable Chowder,
288
Pasta Fagioli (Bean) Soup, 284
Ravioli Soup, 292
Seafood Gumbo, 153
Southern Italian Clam Chowder,
158
White Cheddar Seafood Chowder,
290
Zesty Noodle Soup, 288
Southern Italian Clam Chowder, 158
Southwestern Beef Stew, 90
Southwestern Pasta Sauce, 196
Soutwestern Pumpkin Stew, 46
Southwest Pork and Dressing, 112
Spaghetti Bake, 256
Spaghetti Pies
String Pie, 260
Turkey-Spaghetti Pie, 251
Spaghetti Rolls, 245
Spaghetti Twists with Spicy Fresh
Salsa, 226
Spanish Style Beef and Rice
Casserole, 68
Spanish-Style Chicken & Rice, 6
Speedy Stuffed Peppers, 66
Spicy Beef Stir-Fry, 275
Spicy Peanut Sauce, 211
Spicy Quick and Easy Chili, 92
Spicy Ravioli and Cheese, 174
Spinach
Brown Rice-Spinach Quiche, 313
Chicken Breasts Florentine, 19
Easy Spinach Pie, 97

Spinach (continued)
Garlic Shrimp with Wilted
Spinach, 152
Hearty Manicotti, 174
Italian Sausage Lasagna, 225
Lasagna Primavera, 187
Lasagna Roll-Ups, 163
Lasagne Roll-Ups, 236
Make-Ahead Breakfast Casserole,
294
Mostaccioli with Spinach and
Feta, 200
Paprika Pork with Spinach, 258
Pasta Fagiole, 206
Shrimp Classico, 154
Spinach-Cheddar Squares, 298
Spinach-Cheese Lasagna Rolls,
170
Spinach-Cheese Strata, 304
Spinach Lasagna, 232
Spinach Ziti Casserole, 168
Sunday Super Stuffed Shells,
239
Turkey Florentine Spaghetti Pie,
45
Turkey Manicotti, 243
Turkey-Spinach Manicotti, 242
Vegetable Lasagna: 180, 182
Vegetarian Lasagna, 163
STARKIST® Swiss Potato Pie, 140
Stews
Arizona Turkey Stew, 58
Bistro Burgundy Stew, 90
Black Bean & Pork Stew, 119
Country Chicken Stew, 38
Dijon Lamb Stew, 125
Easy Beef and Rice Stew, 88
Hungarian Goulash Stew, 91
Navajo Lamb Stew with Cornmeal
Dumplings, 122
Old-Fashioned Beef Stew, 88
Ravioli Stew, 292
Southwestern Beef Stew, 90
Soutwestern Pumpkin Stew, 46
Stir-Fried Corkscrew Shrimp with
Vegetables, 154
Stir-Fried Scallops with Vegetables,
158
Stir-Fries, Beef
Beef à la Stroganoff, 278
Beef and Broccoli, 87
Beef Benihana, 84
Beef Oriental, 278
Cantonese Tomato Beef, 280
Five-Spice Beef and Bok Choy,
282
Ground Beef Chow Mein, 80
Hunan Chili Beef, 85
Korean Beef, 284
Mandarin Tomato Beef, 80

Stir-Fries, Beef (continued)
Moussaka-Style Beef and
Zucchini, 82
Spicy Beef Stir-Fry, 275
Teriyaki Beef, 81
Teriyaki Chop Suey, 87
Three-Pepper Steak, 82
Stir-Fries, Chicken
Asparagus Chicken, 36
Chicken and Vegetables with
Mustard Sauce, 36
Chicken Thighs with Peas, 34
Chicken Walnut Stir-Fry, 34
Mandarin Cashew Chicken, 38
Stir-Fries, Fish & Seafood
Creamy Salmon with Green
Beans, 286
Lemon-Garlic Shrimp, 150
Pad Thai (Thai Fried Noodles), 276
Rainbow Stir-Fried Fish, 148
Saucy Stir-Fried Fish, 148
Stir-Fried Corkscrew Shrimp with
Vegetables, 154
Stir-Fried Scallops with
Vegetables, 158
Stir-Fries, Meatless
Eggplant Italiano, 214
Oriental Tofu Noodle Salad with
Spicy Peanut Sauce, 211
Sesame Peanut Spaghetti Squash,
179
Szechuan Vegetable Stir-Fry, 214
Zesty Mixed Vegetables, 212
Stir-Fries, Pork
Hot 'n Spicy Pork, 116
Ivory, Rubies and Jade, 115
Mandarin Pork Stir-Fry, 116
Paprika Pork with Spinach, 258
Savory Pork & Apple Stir-Fry, 113
See the Lite Pork Fried Rice, 115
Sweet & Sour Mustard Pork, 110
Sweet & Sour Pork, 113
Stratas
Cheddar and Leek Strata, 301
Cheese Strata, 302
Chesapeake Crab Strata, 156
Easy Morning Strata, 304
Herb Strata, 302
Italian-Herb Strata, 302
Mexican Strata, 302
Mexican Strata Olé, 301
Spinach-Cheese Strata, 304
Sunrise Squares, 296
Vegetable Strata, 302
String Pie, 260
Stuffed Franks 'n Taters, 94
Stuffed Manicotti, 186
Summer Turkey Lasagna, 231
Sunday Super Stuffed Shells, 239
Sunrise Squares, 296

INDEX

Superb Fillet of Sole & Vegetables, 142
Surfin' Tuna Casserole, 139
Sweet & Sour Mustard Pork, 110
Sweet & Sour Pork, 113
Szechuan Vegetable Stir-Fry, 214

T
Taco Bake, 70
Tacos in Pasta Shells, 241
Tag-Along Tuna Bake, 133
Tasty Turkey Pot Pie, 52
Teriyaki Beef, 81
Teriyaki Chop Suey, 87
Tetrazzinis
    Chicken Tetrazzini, 238
    Sausage Tetrazzini, 238
    Turkey Tetrazzini, 236
Texas-Style Deep-Dish Chili Pie, 64
Tex-Mex Chicken & Rice Chili, 40
Tex-Mex Lasagna, 68
Thai Noodles with Peanut Sauce, 216
Three-Pepper Steak, 82
Tofu
    Oriental Tofu Noodle Salad with Spicy Peanut Sauce, 211
    Szechuan Vegetable Stir-Fry, 214
Tomato, Bacon and Cheese Supper, 96
Tomato-Basil Sauce, 180
Tomato-Zucchini Pesto, 201
Tortellini with Creamy Pesto, 198
Tortilla Chicken Bake, 15
Tuna
    Albacore Vegetable Pilaf, 147
    Angel Hair al Fresco, 270
    Bacon-Tuna Parmesano, 264
    Biscuit-Topped Tuna Bake, 135
    Creamy Scalloped Potatoes and Tuna, 128
    Crunchy Tuna Squares, 143
    Easy Three Cheese Tuna Souffle, 126
    Homestyle Tuna Pot Pie, 136
    Mushroom and Tuna Bake, 144
    Old-Fashioned Tuna Noodle Casserole, 135
    Quick and Easy Tuna Rice with Peas, 145
    Savory Rice Pilaf with Tuna, 150
    STARKIST® Swiss Potato Pie, 140
    Surfin' Tuna Casserole, 139
    Tag-Along Tuna Bake, 133
    Tuna and Broccoli Bake, 140
    Tuna and Pasta Frittata, 145
    Tuna and Rice Skillet Dinner, 145
    Tuna Mac and Cheese, 251
    Tuna Noodle Casserole, 221
    Tuna Pesto & Pasta, 267

Tuna *(continued)*
    Tuna Tortilla Roll-Ups, 132
    Tuna Vegetable Medley, 254
    Tuna, Rice and Biscuits, 143
    Tuna-Swiss Pie, 138
Turkey *(see also **Chicken; Chicken, Cooked; Turkey, Cooked; Turkey, Ground; Sausage**)*
    Arizona Turkey Stew, 58
    Eggs and Rice Dish, 317
    Homespun Turkey 'n' Vegetables, 48
    Manhattan Turkey à la King, 268
    Summer Turkey Lasagna, 231
    Turkey-Olive Ragoût en Croûte, 50
Turkey, Cooked
    Alphabet Turkey Soup, 286
    Colorful Turkey Pasta Bake, 246
    Creamy Creole Turkey Bake, 248
    Creamy Turkey & Broccoli, 55
    Dilled Turkey Noodle Bake, 261
    Easy Turkey and Rice, 55
    Mexican Rice and Turkey Bake, 50
    Mexican Turkey Rice, 57
    One-Dish Meal, 54
    Tasty Turkey Pot Pie, 52
    Turkey and Rice Quiche, 313
    Turkey Cottage Pie, 46
    Turkey 'n Stuffing Pie, 52
    Turkey Olé, 58
    Turkey Parmesan, 44
    Turkey-Spaghetti Pie, 251
    Turkey-Spinach Manicotti, 242
    Turkey Tetrazzini, 236
Turkey, Ground
    CHEX® Under Wraps, 234
    Easy Microwave Turkey Lasagna, 231
    Italian Rotini Bake, 254
    Mexican Turkey Lasagna, 43
    Mexican Turkey Stuffed Shells, 241
    Rice Lasagna, 43
    Turkey Florentine Spaghetti Pie, 45
    Turkey Wild Rice Supreme, 48
    20-Minute White Bean Chili, 57
Turkey Lasagna, 228
Turkey Manicotti, 243
20-Minute White Bean Chili, 57

V
Valley Eggplant Parmigiano, 162
Veal
    French Veal Casserole, 73
    Sunday Super Stuffed Shells, 239
Vegetable & Cheese Platter, 176
Vegetable & Orzo Pasta Sauté, 203
Vegetable-Cheese Frittata, 306
Vegetable Lasagna: 180, 182

Vegetable Risotto, 190
Vegetable Strata, 302
Vegetarian Lasagna, 163
Vegetarian Paella, 172

W
Water Chestnuts
    Beef and Broccoli, 87
    Chicken and Zucchini Casserole, 19
    Chop Suey Casserole, 64
    Crunchy Tuna Squares, 143
    Hot 'n Spicy Pork, 116
    Ivory, Rubies and Jade, 115
    Mandarin Cashew Chicken, 38
    Rainbow Stir-Fried Fish, 148
    Sesame Steak, 79
    Stir-Fried Corkscrew Shrimp with Vegetables, 154
    Sweet & Sour Pork, 113
Weekend Brunch Casserole, 299
White Cheddar Seafood Chowder, 290
"Wildly" Delicious Casserole, 22
Wisconsin Cheesy Pasta Primavera, 208
Wisconsin Swiss Linguine Tart, 165

Z
Zesty Mixed Vegetables, 212
Zesty Noodle Soup, 288
Zucchini
    Albacore Vegetable Pilaf, 147
    Beef Benihana, 84
    Chicken and Zucchini Casserole, 19
    Dijon Roasted Vegetable Soup, 41
    Festive Chicken and Stuffing, 24
    Italian Garden Fusilli, 188
    Italian Rotini Bake, 254
    Italian Sausage Supper, 99
    Lasagna Primavera, 187
    Minestrone, 120
    Moussaka-Style Beef and Zucchini, 82
    Mushroom Frittata, 194
    Mustard Chicken & Vegetables, 265
    Pasta and Vegetable Chowder, 288
    Pasta, Beef & Zucchini Dinner, 273
    Pasta Primavera Casserole, 220
    Pasta Primavera with Roasted Garlic Sauce, 204
    Sole Almondine, 144
    Summer Turkey Lasagna, 231
    Tomato-Zucchini Pesto, 201
    Turkey Parmesan, 44
    Vegetable Lasagna, 180
    Vegetable Risotto, 190

METRIC CONVERSION CHART

VOLUME MEASUREMENTS (dry)

1/8 teaspoon = 0.5 mL
1/4 teaspoon = 1 mL
1/2 teaspoon = 2 mL
3/4 teaspoon = 4 mL
1 teaspoon = 5 mL
1 tablespoon = 15 mL
2 tablespoons = 30 mL
1/4 cup = 60 mL
1/3 cup = 75 mL
1/2 cup = 125 mL
2/3 cup = 150 mL
3/4 cup = 175 mL
1 cup = 250 mL
2 cups = 1 pint = 500 mL
3 cups = 750 mL
4 cups = 1 quart = 1 L

VOLUME MEASUREMENTS (fluid)

1 fluid ounce (2 tablespoons) = 30 mL
4 fluid ounces (1/2 cup) = 125 mL
8 fluid ounces (1 cup) = 250 mL
12 fluid ounces (1 1/2 cups) = 375 mL
16 fluid ounces (2 cups) = 500 mL

WEIGHTS (mass)

1/2 ounce = 15 g
1 ounce = 30 g
3 ounces = 90 g
4 ounces = 120 g
8 ounces = 225 g
10 ounces = 285 g
12 ounces = 360 g
16 ounces = 1 pound = 450 g

DIMENSIONS

1/16 inch = 2 mm
1/8 inch = 3 mm
1/4 inch = 6 mm
1/2 inch = 1.5 cm
3/4 inch = 2 cm
1 inch = 2.5 cm

OVEN TEMPERATURES

250°F = 120°C
275°F = 140°C
300°F = 150°C
325°F = 160°C
350°F = 180°C
375°F = 190°C
400°F = 200°C
425°F = 220°C
450°F = 230°C

BAKING PAN SIZES

Utensil	Size in Inches/Quarts	Metric Volume	Size in Centimeters
Baking or Cake Pan (square or rectangular)	8×8×2	2 L	20×20×5
	9×9×2	2.5 L	22×22×5
	12×8×2	3 L	30×20×5
	13×9×2	3.5 L	33×23×5
Loaf Pan	8×4×3	1.5 L	20×10×7
	9×5×3	2 L	23×13×7
Round Layer Cake Pan	8×1½	1.2 L	20×4
	9×1½	1.5 L	23×4
Pie Plate	8×1¼	750 mL	20×3
	9×1¼	1 L	23×3
Baking Dish or Casserole	1 quart	1 L	—
	1½ quart	1.5 L	—
	2 quart	2 L	—